Keepers of the Ancient Knowledge

Keepers of the Ancient Knowledge

The Mystical World of the
Q'ero Indians of Peru

Joan Parisi Wilcox

ELEMENT
Boston, Massachusetts • Shaftesbury, Dorset
Melbourne, Victoria

© Element Books, Inc. 1999
Text © Joan Parisi Wilcox 1999

First published in the USA in 1999 by
Element Books, Inc.
160 North Washington Street,
Boston, Massachusetts 02114

Published in Great Britain in 1999 by
Element Books Limited
Shaftesbury, Dorset SP7 8BP

Published in Australia in 1999 by
Element Books Limited for
Penguin Books Australia Limited
487 Maroondah Highway, Ringwood, Victoria 3134

Library of Congress Cataloging-in-Publication data
Wilcox, Joan Parisi.
    Keepers of the ancient knowledge: the mystical world of the Q'ero Indians of
Peru/ Joan Parisi Wilcox.
        p.   cm.
    Includes bibliographical references and index.
    ISBN 1-86204-492-9 (alk. paper)
    1. Q'ero Indians—Religion. 2. Shamanism—Peru. 3. Spiritual life. I. Title.
F3430.1.Q47W55 1999
299'.883—dc21   98-56180
                                                                      CIP

British Library Cataloguing-in-Publication data available

First Edition
10 9 8 7 6 5 4 3 2 1

Book design by Jill Winitzer
Printed and bound in the United States by Courier

Contents

Acknowledgments

No book is ever the author's alone. Many people provide inspiration, ideas, feedback, and support. I have been blessed to have had the assistance of many extraordinary people during this project.

My deepest appreciation and love to my family, each of whom has nurtured me in ways untold, and to my friends and fellow adventurers who were indirectly a part of the making of this book. Particular thanks to Eileen—for everything and then some—and to Sandy, whom I recognized as a sister in spirit at first glance and who has always proven herself to be one.

A special thank you, too, to my mother, for being my best friend, my earliest and greatest inspiration, and an exquisite example of strength and unconditional love. Thanks, Mom, for providing emotional and financial support—and for so quickly getting over your fears that I was running off to Peru to join some weird New Age cult.

My heartfelt thanks to Jesse Telles and Anamaria Szendroi for serving as Spanish translators and for expressing their friendship in such nurturing ways. My appreciation, too, to Cristobál Cornejo for translating the many secondary, academic articles that provided background for and confirmation of much of the information in this book. To anthropologist Ricardo Valderrama Fernández I offer my sincerest gratitude for providing the Quechua translations during the Urubamba interviews.

There is no way to gauge the importance of Dr. Juan Núñez del Prado's contribution to this book. Very simply, it would not have been written without him. From my first meeting with him, which took place in the Dreamtime, I knew Juan would be more than a friend and teacher to me, he would be a mentor. He has proven that to be true in more ways than he knows. He has also demonstrated that a sharp intelligence and a keen skepticism can happily coexist with humility, integrity, and a deep spirituality.

It also is impossible to adequately acknowledge my husband, John, for his unconditional support and love. It is largely your spirit, John, that has so magnificently scripted our story together, through all its challenges and triumphs.

Thank you to Tchir, partner of the heart, who introduced me to my agent, William Gladstone. Thanks, Bill, for believing in the timeliness and value of the Q'ero's message, and for shepherding the manuscript into the hands of Roberta Scimone at Element Books. Roberta's vision for this book mirrored my own, and I deeply appreciate her holding the space for that vision despite enormous pressures to the contrary. Thanks, also, to Barbara Neighbors Deal for her insightful suggestions.

Finally, I thank the Q'ero, the keepers of the ancient knowledge, who have become more than teachers to me; they've become friends, brothers and sisters in spirit. Anything that touches your heart and stirs your spirit in this book comes first from them, a gift to you from your brothers and sisters in the Andes.

The making of this book was a complicated project that spanned geographic boundaries, cultures, and languages. Many times it seemed as if we were also bridging vast stretches of historical and mythical time and, indeed, stepping outside of time itself. The words, knowledge, and wisdom of the Q'ero and their students that I have been able to record for you here are the result of many people opening their hearts and their spirits to you, directing the finest energies from the *hanaq pacha* (upper world) to the *kay pacha* (middle world) for your understanding and use. Any errors that occur I suspect are stray signals from the *ukhu pacha* (lower world)!

Preface

I have been given a great gift: to be, in some small and modest way, the conduit for the message of the Q'ero mystics of Peru, to provide the vehicle through which these shamans can speak of their tradition and reach out to a world in need of reminding that we are all spiritual and energetic beings in the Great Web of Being. Theirs is a cosmology that is life-affirming and self-empowering. The larger Andean mystical-shamanic tradition (see Appendix I), within which the Q'ero work, is one that has a keen applicability beyond the high snow-peaked mountains of central Peru. Indeed, when you read the Andean prophecy about the potential spiritual evolution of humankind, a prophecy that is unfolding at this very moment and to whose fulfillment you can contribute, you will feel the import of this gift for yourself.

I spent many hours considering how to best assist the Q'ero to reveal their metaphysical world. As I pondered the challenge before me, I was reminded of the dilemma of Thomas E. Mails, who wrote the biography of the Lakota elder Fools Crow and of the Hopi "Elderly Elders." He said, answering a critic who claimed Mails as a writer was too intrusive in his books, that it is impossible to make a direct translation from a foreign language, such as Lakota or Hopi, to English. Moreover, Mails said, "The writer is forced to do interpretive writing. In other words, he has to put what the informant says in his own words, and in words that his English audience can understand."[1] Mails's words ring true of my own experience with the Q'ero. Stepping up the rungs of the language ladder—from English to Spanish to Quechua—and down again was a dizzying and hazardous climb, one fraught with missteps that often left me tumbling down to the ground of confusion. Thankfully, I had the assistance of two esteemed anthropology professors, both of whom are fluent Quechua speakers and expert at interviewing indigenous peoples. One, Juan Núñez del Prado, is an initiated *paqo* himself. Still, I faced another hurdle that Mails speaks to when he says that anyone who has ever been "invited by some great holy man to do his biography . . . would have learned on the first day they sat together that the information would not flow freely out of his informant. The informant might want to do a book, but he wouldn't have the remotest idea about what doing this entails. Informants are not faucets whose handles can be turned to obtain flowing lyrics." True, true, true.

We in the West are expert talkers. We are eminently verbal and analytical, and we are predisposed to philosophizing. I can attest that the Q'ero are not. They are taciturn, and extremely concrete and pragmatic thinkers. As eager as they were to tell their stories and share their mystical cosmology, the flow of their words was often dammed, and I would have to steer around the dam in order to once again find the course of the stream or pry the blockage loose to get the water trickling again. The maneuvering was worth the effort. However, I relate these difficulties because they are not hidden or written out of this book. Indeed, in my mind they are an important part of the message. It is my belief that the reader who is likely to pick up this book is also the reader who is, and no doubt has been for some time, on a personal spiritual journey. You have probably attended workshops and read widely in the perennial philosophy, and thus you are an expert in the narrative of mysticism. You by now intuitively know how it is supposed to sound. But what this book will demonstrate is that when you are face to face with the mystics, you may be shocked at how different the narrative can be. I suspect that just as Fools Crow was not quite as articulate or cohesive as Mails made him out to be on paper, so don Juan Matus was not as eloquent as Carlos Castaneda made him sound. Mails relates a telling anecdote about Fools Crow's reaction to hearing the words of Black Elk read to him from John Neihardt's classic, *Black Elk Speaks*. Fools Crow flatly proclaimed, "That is not my uncle, Black Elk." I predict that many of you may have much the same reaction as you read this book, especially those of you whose only exposure to Peruvian mysticism has been through fiction, such as *The Celestine Prophecy*, or Western teachers of Andean mysticism.

Considering such pitfalls, I decided in this book to risk continuity of style in order to balance my role as *interpreter* with my role as *recorder*. I recognize my duty as a writer and as a paqo— an initiate and practitioner of the Andean path—to introduce you to and establish the framework for the world of Andean mysticism. But I also want you to be able to hear the Q'ero, just as they sounded to me and as they would sound to you if you were speaking with them. I want you not only to be my companion along the path of Andean mysticism, but also to be looking over my shoulder as we sit in circle listening to the Q'ero tell us about the joys and fears they experienced during their initiations into the sacred priesthood; about heavy and light energy and all the other specifics of the *kawsay pacha*, the world of living energy; about the journey to the land of the dead and beyond. I want you to hear their voices, not mine, and to get a feel for the rhythms and cadences, the brevity and intensity, of a Peruvian story told by an Andean master paqo. In order to allow the reader to vicariously experience the Q'ero—to, as it were, see through their eyes and feel with their hearts—I have, in Part II of this book, reproduced my interviews with the Q'ero as closely as possible to how they actually happened, with the give and take and verbal asides that occur between interviewer and interviewee. My own questions and difficulties in understanding are not glossed over. I am a fellow seeker, no doubt experiencing a spiritual journey similar at heart with yours. I claim no special insight.

First, however, in Part I, I provide you a comprehensive overview of the Peruvian mystical system as it is practiced in the mountains of south-central Peru. These somewhat complex, more encyclopedic chapters are a primer on Peruvian mysticism and provide the fundamental and necessary context for understanding the Q'ero interviews and for completing the exercises in Part III. The information provided in these chapters reveals a mystical-shamanic tradition that is millennia old and yet thrives robustly to this day in the hearts and minds of the Andean people. As you will quickly discover, it is not the shamanism of Carlos Castaneda or Lynn Andrews or even Victor Sanchez. You won't find shamanic or psychotropic-induced journeys to other dimensions or to realms inhabited by inorganic beings. Instead you will find an eminently pragmatic sacred tradition that provides tools for living in harmony with nature, with the spirit realms, and with your fellow human beings. This is a system replete with practices whose goals are to provide ways for all of us to live with well-being in the challenging world of flesh and blood, and yet to live simultaneously as energy beings who are in continual interchange with the kawsay pacha, the universe of animating energy. It is also a cosmology that looks forward with hope and optimism to the conscious evolution of humankind. It is my hope that you will take your time in these opening chapters, absorbing the fundamentals of Andean cosmology and its unique blend of utilitarianism and utopianism, of pragmatism and mystery.

In these opening chapters, I necessarily write as interpreter of the Andean mystical system and as a paqo initiated into that system. In the interview chapters of Part II, I allow you to eavesdrop on the Q'ero as they talk about themselves and the world of Andean mysticism. Part III, however, is where you may, if you are so moved, put these shamanic practices into use in your own life. The exercises of Part III are offered with the hope that you may find greater well-being as a human being and as a spiritual being through an enhanced interaction with the kawsay pacha. These exercises demonstrate the wide applicability of Andean mysticism. You don't have to travel to Peru to be an "Andean" mystic, you have only to believe, as Andeans do, that you are in energetic interchange with the world of living energy. These exercises help you attune to and gain control of your own energy body and begin to put into use the practical, spiritual, and energetic "tools" of an Andean shaman.

I did not consider how to organize this book in a vacuum. Actually, the reverse was true. During the drafting stage of this book, I experienced considerable pressure from colleagues and potential publishers to introduce you to the Q'ero and to Andean mysticism by relating my own adventures along the sacred path, focusing on the mysterious, the otherworldly—those experiences with the metaphysical world that readers have come to expect in books about shamanism and mysticism, for instance in the works of Castaneda, Andrews, Sanchez, or other metaphysical adventurers. But I decided that, ethically, I could not make the "unusual" the focus of this book. I decided I would not write to the lowest common denominator of the metaphysical—the impulse for the enigmatic—because I have learned that real spiritual work, mystical, shamanic, or otherwise, is not practiced in the otherworld, but in the here-and-now, in the harried, anxiety-filled, self-interested world that most of us wake up to every day. It is this world that is most affected, most transformed by metaphysical training. It is this world that immersion into the mystical reveals to be the nemesis, the trickster, the chimera. It is this world—which seeks to ground us in our bodies and limit our vision and subvert our belief that the cosmos is alive and conscious—that demands to be transformed by first transforming ourselves.

But such alchemy is not wrought only from a magical encounter with a nature spirit high on a snow-capped peak or the experience of slipping the bounds of space-time under the influence of a psychotropic drug during a jungle ceremony. What is truly transformational and magical is knowing that every moment, no matter how seemingly mundane, is pregnant with wonder, *and then fully living that moment.* The metamorphic instant occurs instead when you can pull back the curtain of the most intensely "supernatural" experience and recognize the fat man with the fancy hat as the wizard who only plays at being a wizard because he has forgotten that he already is a wizard. That wizard is, of course, you—and me, and him, and her. . . .

However, it is no doubt true that the more spectacular and out-of-this-world our experiences, the more we are inclined to question the rules about reality we have all been force-fed since birth. It is true that I have had plenty of wild and woolly experiences: I have merged consciousness with *Mama Killa,* the moon; I have seen and dialogued with spirits, including an Inka, who patiently showed me how to "walk the rocks" along the Inca Trail and who told me the story of the Hummingbird King.

I have felt energy, and seen it—a streak of brilliant blue light whipping across time and space in the sacred ruins of Machu Picchu. These experiences kept me off balance enough to recognize my own complacency and complicity in buying into the scientific-materialist belief system. Although I have seen and felt these things, they are not especially important parts of my journey along the Andean path. They are not the tools I have learned to use in order to live life consciously. *To live life consciously.* That is what the practice of mysticism or the choice of a spiritual path is all about. It is not only about nonjudgment, unconditional love, forgiveness, patience, developing intuition, interacting with the energy that animates the cosmos, including your own. It is also about being *conscious* of your every action, thought, feeling, emotion, intention, intuition, dream, and vision. It is about *bridging* worlds, not being immersed in either the mundane or the magical; and it is about having the courage to leap from the bridge into multidimensionality with your eyes open and no bungee cord attached to your ankles. It is about conscious fluidity.

In *practice* being a shaman or a mystic is about living the principles of your spiritual path every day in your own humble way, not running to exotic places in search of unusual experiences. It is not the Hollywood moment, but the state of your being during rush hour traffic or after spending hours with a crying child or when you've just burnt the last piece of toast. It is about not only recognizing the miraculous in the seemingly mundane, but experiencing the miraculousness of the mundane.

And so when I decided to write about the Q'ero, for reasons that will become clear in the Introduction to this book, I had to make some crucial choices. In addition to the narrative and organizational decisions I have already discussed, I chose to make the following decisions for the following reasons, reasons that have everything to do with you—the reader. I chose to keep myself out of the book as much as possible. This book is not about me, it's about the Q'ero, keepers of the ancient knowledge of Peru. I decided to expect my reader to look beneath the razzle-dazzle in order to appreciate touching a culture untainted by Western mystical expectation. What is a Peruvian mystic really like after all the Western students and tourists have gone home? I cannot tell you—not really. I can tell you my experience of the Andean path and the paqos I have worked with, but my experience may not be your experience. However, the Q'ero *can* tell you. In their *own* words. The Andean tradition is theirs, part of every fiber of their being. It is the tradition of their fathers and grandfathers, of their ancestors back to a time beyond the count of a calendar. The knowledge that the world is a world of living energy is carried in their genes, entwined in the spiral of their DNA. It is not a premise to be proved or disproved, as it necessarily is for many of us. And yet the Q'ero struggle, just as we do. If nothing else, this book will somewhat demystify the mystics. For they reveal themselves as human, vulnerable, subject to the same fears and foibles as the rest of us. If you are curious about what the mystics of Peru *really* think and feel and practice, then you have picked up the right book, for within these pages a mystical tradition is revealed from the *mystics'* own perspective. This is a perspective that I find wholly underrepresented in the popular marketplace. So, as I address your possible expectations, I am trying to be as honest as I can with those of you who may have an appetite only for dessert. I would like to suggest that you will find more sustenance with the main meal, despite its perceived lack of culinary flair. Like the Q'ero, you will eat potatoes, not filet mignon!

The decision to reproduce the interviews was complicated by the fact that there were several people present for most of them. So that readers can clearly follow the conversations, I have introduced the people who appear in this book, and explained their relationships, below.

I have worked with the Q'ero or their mestizo students since 1993, yet I met with the Q'ero only once for *structured* interviews: for four days in Urubamba, Peru, in July 1996. Accompanying me to Peru were two close friends who are also paqos of Andean mysticism, Anamaria Szendroi, who helped with the Spanish translations during the interviews, and Sandra Corcoran. Present for the entire four days of interviews, they also have an important presence in the middle section of this book. Also present in Urubamba was Dr. Ricardo Valderrama Fernández, an anthropology professor at Universidad Nacional San Antonio Abad del Cusco and a recognized expert in recording the oral histories of the Andean indigenous peoples. He provided the Quechua translations during the interviews. Dr. Juan Núñez del Prado, a professor of anthropology at Universidad Nacional San Antonio Abad del Cusco and an initiated *kuraq akulleq* (fourth-level paqo, or master shaman) in the Andean mystical priesthood, was also present. He not only handled all the logistical arrangements in Peru, but he provided translation assistance and expert commentary during the interviews. Juan is one of the most powerful of all teachers of Andean mysticism, uniquely blending an immense intelligence with a boundless love and a profound respect for the mystical tradition that has so transformed his own life. To my mind there is no better—or rarer—combination of attributes in a teacher. He is truly a collaborator in this book.

Below is a list of the Q'ero who participated in the Urubamba interviews, their ages, titles, and the particular village in Q'ero at which they were living at the time of these interviews:

Don Mariano Apasa Marchaqa, 48, kuraq akulleq from Qollpa
   K'uchu
Doña Agustina Apasa, 38, pampa mesayoq and don Mariano's wife
Don Juan Pauqar Espinosa, 42, alto mesayoq from Chua Chua
Don Agustín Pauqar Qapa, 32, pampa mesayoq from Q'ero Totorani
Don Juan Pauqar Flores, 56, from Chua Chua, pampa mesayoq and
   often an adviser to don Manuel Q'espi and other paqos
Don Julian Pauqar Flores, 47, from Chua Chua, don Juan's brother,
   also a pampa mesayoq; served as "president" of Q'ero in 1994

I met with don Juan Pauqar Espinosa and don Agustín Pauqar
Qapa again in October 1996, on the Hopi reservation in Arizona,
during the first trip ever by a Q'ero to the United States. During
this trip they met with their northern brothers, the Hopi, and
joined the "energy bubble" of South America with that of North
America at the San Francisco Peaks, the most sacred site of the
Hopi. While I did not formally interview them at any length during this trip, I did get a chance to hear their initiation stories
again and to clear up some ambiguities and discrepancies.

    I also worked extensively with the Q'ero in 1997, while
undergoing the ten-day kuraq akulleq initiation, the Hatun
Karpay, and while participating in research with Don Wright
about Peruvian whistling vessels.[2] The Q'ero I've specifically
worked with, besides those named above, have included José
Q'espi Marchaqa, Martín Pauqar Qapa, Martín Q'espi, Lorenzo
Q'espi Apasa, Humberto Sonqo, Guillermo Sonqo, Turibio
Q'espi Lonasqo, Benito Apasa Lonasqo, Isidro Q'espi Marchaqa,
Modesto Q'espi, don Sebástian, and don Bernadino,[3] some of
whose stories are recorded in this book. However, there are three
other paqos whose presence permeate this book. One I have
worked with; the other two are deceased and I know of them only
through their reputations and the work of their students. These

three masters are don Manuel Q'espi and don Andreas Espinosa, of Q'ero; and don Benito Qoriwaman, of Wasau. Don Manuel is a kuraq akulleq and the eldest paqo in Q'ero. He is also the son-in-law of the famed kuraq don Andreas Espinosa. I have briefly visited don Manuel's village of Chua Chua and there received the *Karpay Ayni* initiation from him while sitting on a pile of tiny frozen potatoes in his hut. I have also worked with don Manuel several times over the last several years in and around the Sacred Valley.

Don Andreas Espinosa, who died in November 1981, is still spoken of in Q'ero with reverence as one of the greatest paqos of modern times. He not only helped teach and initiate most of the Q'ero paqos interviewed for this book, but he was a primary teacher to and profound influence on two of my mestizo teachers, Américo Yábar and Juan Núñez del Prado.

Don Benito Qoriwaman, who died on April 8, 1988, was a recognized master of the Waskar lineage who lived and worked in the "town of sorcerers" just outside of Cuzco. He was a friend to don Andreas, spent a considerable amount of time in Q'ero, and also profoundly influenced both my mestizo teachers.

Finally, I would like to introduce one other paqo whose presence permeates this book—Américo Yábar. He is a mestizo who was trained and initiated as a kuraq by the Q'ero. He teaches Andean shamanism around the world, and I have the good fortune not only to have been trained by him, but to call him friend. I traveled with Américo and four other women paqos around Peru and Bolivia for two weeks in June 1995, and much of what I learned during that time I have passed on in this book in Américo's own unique and highly poetic voice.

Finally, a note about the Quechua spellings. Quechua, the administrative language of the Inkas and the indigenous language of Peru, historically was not a written language, but it has been transliterated by historians and scholars. There are various "official" Quechua dictionaries, and for this book I primarily relied upon the 1995 first edition of *Diccionario Quechua* published in Cuzco by the Academia Mayor de la Lengua Quechua, and the advice of Ricardo Valderrama and Juan Núñez del Prado. For example, "Inka" is spelled with a "k" rather than the Castilian "c." In addition, I have not used the proper plurals for Quechua words. In Quechua the plural is indicated by the suffix *-kuna*. A few examples: the generic term for an Andean mystic is *paqo* and a mountain spirit is called an *Apu*. The plural of these terms would be written, respectively, as *paqokuna* and *Apukuna*. For the sake of clarity with readers, however, I have chosen to follow the convention of many other English-language authors and write the plural of Quechua words with an "s" suffix: *paqos* and *Apus*. (Refer to the Glossary for definitions and approximate pronunciations of selected Quechua terms used in this book.)

Introduction

The writing of this book began long before I ever picked up a pen, turned on a tape recorder, or switched on a computer. It's difficult to decipher exactly where the first seeds were sown. This book may have germinated at midnight, January 1, 1994, during a New Year's pipe ceremony, when I prayed with the *chanunpa* that I would walk the Inca Trail, the road of the shamans, to Machu Picchu with my closest friends, whom I had met during my journey along the Andean path.

Or perhaps it began high in the mountains of Peru, when a Q'ero *kuraq akulleq*, or master shaman, named don Mariano Apasa Marchaqa agreed to come down from his village to meet a group of spiritual seekers from the United States.

Maybe it really sprung into being in a run-down hacienda, in August 1994, at the completion of the now very real Inca Trail trek, when, exhausted and sore, I sat on the cold floor of a shadowy room in a circle with twenty-six fellow trekkers, two teachers, and two Q'ero shamans—and one of those teachers called my name. . . .

Salqa Wasi, which means something like the house of the "undomesticated" or "wild" energy, is located in the village of Mollomarqa, in the Andes mountains of Peru, about halfway between Paucartambo and Q'ero. The compound of three rather dilapidated stucco buildings is the ancestral home of Américo Yábar, one of my teachers. A mestizo, Américo has been trained by the Q'ero and initiated as a kuraq akulleq in the Andean mystical hierarchy. Salqa Wasi was in the process of being turned into a place of learning, where the North American and European students of Américo, and of his colleagues who teach Andean shamanism, could come to meet with and be trained by the Q'ero. I had come here with my husband and twenty-five others, all of whom had walked the Inca Trail and worked energetically at Machu Picchu under the tutelage of Alberto Villoldo and Américo, teachers of Andean shamanism. We had been joined in Cuzco by two Q'ero mystics: don Mariano Apasa Marchaqa, a kuraq akulleq, and don Juan Ordoñus, a *pampa mesayoq* (keeper of the earth rituals) and assistant to don Mariano.

On this night, our second at Salqa Wasi, we gathered in a circle, sitting on stiff alpaca furs on the wooden floor of the frigid great room. Two sputtering candles, precariously balanced in pools of melted wax atop overturned aluminum cans, cast the room in a gauzy yellow glow. Against one wall, at the "head" of the circle, sat Alberto, don Mariano, Américo, and don Juan. They had just completed a *despacho* ceremony, a ceremony of thanksgiving to the nature spirits and a divination of our group's energy. Two of our group, Jessie and Lynne, had been instructed to go outside with don Juan to build the fire in which the despacho bundle would be burned as an offering. When they returned, don Juan reported that the smoke had risen straight and had been filled with refined energy. Our offering had been accepted by the *Apus*, the spirits of the mountains.

Now Américo, who spoke Quechua—the indigenous language of Peru—whispered with don Mariano, who sat statuelike under his red ceremonial poncho. Through Alberto, who translated Américo's Spanish to English, Américo announced that five "students" would be called forward. I, and I'm sure everyone else in the group, had no idea what being "called forward" entailed. Alberto began by calling Lynne. She scooted forward a few feet until she was squatting on her knees before don Mariano. He stared intently into her eyes, selected a stone of power—called a *khuya*—from his bundle of personal ritual objects, and began to speak, to give what I can only characterize as an energy reading. Américo translated to Spanish and then Alberto translated to English as don Mariano, placing the khuya in Lynne's palm, told her it represented the "head," a stone of transmission of the mystical lineage that she should guard and protect. She was admonished never to lose the stone or to give it away. Jessie was next. Don Mariano also placed a khuya in her palm and then praised her for her intelligence, strength, and power. As Jessie retreated to the periphery of the circle, Sandy was called forward, given a power stone, and acknowledged simply and beautifully as a woman of pure heart. Then I heard my name called. Like everyone else, I suppose, I had been secretly hoping to be called forward, to be acknowledged by don Mariano. But when it actually happened, a wave of apprehension passed through me. For a second I wondered if I dare interact eye to eye, energy body to energy body with don Mariano, who seemed, in the smoky glow of the flickering candles, powerful and enigmatic.

I moved the few feet forward to sit before him and nervously raised my eyes to meet his. They were black beyond expression, and unsettling. I felt him place a small khuya in my open palm, and glancing down I saw a white stone, about an inch and a half long, barrel shaped, and deeply pitted with dark spots. Then don Mariano began to speak, his eyes unwavering, locked onto mine. "You have much work to do in order to gain control of your energy." My mind whirled. *Oh my god*, I thought, *everyone else was praised and I'm being criticized.* I cut off the self-involved thought, but I felt vulnerable, exposed. Now, when I most needed to, I couldn't control my attention, never mind my energy body. "You must work hard," don Mariano continued. "If you succeed, then the way will be open for the word to flow forth. You will bring the word of Q'ero to the world." I flinched in surprise, not so much at his prediction, which barely registered at the time, as at the fact that he had seen who I was, he had somehow known I was a writer. How could he know that? I hardly knew Américo and it was obvious that Alberto was spontaneously choosing people to call forward, so it didn't seem reasonable that they could have prompted don Mariano with information. My skeptical, rational mind was in a whirl. This wasn't simply a blessing from a shaman; don Mariano actually knew something very concrete about me—from my energy field. I wondered what else he was seeing.

Then I heard Américo and Alberto translating once again: don Mariano was counseling me that when I sit down to write I should think about him, call to him to come and assist me, and he would. As I stumbled back to my place in the circle, my husband, John, was being called forward. I barely heard don Mariano's prediction about a new job path he would soon embark upon.

The next day I spotted don Mariano sitting on the lawn behind the hacienda's main building with Pépe, who had been one of our guides on the Inca Trail. I cautiously approached, wary of interrupting their conversation. Pépe smiled and waved me forward. He translated as I thanked don Mariano for the gift of the khuya. Then I asked permission to ask a question. Pépe translated for me: "What did you mean when you said I would bring the word of Q'ero to the world?" What I was really asking, but was afraid to, was, "Do you *really* mean I will one day write about the Q'ero? Can that be possible?"

Pépe listened intently to don Mariano's reply and then translated: "'Do your work. Work hard to master your energy. Learn to extend your energies up to the Apus, and I will meet you there and give you much information.'" At a loss for words, I thanked don Mariano and rose to leave. Don Mariano spoke again, and Pépe caught my arm. "There is more. He says that he blesses you, your family, your house, and your job."

• • •

So went my first trip to Peru. At that time I had been studying shamanism and the Andean mystical tradition for little more than a year, having been attracted to this realm of exploration through reading the autobiographies of various spiritual adventurers. I have always been an avid reader, especially about metaphysics and the perennial philosophy, and at the time of my introduction to shamanism I had recently left a doctoral program in literature. But I have never been the outdoors type, preferring the intellectual world to the physical, so I was caught off guard by the psychic pull I felt toward shamanism, which is a perceptual practice grounded in intense, personal interaction with the natural world. The more I read about shamanism, however, the more I wanted to know—and the more I wanted to *experience* this world of living energy myself. Although I had been meditating for nearly twenty years, my practice of mantra meditation had been rather undisciplined and sporadic. Meditation had helped me make significant positive changes in my life, attitudes, and perceptions, but I sensed shamanism could do what meditation alone had not: help me embrace Oneness but also help me live fully and divinely in the physical. So I began by stepping out of my mind and into my body. I slowly acquainted myself with the natural world, first by taking lazy walks in the state conservation lands around our home and then by sharing increasingly ambitious hikes with my husband. I tried to be aware of my surroundings, not just to see, hear, and smell the natural world around me but to shift my perception in order to experience my interconnections with it. I have always been very intuitive, experiencing what are commonly called psychic experiences, but my immersion into the physical precipitated a whole new kind of awakening. I felt whole—a fusion of body, mind, and spirit—for the first time in my life. It seemed a natural transition, then, for my husband and me to "intend" our meditations toward meeting teachers who could guide us into the multidimensional realms of the shamanic universe. We were particularly interested in Andean mysticism, although if I had been asked at that time to explain why this particular metaphysical tradition of all traditions was the one that called me, I would have been hard pressed to answer. Very simply, the Andean concept of *ayni*—reciprocity—seemed a beautiful way to engage the world, and the Andean concept of nature spirits— *Pachamama*, Mother Earth; *Mama Killa*, the moon; *Inti*, the sun; and the *Apus*, the spirits of the mountains—seemed as familiar as family. The pull of Peru was as intense as any impulse toward home I had ever experienced while living away from my family in various places in the United States.

One day, a few months into this new shamanic pursuit, I received a complimentary copy of a New Age magazine. As I flipped through, my gaze fell upon a small ad for a workshop on Inka shamanism. My husband and I attended, and, to be truthful, it was not a very successful weekend for me. But a curious series of synchronicities, too complex to explain here but involving eagles, my deceased father, and my deceased best friend from graduate school, convinced me that there was

something about the weekend and its shamanic work to which
I had not been attentive. So I decided to give the workshop
route another try and continued to work with this teacher.
Before long, my husband and I were intensely involved with him
and volunteering our time to the educational organization he
founded and through which he conducts his shamanic training.
We worked with him for a year and a half, and during that time
we became well-grounded in his synthesis of North and South
American shamanism. Through him, we met other teachers,
such as Américo Yábar, and many others who would become
lifelong friends along the path, and we dreamed of traveling to
Peru.

Now, we had just completed the Inca Trail trek and met the
Q'ero for the first time. My two weeks in Peru had been, quite
literally, eye-opening, enabling me to perceive the world of
spirit—the kawsay pacha—and to connect with my energy body
in new ways that were deeply nurturing and liberating. However,
although I was satisfied with my slow but steady progress upon
the sacred path, I was growing steadily more unhappy with my
teacher and what I perceived as his inability to truly "walk
his talk." Soon I was to be very grateful to don Mariano for his
blessing, for less than five months after this trip to Peru I made
the decision to seek out new teachers and new levels of training.
By parting ways with this teacher, however, I had broken my primary—my *only*—link to Peru, and I wondered how I would ever
continue to be trained in the Andean tradition. Over many
months I reached deep within myself to maintain a solid and
trusting center, and I consistently practiced shamanic techniques to stay connected with my energy body, to cleanse it of
heavy energy, and draw into it the refined energy of the *hanaq
pacha*, the upper world. Every night I slept with the khuya, the
stone of power, don Mariano had given me, and I routinely did

ceremony to call in new teachers and new pathways back to Peru and to the Q'ero. Soon doors did begin to open, new teachers did appear—sometimes by the most amazing "coincidences." I learned a huge lesson in trusting Spirit and in walking *my* talk.

By May 1995, I was back in Peru: I spent a month there, training and traveling to sacred sites with two different teachers, Juan Núñez del Prado and Américo Yábar. With Juan and seven others, I found myself on horseback headed for the Q'ero villages and the Q'ollorit'i festival, a sacred festival held at the base of a glacier that is an ancient site of initiation for *paqos*, practitioners of the Andean mystical tradition. After Q'ollorit'i, I and four women friends, all paqos, worked in the Sacred Valley around Cuzco with Américo Yábar. We then traveled to Nazca and to the Islands of the Moon and Sun in Lake Titicaca. Nearly everywhere I and my companions went, there were Q'ero to teach us, including the two noted Q'ero kuraqs don Mariano Apasa and don Manuel Q'espi. The evening of the summer solstice of 1995 found me and my fellow paqos sitting under the stars at Pikillaqta with Américo and six Q'ero mystics, old and young, who performed a despacho ceremony, gave us two *karpays* (energetic transmissions or initiations), and then told us magical stories about the puma, the rainbow, the condor.

During the next year I wrote about what I learned, often collaborating with others who walked the path with me. When I sat down to write I would throw my energy filaments up to the Apus to draw upon don Mariano's energy. I must have succeeded, for my writing was being published and a diverse range of people were contacting me, expressing interest in the Q'ero cosmology. The word of Q'ero was beginning to be told, through my efforts and those of a few others. But it was obvious that a project of a much more in-depth nature was needed, and soon. My intuition and instincts were telling me that time was working against the Q'ero.

One reason for my concern is that there are few kuraq akulleqs left in Q'ero. One of the most respected, don Manuel Q'espi, is in his late seventies. When he passes, one of the last of the Q'ero paqos who live relatively isolated in the mountains will be gone. Another reason is that the younger paqos, such as don Mariano and others, who are in their forties and fifties, have increasing contact with foreigners through teachers from the United States who bring their students to Peru. As more and more spiritual seekers travel to Peru and as the Q'ero seek to alleviate their grinding material poverty by accepting foreigners' money and goods, the integrity of the mystical tradition is subject to enormous pressure. In addition, as this spiritual tradition is translated for consumption by other cultures, it is subject to inevitable dilution.

Although I acknowledge the wise advice Juan Núñez del Prado once gave me that it is patronizing to "sentimentalize the Indians," the fact remains that the Q'ero have little experience with outsiders. The first anthropological expedition to Q'ero was mounted in 1955, by anthropologist Oscar Núñez del Prado, Juan's father. Being the analytical scientist, he had only passing interest in the Q'ero mystical tradition, although he recorded many Q'ero myths and stories and documented their cosmology. But times, and anthropologists, have changed. Unfortunately, for many tour operators and shamanic workshop teachers, indigenous spiritual wisdom is a much sought-after commodity. The Q'ero, who have lived relatively isolated in villages high in the mountains, venturing out only as far as Cuzco, are stepping into a world whose values they can barely fathom. I find it unsettling to imagine how their lives, and perhaps their spiritual practices and beliefs, will change under the increasing encroachment of foreign contact.

I am not an alarmist. The mystical system will live on, as it has for countless centuries, because these beliefs and practices, which are so provocative and liberating for us, are simply everyday life for a Q'ero farmer, as natural and necessary to him as his own breathing process. But if history is our teacher, we have cause for concern. In the sixteenth century the Spanish conquest of Peru introduced not only new political and cultural realities, but a new religious authority as well. Catholicism infiltrated every aspect of Andean life, weaving itself deep into the fabric of indigenous spirituality. The Q'ero did not escape this influence, as the stories that follow make clear. Today, new ideologies threaten. Over only the few years I have been studying in Peru, I have seen evidence that this mystical system and some of its teachers risk being compromised. It has become apparent that anyone who ventures to Peru today must do so with his or her eyes open. There are some exquisite teachers whose integrity is beyond question, but there are others for whom the mystery of the Andes is simply good ad copy.

As a foreigner trained in the Andean, and Q'ero, mystical system, I include myself as part of the dilemma I have just outlined. As a writer, particularly, I am in a catch-22 position. Therefore, I must consciously and frequently take a "time out" to evaluate as frankly as possible my actions, words, motives, and heart space. I am selective about the teachers I work with in Peru, and about whom I recommend to others. And I always caution spiritual seekers to understand how belief systems must be translated from culture to culture, and that we cannot, as North Americans, ever "become" a pampa mesayoq, alto mesayoq, or kuraq akulleq, even though we can be initiated to these levels of the mystical "priesthood" and have access to the same energies associated with them.

Despite the potential pitfalls, the fact is that the Q'ero are having increasing contact with foreigners, a contact they mostly desire and welcome. As I worked with my mestizo teachers and the Q'ero, I began to see that, to ensure the accurate representation of their mystical system, a way had to be provided for the Q'ero to speak to outsiders in their *own* words. Theirs is a mystical system that has a depth and beauty equal to any spiritual cosmology in the world. And the Q'ero paqos themselves are complex and irresistibly interesting. There had to be some way for those of us who don't speak Quechua, and who can't continually travel to Peru, to get to know the Q'ero not only as respected mystics but also as multifaceted and vulnerable human beings. There had to be a way to demystify the Q'ero belief system by disengaging it from the worst of the New Age excesses while at the same time preserving its relevance, truth, and integrity. As the idea for this book took form in my imagination, I prayed, performed ceremony, and put out tentative feelers to my Peruvian teachers. I listened to the spirit energies and was alert for their synchronistic messages. It became clear that there was one formidable hurdle I had to overcome—my belief in myself. Could I really pull off such a project? Could I face another horse trip into the mountains? How would I fund such a project? How would I ever deal with the language barriers? How would I get sustained access to the Q'ero? Would the Q'ero even want to talk? As I envisioned the book and formulated a plan for making it a reality, I relied heavily upon Spirit to guide me through the logistical minefield and upon close friends to buoy me with much-needed support and encouragement.

Finally, in early 1996, I worked up the courage to telephone Juan Núñez del Prado and Américo Yábar to explain the idea for this book. But overcome with self-doubt, I hung up the phone before I even finished dialing. I was petrified. Who did I think I was to attempt such a project?

But Spirit persisted in sending me unmistakable messages that this book was my destiny, and finally with the translation help of two friends, Anamaria Szendroi and Jesse Telles, I was able to fully explain my project to my teachers via telephone and fax. Américo expressed immediate interest and support, but ultimately he was too busy traveling and teaching to undertake the project with me. Juan, however, was not only enthusiastic, but he offered to lend me whatever assistance he could. He voiced his opinion that my desire to undertake such a daunting project was a direct result of the energy I had touched, and that had touched me, at the sacred festival of Q'ollorit'i. "Your group was the first I took to Q'ollorit'i with the express purpose of receiving the spiritual sustenance of the Inkas," he explained. "Many Westerners have gone there to investigate the culture, others out of curiosity, and still others with the intent of receiving the spirit of the mountain. But yours was the first group that went as true pilgrims, totally conscious, and with the intent of touching the heart of the prophecy."

Soon the project took on a life of its own. My husband enthusiastically encouraged me to empty our bank account to pay for the research expenses for the book. Juan and I logged hours on the phone, working out the formidable logistics and costs. After months of discussion and planning, in June 1996, Juan arranged for a messenger to ride on horseback the two days to Q'ero, for there are no roads on which vehicles can pass, to explain the project and invite the Q'ero to speak. The Q'ero enthusiastically accepted my invitation, and you are about to read their words and the words of their mestizo students. This is their book. Although technically I am its author, my role more accurately is as conduit. This book is my service to my teachers, my gift of *ayni*—of reciprocity and thanksgiving—for their selfless teachings, support, and empowerment.

I was fortunate during this project to have the assistance of many gifted people, who are acknowledged elsewhere in this book. However, it is primarily through the efforts of Juan Núñez del Prado that the Q'ero paqos who participated in this project entrusted me with their stories, bestowing upon me as a gift the privilege of preserving within these pages a small but significant portion of their personal history and mystical knowledge. This is a gift I have accepted, and which I share with you, with the deepest humility, the profoundest sense of responsibility, and boundless joy.

And so don Mariano Apasa's prediction is fulfilled. The most respected mystics of the Peruvian Andes, the keepers of the ancient knowledge, speak.

Keepers of the Ancient Knowledge

Part I

The Kawsay Pacha: The World of Living Energy

IT WAS MAY 1997, and the sun was setting over the grand ruins of Ollantaytambo, the Temple of the Wind. Modesto Q'espi and Isidro Q'espi Marchaqa, young Q'ero pampa mesay-oqs-in-training, had just released sacred coca leaves into the wind. Earlier, I, too, had performed this prayerful ritual, gently blowing my finest energies through my breath into the coca leaves. Then, standing on the uppermost platform of the temple and facing into the wind, I had raised my hands above my head and let the coca leaves flutter into space, the wind carrying my energy and prayers into the cosmos. Now, the ceremony complete, I stood off to the side, observing don Modesto. He was tiny, about five feet tall, as most Q'ero are. Lithe and handsome, he carried himself with dignity, moving with grace and gentleness despite his withered right leg. I watched as he turned his youthful, brown face up toward the pink-hued sky, where Mama Killa, the moon, was visible even as Inti, the sun, was sinking behind the mountains. Juan, my teacher and a fluent speaker of Quechua, listened as Modesto pointed toward Mama Killa and told a brief story. Juan waved me over. "He knows Mama Killa," he explained. "He just told me that one day Mama Killa embraced him, carried him into the sky and back in time, to a time before the Runa, human beings, walked the earth." I was taken aback. Since I had met Modesto, only days before, I had, inexplicably, felt a strange and subtle connection with him, and now I understood why: I, too, had been embraced by Mama Killa. Years ago, on my first trip to Peru, I had immersed myself in the sacred, ancient baths at Aguas Calientes under the moon and stars. Sometime during my meditation I had left my body, and my spirit had been drawn by the luminous arms of Mama Killa into her energy field. Tranquility. Sweetness. Expansiveness. Limitlessness. Stillness. Grandeur. I had no words to describe the exquisiteness of the experience. Now, the memory alone was enough to raise goose bumps. I asked Juan to inquire of Modesto if Mama Killa had spoken to him, bestowed any teaching upon him. Juan asked the question and replied, "No. He says she was silent. And the world that existed before the Runa also was silent." I restrained my impulse to reach out to Modesto and hug him. Instead, I asked Juan to tell Modesto of my own mystical union with Mama Killa. As Juan translated, Modesto's eyes remained fixed on mine. His face was unreadable, absolutely expressionless, but his eyes were bright and intense. When Juan finished my story, Modesto reached up and embraced me, tenderly patting my back as he whispered in my ear. Juan, leaning close, translated: "You are my sister. My sister of the moon."

Chapter 1

In the Land of the Inkas: An Overview of Andean Mysticism

"The Q'ero live up where the rains begin, where the clouds originate," says Q'ero-trained mystic Américo Yábar. "They live in the ravines, where the pumas also live. They live where the children grow up enfolded with the natural, cosmic vision." To anyone who has made the arduous horse trip to Q'ero, Américo's words ring true, for the mist-shrouded villages of Q'ero step up the slopes of the central-southern Andes, from the lowest village at the subtropical level, to the picture-post-card-pretty ceremonial village of Hatun Q'ero at about 11,000 feet above sea level, to Chua Chua, a cluster of twenty or so huts at more than 14,500 feet. Throughout the year, the five hundred or so Q'ero migrate from village to village according to the cycle of planting, from sowing the corn at the lowest level to planting potatoes and herding alpaca and llama at the highest. Despite the utter normality of their agrarian life, a life of relentless toil and precarious subsistence not unlike that of most other indige-nous peoples of the Peruvian Andes, the Q'ero are different, distinct, set apart from their contemporaries because they, more than any other indigenous population in the Andes, have pre-served the ancient spiritual practices. "The Q'ero people," describes writer César Calvo, "to this day dress like Inkas, con-verse like Inkas, and live like Inkas. . . ."[1] Calvo was writing in the early 1980s, but today, more than fifteen years later, the

Q'ero mystique remains. They no longer live in such stringent isolation, yet the Q'ero retain their reputation as the keepers of the ancient ways, as having preserved the indigenous belief system not only of the Inkas but of those who came before them. They call themselves the "grandsons of Inkarí," the mythical first Inka, who founded the *Tawantinsuyu*, the Inka empire, and who bequeathed to the Q'ero the mystical tradition. The Q'ero mystics are the most respected *paqos*, or practitioners, of the Andean mystical path.[2] Paqos from all over the Cuzco area, even though they may have been fully initiated by teachers from their own region and lineage, still journey to Q'ero to receive the *karpays*—the initiation rites—from Q'ero elders.

Although the Q'ero are recognized masters of the Andean mystical-shamanic tradition, the tradition itself is widespread and flows deep within the veins of the indigenous population. In order to understand not only the Q'ero, but all native Andeans, one must first attempt to see through their eyes and feel with their hearts a nature that is alive and responsive, in which spirit suffuses the physical world, from the highest, snow-capped peak to the deepest, vine-tangled jungle. From the *alto mesayoq* who makes a ritual coca offering to an *Apu*, the spirit of the mountain, before he seeks its counsel, to the villager who spills a few drops of *chica*[3] on the ground to slake Mother Earth's (*Pachamama's*) thirst before his own, to the pregnant woman who claims the rainbow impregnated her when she inadvertently saw its reflection in the river, Andeans share an interconnectedness with the cosmos that is at once humble and profound.

Andeans are born into a world that they believe is as conscious of them as they are of it. "The great message of the Andes, the greatest belief of the Andes with respect to humanity," claims Américo Yábar, "is our approximation of spirit with nature, with Pachamama, with the wind, sun, and stars. This is the constant invitation of the Andean world—that the world is populated by spirit." This invitation toward consciousness of a living cosmos should be accepted by all people, he says, because "there are no better teachers than life and the spirits of nature, for theirs is an open language. Through them we become aware of how entrapped we are by our [rational] minds. Through them we can also become aware that every decision is one of feeling, speaking, and moving on this planet with heart."

To immerse yourself in the mysticism of Peru, it is necessary to divest yourself of mind and center yourself in heart. I first glimpsed this truth during my first meeting with don Mariano Apasa Marchaqa, when he predicted that one day I would write this book. It has taken more than three years for me to move from my head to my heart, the space from which this book flows, but for another of my Q'ero-trained teachers, Juan Núñez del Prado, this lesson was taught on his first meeting with a noted kuraq akulleq, don Benito Qoriwaman. Juan says, "It all began for me when I was very young, doing my academic work. I was trying to do a report about social structures and I was working in a little town near Qotobamba. At that time I was totally a rationalist and an atheist. For me the [supernatural] beliefs of the Indians were just another religion.

"But then I had the opportunity to go work in several communities, almost all in this area, and I discovered that there was a very structured system of beliefs, of supernatural beliefs, that were applicable to a large area and not only to one or two little communities. It was a much broader system than I thought, and I discovered it belonged to a greater area of the Andes. My interest was raised, so I asked my mentor to change my special research area from the study of social structures to that of the religious system. I thought there must be something special going on to preserve such an ancient system until these modern times. So I returned back to Cuzco to study, to look for the structure of that religious system. What I found was amazing!

"I found a very complex structure of 'priests.' These shamans were practicing mysticism: they were on the shamanistic path, where you depend only on your personal experience. I discovered a kind of underground church—with 'priests,' initiations, practices, and prophecies.

"Of course, as an academic, my first thought was of gaining prestige through uncovering and explaining this system. For that reason, I sought to meet the highest priest in the hierarchy. I learned that there were two masters in the valley, one in the north and one in the south. I met the master of the north, and he taught me many things. Then I began looking for the other master, the master of the south. One day I met a fat, little man; he was an Indian, dressed in dirty clothes, and he lived in a little house, very little and uncomfortable, and the name of that man was don Benito Qoriwaman.

"At that time I couldn't speak Quechua well, so I hired the services of an assistant, Manuel, to serve as translator. I took him with me to meet with don Benito. We also carried traditional gifts for the master—a bottle of *pisco* [alcohol] and a little packet of coca leaves. When we met with don Benito, he had an incredible twinkling in his eyes, and he invited us into his house to share these gifts. We sat at a little table, and he poured a little cup, the size of a shot glass, of pisco. As we began our talk, don Benito passed the little cup of alcohol. We drank that and we start talking, using the assistance of the translator, Manuel. Soon, don Benito passed another tiny cup of pisco, and then he started to talk directly to me, instead of to Manuel, using a mix of Spanish and Quechua. I talked with him in Spanish and used the few Quechua words I knew. Then he passed the third cup of pisco.

"After the third tiny cup, he looked me in the eyes and he started to talk to me in a very strange language, not Spanish, not Quechua, not Chinese—not any language I recognized then, or since. The incredible thing was I could understand everything he said. What's more, I could speak this same strange language—fluently! We had a long talk, two hours of talking like that. And what was even more strange was that I could see what he was talking about, as if there were a movie camera in my brain projecting images!

"But during that time, everything seemed normal. I asked don Benito many things, and he provided me a lot of information. It was like reading a book in two hours. It was fantastic!

"Finally don Benito brought the meeting to an end. I got up to leave, and that's when I discovered that Manuel was totally drunk. He could usually drink a bottle of whiskey without feeling the effects—it's like lemonade to him. But at that moment, he was completely drunk, from three tiny cups of pisco! I had to carry him out of don Benito's house, and as I was carrying him, I 'woke' up—or something like that. I suddenly knew what had happened, and I knew that something very, very strange had happened there.

"After that, my intellectual paradigm was blown. Before that experience I was an academic, doing intellectual research. After that experience, I became a disciple of don Benito. I discovered he had something very, very, very important to teach me. That experience changed my life."

THE CONSCIOUS WORD

Juan's training, like my own, began with instruction in sensing the energies of the *kawsay pacha*, the world of living energy.[4] For an Andean paqo, the world of nature is alive and responsive,

and the cosmos is a vibrating field of pure energy. Andeans recognize two fundamental types of energy: *sami*, refined energy;
and *hucha*, heavy energy, which is produced only by human
beings. We each are in constant interchange with these energies, in a reciprocal relationship with the kawsay pacha called
ayni. Ayni is the seminal operative principle of behavior and of
being in the Andes. In the social structure, ayni operates as a
system of communal, shared labor, where, for example, farmers
help work their neighbors' fields. Ayni is also a guiding moral
principle, similar to the Christian concept "do unto others as
you would have them do unto you." In this light, ayni operates
as a moral code, a code of personal conduct. Within the mystical cosmology, however, ayni takes on even greater significance,
for it is an implicate, creative principle of the natural world. In
the kawsay pacha, the world of living energy, you are in constant interchange with either heavy or light energy. You mediate
this energy through your energy body, called the *kawsay poq'po*,
which means "energy bubble" in Quechua. Your *poq'po* surrounds and connects with your physical body, and you mediate
energy through it at a chakra-like center near your navel. This
"spiritual stomach" is called the *qosqo*. Like your physical body,
your energy body, or poq'po, has a skin, an outer layer that acts
as a filter and protective barrier. I will discuss the poq'po in
more detail in the next chapter, but the important point for
now is that it is through this energy body that we interchange
energy with other people and with nature spirits in acts of ayni.
Because we are fundamentally energy beings and we live in
a world of living energy, we can never act outside the sphere
of ayni's influence—we can only be conscious or not of its
operating force in our lives.

In the Andes, the kawsay pacha is dominated by two primary spirit energies: *Pachamama* and the *Apus*. Pachamama,

the Earth, is the first Mother, the true Mother, the spirit Mother. From her we have all been given form and substance, and it is largely her will that determines the quantity and quality of our worldly sustenance. It is to her, and to the spirits of the rain and the hail and the other elements that exist within her domain, that Andeans owe the very conditions of their lives. Therefore, every action they undertake is necessarily an act of ayni, or reciprocity, with Pachamama. Before any food is eaten or liquid is drunk, a portion is offered to the Earth Mother. Before a spade is thrust into a field or before a river is crossed or before a thousand other mundane actions are undertaken, an offering is made to the Mother. Every day Andeans perform countless acts of thanksgiving or propitiation to Pachamama, and every day Pachamama bestows her gifts—a healthy child, a multiplying alpaca herd, a productive harvest—or metes out her challenges.

Pachamama also provides multitudinous reference points from which Andeans orient their lives, both physical and spiritual. The natural formation that is physically closest to the place of your birth—be it a mountain, a river, a lagoon, a rock outcrop, whatever—is called your *itu*. According to América Yábar, the itu is the sacred physical space into which you enter this world and the energetic space that first touches the energy filaments of your body. From that first energetic touch, you are part of a physical and spiritual interchange with the living power of nature, with kawsay—the animating energy. Itu actually is the Spanish term for this energy place. The ancient Quechua term is *saiwa*. To be precise, if the natural formation is considered composed of "masculine" energy, it is called an itu/saiwa; if it is considered feminine, it is called a *paqarina*. Sometimes the term itu is used generically to refer to any energy that is dominant at your place of birth or during your formative years, but in reality everyone has both an itu/saiwa and a paqarina associated with his or her place of birth.

In central and southern Peru, the itu is most often a mountain, but a mountain is rarely simply a mountain. It is an Apu—a sacred being, a lord that not only gives presence to the physical mountain but that controls the dialogue with the paqos who are in "service" to it. All paqos are in service to one or more Apus, which comprise the highest level of nature energy and are the most important spiritual guides within the Andean shamanic system. It is through the Apus that the paqos receive wisdom, counsel, and healing knowledge. There is a clear distinction to be made, however, between "service" and "servitude." As Américo explains, "Every living thing in the universe has a relationship of service. To know, first you must serve. This vocation of service doesn't mean that you take an attitude of servitude or you submit your energy to others—absolutely not. But a teacher has to feel whether or not you can serve by visualizing your command of energy." An Apu, then, calls upon an Andean paqo, offering to be his master, only when the Apu itself has determined that the paqo's command of his personal energy is commensurate with the Apu's own power.

Even when you are working at the most elementary level of the Andean mystical system, ideally you should pay homage to the Apus, the lords of the mountains, and begin to develop a dialogue with them. It is customary, upon arriving in Cuzco, to make an offering to the Apus, asking their permission to work in the area and for a blessing to aid you in your work. I remember stopping along the Inca Trail, during the very first day's trek, to "introduce" myself to the Apu Veronica, under whose gaze I was hiking, and to ask her assistance in the physical challenge I knew lay before me. Veronica is this Apu's Spanish name. Its ancient Quechua name is Waqaywillka, which in the mystical system translates to the Mountain of Black Light, the black-light energy being one of the most powerful in the Andes. After my appeal to Apu Veronica, I felt protected during what turned out to be an excruciatingly painful trek, and just when I thought I could not take another step, an apparition appeared to teach me how to "walk the rocks." A gift from Apu Veronica? Who knows? I simply know that after my "lesson" by this phantasmagoric Inka, I flew down the steepest part of the trail without hesitation or fear, making up hours and miles so that instead of walking dead last, as I had been for three days, I ended up following the first group of trekkers, the leaders, through the Gate of the Sun into Machu Picchu.

Paqos interact with Apus in magical ways that widely affect the lives of those around them. They may call upon an Apu for a blessing, for good weather for crops, to impart healing power, or for protection. The Q'ero tell several stories that describe the awesome powers of these lords of the mountains. In Urubamba, don Juan Pauqar Flores told us about a powerful Q'ero alto mesayoq who, in his words, was "almost as God." The story was told to him by his grandmother, but the other Q'ero had heard other versions of it as well, and each contributed details.

This alto mesayoq's name was Garibilu Q'espi, and he lived in the late nineteenth and early twentieth centuries. He was a master who could invoke the power of the Apus for any purpose. In his time, the story goes, disease and pestilence, such as smallpox, had come to Q'ero. Although the diseases were recognized as having been transmitted from mestizos traveling through the area, the Q'ero energetically attributed them to a particular Apu, who was the "owner of all the sicknesses." Many people were dying, don Juan reported. "They were dying in the fields and near the rivers, falling like mice. Only a few children survived—the children who drank the milk from their dead mothers, only they survived."⁵ The situation throughout Q'ero was desperate. There were so many sick and dying people that there were none to remove all the bodies. "When the animals came, the pumas and other carnivores," don Juan explained, "the people still living could not prevent them from eating the dead people."

Soon Garibilu Q'espi himself fell sick, from yellow fever, which had been sent by this same Apu. He became desperately ill, even suffering from convulsions. But Garibilu Q'espi was a great paqo, and he recognized that the Apu had sent the yellow fever as a tool. In the Andes, everything, even disease, has an energetic connection, and in this case, the yellow fever sent by the Apu as a sickness became, in the hands of a master paqo, a tool that was ultimately used for the good of the community. Don Garibilu recognized that the yellow fever had the power to save Q'ero, so he gathered all his power and used this disease to "eat" all the other pestilences in Q'ero.⁶ Using his energy body, he energetically incorporated all the diseases into his own body and, using his qosqo, or spiritual stomach, he "digested" them through the power of the yellow fever. Then he turned toward the Apus and invoked their names, including the one responsible for the diseases. To these Apus he commanded, "You will take this pestilence back!" The Apus complied, taking back the yellow fever, and with it all the other diseases that were ravaging Q'ero. Soon don Garibilu and the others recovered, and Q'ero was saved from extinction.

"In this way," don Juan concluded, "a new thing was done by this alto mesayoq, Garibilu Q'espi. This was a good, ancient [kuraq] akulleq."

The Q'ero also attribute the Apus with saving them from the Spanish conquistadors. In 1532, Francisco Pizarro and approximately 168 men managed to conquer the Inka Empire, a nation of millions.[7] The story of the Conquest is told and retold in many fine accounts, but there is one battle that may not be recorded anywhere in the history books. It is the battle for Q'ero, waged by one great alto mesayoq with the help of his Apu against a contingent of Spanish soldiers, and it is the one battle the Spaniards lost. The following story was told jointly by don Juan Pauqar Flores and don Agustín Pauqar Qapa.

At Wiraqocha Pampa, a highland plain not far from Q'ero, the story goes, an alto mesayoq was tending his llamas when he spotted Spanish soldiers. This alto mesayoq, named Garibilu Q'espi,[8] left his llamas and escaped undetected up the mountainside, headed as fast as he could toward the lower villages of Q'ero. He alerted everyone he saw along the way to the imminent arrival of the Spaniards, and these Q'ero fled in terror. When the Spaniards finally entered the first Q'ero village, they found it empty, and they found themselves in trouble, for there was no one to give them food and water and other supplies that they desperately needed.

Meanwhile, the Apus began calling to Garibilu Q'espi. They instructed him to follow their directions in order to save Q'ero. "You must go to the mountain above Wiraqocha Pampa," they told him. "There, you must build a *saiwa* [a column of stones]. When you leave, we will kick the saiwa, and the stones will fall on the Spaniards."

"When the Spaniards came," don Agustín explained, picking up the story from don Juan, "they made a lot of abuses. They killed many animals and made their bones into their staffs. There were mounds of bones in Q'ero. Seeing that, our grandfather [ancestor], this alto mesayoq Garibilu Q'espi, climbed to the highest hill." There he followed the Apus' instructions, building a giant column of stones. When the Spaniards came back down through the pampa, don Juan and don Agustín explained, the Apus did just what they promised. "Three clouds became clean in the sky and produced lightning. The lightning struck the saiwa, and all the hills fell down and crushed the Spaniards. Only a few soldiers survived, only those who were high up the mountain."

Don Agustín shook his head slowly, seriously, considering don Garibilu's feat. "If there had been more Spaniards, surely they would have killed all the Q'ero. After this [battle], the Spaniards decided to never return back to Q'ero. They came nevermore," he said. "If these things had not happened as I say, we would not be here."

As don Agustín fell silent, don Juan leaned forward and spoke softly, as if he were revealing a secret. "The proof of this battle was found by Martín Waman, who died long ago. He found a piece of a Spaniard's gun at Wiraqocha Pampa. This thing really happened! This alto mesayoq, Garibilu Q'espi, must have been a powerful paqo, because through his invocation the Apus made the stones fall onto the Spaniards." Then don Juan concluded with a characteristic Q'ero flourish, invoking a modern simile and provoking a hearty laugh all around: "Garibilu Q'espi defended the Q'ero like a lawyer defends a client in the courts!"

As the most powerful nature energies, Apus are the tutelary spirits of the paqos. A potential paqo is first called to the sacred path by receiving the call of an Apu through its manifestation, the *estrella*. Although *estrella* is the Spanish word for star, when paqos talk about their estrella they are referring to the "call" of the Apu, and in some cases to the physical representation of the spirit of the sacred mountain to which they are aligned and in service. Because a paqo may be called by more than one Apu, he or she[9] may have several estrellas. According to Juan Núñez del Prado, the paqos' use of this term may have been borrowed from the Conquistadors and their colloquialisms, *buena estrella* and *mala estrella*, meaning, respectively, good luck and bad luck. To be called by an estrella means that a paqo has found his luck, his guiding spirit. An estrella, as representative of an Apu, may materialize in any of many possible forms, both human and animal, such as a hummingbird, bull, condor, or puma. However, it most frequently appears to a potential paqo in a dream or a vision as a man in white or shining clothing. To refuse the call of an estrella may imperil not only that person's life or soul, but his family's as well. Once accepted, however, the estrella becomes the conduit through which the paqo communicates with the Apus. As a paqo becomes more powerful, so do his estrellas, because he is able to dialogue with more and more powerful Apus. As the power of his Apus increases, so does the paqo's ability to empathize with larger and larger groups of people, and so his ability to "push the kawsay"—to consciously influence the world of living energy in service to others—grows on a commensurate scale.

There is a hierarchy of Apus, each level distinguished by the relative strength and range of its influence. The least powerful are the *ayllu Apus*, mountains which influence a small community. *Ayllu* is a kinship term in Quechua that refers to a group of people joined by blood or communal ties. Just as an ayllu is the smallest civic unit in the Andean, so an ayllu Apu is a sacred mountain that influences the smallest geographical area. Examples are the Apus Pukin and Pikol, which govern the San Jerónimo and Santiago neighborhoods of Cuzco, respectively. Next is the *llaqta Apu. Llaqta* means "town" in Quechua; thus a llaqta Apu influences a geographical region that encompasses a group of towns or villages. The Apus Saqsawaman[10] and Wanakauri are each llaqta Apus. Finally, there is the *suyu Apu*, which is an Apu that influences a large region; the word *suyu* means "quarter" in Quechua. Apu Ausangate and Apu Salqantay are suyu Apus. The first three levels of the alto mesayoq path correspond to the three hierarchies of Apus and so are named after them.

THE ANDEAN MYSTICAL PATH

In the Andean priesthood, there are two mystical paths—that of the *pampa mesayoq* and that of the *alto mesayoq*. When a person receives an estrella, he or she must determine, often with the help of an experienced paqo, whether the call has been to the path of the pampa mesayoq or to the path of the alto mesayoq.

Pampa mesayoqs are expert ceremonialists, the keepers of the earth-based rituals and knowledge. They are healers, with a "thorough knowledge of herbal medicines, divination, and magical diagnostics."[11] They are expert at coca leaf divination and may use the coca leaves to diagnose illness and to determine the proper cure. Pampa mesayoqs are masters at making *despachos* and performing the ceremonies connected with them. A despacho is a ritual bundle, made of white paper, that is filled with dozens of natural items—from seeds to incense to candy to starfish arms to flowers—and then buried or burnt as an offering to Pachamama or the Apus, or used for healing or for some other specific purpose. There are more than two hundred different kinds of despachos, and although a single pampa mesayoq is not expected to master the intricacies of every type, he or she is expected to master their basic uses as thanksgiving offerings and healing tools. Despachos are also used in divination: the color and direction of the smoke that rises as they are burned often reveal the state and condition of the energy body and heart of the person or group for whom the despacho was offered.

Although pampa mesayoqs primarily are in service to Pachamama, they also serve the Apus, often having several different estrellas. The pampa mesayoq acts as a conduit, on behalf of the person who has sought his or her service, for the healing or divinatory energy of the Apus, and he receives important indirect counsel from his estrellas, usually in dreams or visions. However, a pampa mesayoq as a rule does not have *direct* communication with supernatural energies. That is the province of the alto mesayoq.

Like pampa mesayoqs, alto mesayoqs are called to the path by receiving an estrella, and they undergo rigorous initiations and apprenticeships, often more than a decade long. They acquire the same knowledge and many of the same skills as pampa mesayoqs, but then the paths diverge, for alto mesayoqs go on to experience the nature energies and spirits *directly*. They can dialogue directly with the estrellas of the Apus to which they are in service, and their power is commensurate with the levels of these Apus. Therefore, the lowest level of the alto mesayoq hierarchy is the *ayllu alto mesayoq*, who incorporates the power of the tutelary spirits of ayllu Apus. Next is the *llaqta alto mesayoq*, and then the *suyu alto mesayoq*, each in service to that respective level of Apu.

The culminating level of alto mesayoq is the *kuraq akulleq*, which means "elder chewer of coca leaves." In Q'ero, as of 1998, there were only two kuraq akulleqs, don Mariano Apasa Marchaqa and don Manuel Q'espi, although don Juan Pauqar Espinosa, a suyu alto mesayoq, is a powerful paqo who is on his way to gaining kuraq stature. Kuraqs have the capacity not only to incorporate the energetic power of Pachamama and to engage the tutelary energies of the most powerful Apus, but they can also touch the energies of the cosmos and work these energies on a truly planetary scale. Kuraqs are also sometimes called *hanaq qawaq*, which means "highest seer," because they can access the most refined energies, which come from the *hanaq pacha* (the upper world). Some rare kuraq akulleqs are even said to be able to summon the Creator itself, who is called *Kamaq* at a universal or cosmic level and *Pachakamaq* or *Wiraqocha* when referring to the creator of the world. A kuraq akulleq's estrella is often called *Taytacha*, which is the manifestation of the divine within the physical. This is generally a term of respect and affection: *tayta* is the formal word for "sir" or "master," and *cha* is the suffix for the diminutive, so *Taytacha* also indicates a partial or specific manifestation of the infinite divine into the physical. *Pachakamaq* and *Wiraqocha* are ancient Taytachas, creators of the Earth. Since the introduction of Christianity, God or Jesus Christ has replaced them in many areas, and one often hears paqos and others appealing to the *Apu Jesucristo*. This Creator energy also finds its equivalent in such distinctively Andean manifestations as the Lord of Q'ollorit'i and the *Taytacha Temblores*, the Earthquake Lord.

THE THREE WORLDS

Paqos are experts at mediating the energies of the three worlds of Andean cosmology: the *hanaq pacha*, the *kay pacha*, and the *ukhu pacha*. The hanaq pacha is the upper world, the multidimensional realm comprised solely of sami, the most refined energy. In Christian terms it is heaven, the abode of God, Jesus, and the angelic spirits. In psychological terms it is the super-conscious, and transpersonally it is the sphere of the visionary and the prophet. Its Andean totem is the condor or the hummingbird, which are the messengers of spirit.

The kay pacha is this world, the physical world. It is Earth and Gaia. It is the world of spirit made manifest, and the sphere of consciousness, ego, and identity. The kay pacha is comprised of both sami and hucha, the light and heavy energies, respectively, because we humans, the dominant occupants of the kay pacha, sometimes act with ayni and sometimes do not. Its Andean totem is the puma (jaguar), whose majesty emerges from the juxtaposition of beauty and danger, of grace and fear, of instinct and will.

Finally, there is the ukhu pacha, the lower world, which is comprised solely of heavy energy. The ukhu pacha is not akin to the Christian hell: the *ukhupacharuna*—people of the lower world—have not been judged and sentenced to a world of suffering; instead, they occupy the heavier energetic realm only because they have not yet learned to live in ayni.[12] Heavy energy is not negative, bad, or dark energy, as will be explained in the next chapter. It is, instead, simply incompatible or disharmonious energy. The ukhupacharuna, therefore, generate disharmonious energy, heavy energy, because they have not yet learned how to live in reciprocity with others. At a psychological level, the lower world is the interior world, the sphere of the unconscious, the domain of the dreamtime. Its Andean totem is the snake, symbolizing the threatening yet potentially transformative nature of the deep.

Andean paqos access energy from all three worlds, yet they do not generally "travel" the three worlds as do the classical shamans described by such ethnologists as Mircea Eliade. Andean paqos work with visions and dreams, but they do so without the aid of hallucinogens, drumming, or ecstatic dancing. There are several shamanic systems indigenous to Peru, found mostly in the jungles or along the northern coast, in which psychotropic drugs, such as ayahuasca or San Pedro, are used. The Q'ero, however, do not utilize any of these means to access the world of spirit. Instead they work in the dreamtime or use nature rituals—centered mostly around working with coca leaves, despachos, and their *mesas* (bundles of sacred objects)—during which they open a dialogue with Pachamama, the Apus, or other spirits. Over a long apprenticeship they learn to read the coca leaves, to open a dialogue with their Apus through the power of their mesas, and to receive counsel from the living world of nature. At any point along his path, a paqo is free to pass on his knowledge to others, although it is usually the most experienced, and thus the most elderly, paqos who accept apprentices and who transmit the *karpays* to other paqos. A *karpay* is an initiation ritual or an energetic transmission of the teacher's own power and his spiritual lineage. It is a doorway, an opening to the sacred power, and thus each paqo is required to grow into the power in his own way. The path of a paqo is decidedly personal, although the body of mystical knowledge and the ritual, shamanic practices are fairly uniform. As with most mystical traditions, an Andean paqo acquires knowledge and wisdom through personal experience. If a teaching is not grounded in personal experience, it does not hold much value for an Andean paqo, and so apprentices are encouraged to place greater trust in their own experiences than in the words of their teachers.

Paqos work energetically, either individually or in groups, within the realms of the three worlds, facilitating the flow of ayni between all three by creating a ley line of light, an energetic column called a *saiwa*. Andean prophecy, as discussed in chapter 3, envisions a time when these three realms will coalesce into one: the hanaq pacha and ukhu pacha merging with the kay pacha to create one paradisiacal world here on Earth. We can each contribute to this spiritual transformation by living in ayni ourselves and by mediating the heavy and light energies of our own world. By cleansing ourselves of heavy energy, we facilitate the energetic evolution of our species.

THE ANDEAN PAQO'S TOOLS

One of a paqo's primary tools is the *mesa*, which means "table" in Spanish. In the mystical framework the mesa is a *mesa de altar* and takes the form of a ritual bundle that contains the paqo's most sacred objects, much like the medicine bundles of North American Indians. When the fabric bundle is opened, it becomes the "altar" upon which the mystic's tools are arranged for use in a healing or divination or other work. Q'ero mesas are very simple, although the mesas of mystics from the north coast of Peru can become quite elaborate. In the Andean regions, the sacred objects within a mesa are most often *khuyas*, or stones of power. The word *khuya* actually means affection or love, and these power stones are ones that are infused with a paqo's most refined energy, empathy, and impulse toward service to others. A mesa, however, may contain many other power objects, such as meteorites and crystals; shells; animals parts, such as a feather or a claw; and a cross. Generally, paqos carry one mesa, but they may have several. For instance, mesas are sometimes distinguished as belonging to the "left side" or the "right side" of the mystical work. The right-side mesa is the primary mesa, filled with khuyas passed on from teachers and colleagues and collected from sacred sites and power spots. The right-side mesa connects the paqo energetically with these masters and sacred sites, and through this mesa the paqo "pushes the kawsay" of the mystical lineage. A left-side mesa is one with a more specific, practical purpose, such as healing or conferring a specific initiation. Paqos "charge" their mesas by exposing them to the energies at sacred sites, by having especially powerful paqos bless them, and by occasionally "feeding" the objects within them by sprinkling them with *pisco*, a 100-proof alcohol made from grapes that is widely used in Andean ceremony.

The khuyas in a mesa may serve only one function or they may have many, often quite diverse, uses. During the interviews for this book, I was given a khuya from don Julian Pauqar Flores's mesa. As he gave it to me, he explained: "As you take this khuya, know it possesses the power to suck out hucha [dense or heavy energy]. Also impurities and difficulties. It will cleanse any hucha from your mesa that may accumulate there. Also with this stone you can awaken the Apus and Pachamama. Always work with it and feed it on August 1 [the first day of the Andean sacred year] because this is the day Pachamama and the Apus awaken. Call the Apus and Pachamama to you and declare your new intentions by saying, 'I am what I speak, not what I have spoken.' This stone is also a stone of activation; its power is an activating power. When you are very busy and you cannot remember everything, do the ritual with this stone." The ritual for the stone involves dipping it in lake or river water before using it to cleanse my energy body and repeating a simple incantation during the cleansing. I was warned never to use the khuya on myself and another person on the same day.

There is still another use for this khuya, one for blessing and protecting a person who is about to take a trip. The person who is about to embark on a trip should ideally be naked, don Julian explained, but if that is not possible, at least his or her arms and legs should be bare. The person should face the direction in which he or she will be traveling, and as I cleanse him or her with the stone, again after dipping it in lake or river water, the traveler should intone: "May the path that I take be walked. May the word that I speak be spoken. May the wish that I make be wished. May the walk that I do be done." Finally, don Julian cautioned me, this ritual must be performed before the day of departure, never on the actual day itself. As you might suspect, of several powerful khuyas in my right-side mesa, this is the khuya with the most uses.

In addition to a mesa, no Andean paqo is without his *ch'uspa*, a woven or llama skin pouch with a long string strap in which the paqo carries coca leaves. Coca is ubiquitous in the Andes. Peasants chew it, with a small piece of lime-ash to enhance its stimulating effect, because it not only suppresses their appetites, which is valuable in a society where food is precious, but it also stimulates their hearts and helps them endure working at high altitudes. Tourists are routinely served coca tea to help them acclimate to altitude. But coca is more than a medicinal; it is the sacred plant of the Andes, and there are many ways that it is used ritually. Almost everywhere in the Andes, one can observe the social exchange and chewing of coca, called *hallpay*.

When coca is used in ceremony, in a sacred context, the act of choosing the leaves and chewing them is called *akulliy*. *Akulliy*, which is pronounced rather like "ak-wee," is the Quechua verb from which the title for the highest level of the Andean priesthood—kuraq akulleq—is derived. (As you may remember, kuraq akulleq means "elder chewer of coca leaves.") The practice begins by first forming a *k'intu*, which is a grouping of three perfect leaves overlaid one atop the other. Many times a person will make a prayer of thanksgiving by gently blowing the prayer through the leaves before feeding the k'intu into his or her mouth. There are three ways that a paqo prays with or interchanges energy through the medium of a coca k'intu, each method evoking a distinct intention on the part of the paqo. *Samiy* is a gentle blowing through the k'intu by which the paqo imparts refined energy. *Samay* describes a strong breath that imparts an energizing influence to that which it is directed. Finally, there is *phukuy*, which is a breath used specifically to establish an energetic connection between two persons or two entities, such as the paqo and an Apu. After the prayer has been made using the k'intu, the k'intu is fed slowly into the mouth and chewed or else it is used as a ritual offering, such as in a despacho. The number of k'intus made for a despacho varies with the specific use of the offering. Generally, twelve k'intus are placed in a circle around the center of a despacho to the Apus, whereas eight are used in a despacho to Pachamama. However, the number and placement of k'intus in a despacho is a complex, and often personal, art form.

Coca leaves are also used for divination and for healing. In divination, the person who is being "read" takes a large handful of coca leaves and lets them fall randomly onto a cloth, or the coca leaf reader throws the leaves after the person being read has infused them with his or her energy. The reader than divines the answer to the person's question in the arrangement and condition of the coca leaves. For instance, a folded or torn leaf may signify ill fortune, whereas one that is tinged gold around its edge may signal good fortune, although these examples are gross oversimplifications of the art of coca-leaf reading. Coca readings can be very specific. For example, in a coca leaf reading I was given by Q'ero alto mesayoq don Martín Pauqar Qapa, one small group of folded and overturned leaves indicated there was a person who was trying to prevent the publication of this book. But another, adjoining group of leaves, which were facing up and were in a much healthier and more perfect condition, indicated I would prevail in this energetic and intentional struggle.

In healing, a patient's coca leaves may be read to determine the nature of the disease and the best cure. Otherwise, the coca leaves are most often placed in the healer's mesa, and the mesa is passed over the ill person's body in order to cleanse his or her energy body. The coca helps the healer "pull out" *hucha*, or heavy energy, and impart *sami*, or refined energy.

Sami and hucha are fundamental energy concepts of Andean mysticism and as such I have devoted a separate chapter to discussing them. Let me close this overview of the Andean mystical world, however, by relating a story that beautifully illustrates the stance of a Q'ero mystic in relation to the kawsay pacha, the cosmos of animating energy. This simple yet profound story prepares us to move in the next chapter to a deeper discussion of our own responsibilities as energy beings. I said toward the beginning of this chapter that to immerse yourself in Andean cosmology you must shift your awareness from your mind to your heart center. The following story, told to me by Américo Yábar, poignantly illustrates how difficult it is for some of us in the West to make that perceptual shift, and yet how different our world might be if we could all only do so.

Several years ago, Américo agreed to meet with a noted neurosurgeon and a contingent of physicians and anthropologists who were studying indigenous healing practices. He brought with him one of his teachers, a kuraq who rarely left his village high in the Andes. Américo did not identify the kuraq as Q'ero, although he well could have been since Américo was trained primarily by Q'ero paqos. In any case, the meeting recounted below took place in a hotel in Cuzco, where the neurosurgeon spent considerable time quizzing Américo about his healing techniques and those of the Andes region. He then turned his attention to the kuraq.

"The doctor asked the shaman," Américo said, lowering his voice and speaking in a mock serious tone, "'So, what it is you do?' The shaman did not answer the doctor right away, and the doctor repeated his question. Again, the shaman did not answer. After several queries, the shaman finally said, 'If that question interests you so much, *you* must be the one to answer it.'

"The doctor said, 'I am a neurologist. I can open your head and take out a tumor the size of a nut. Then I can sew your head closed again, and you will be able to walk. Can you do that?'

"The kuraq carefully considered the surgeon's words for a few minutes, then he shook his head and said no, he could not. 'I cannot do those things,' the kuraq admitted, 'but when you are dying, when you are growing cold and the doctors have given up on you, then I can go out into the cosmos and bring back your soul [anima]. I can put it back into your body, and then you may walk away again. Can you do that?'"

Chapter 2

Children of the Sun:
Engaging Your Energy Body

"Our work as humans," says fourth-level Andean priest Juan Núñez del Prado, "is to have a complete life, to have a real relationship with the *Pachamama*, with Mother Earth, to have a real relationship with everything in the world, with *everything*." We can have a "real" relationship with everything, because everything, including ourselves, has *kawsay*— the vital, animating energy of existence. According to Juan, not only the trees, rivers, and mountains have kawsay, but "even the Empire State building has its own power. The problem is how to establish a good relationship with that [person or place]." Juan's use of the word "power" raises an important point for Westerners—for all Westerners, not just those of us living in mystical relationship with the universe. Juan says, "In the Western tradition we are afraid of the word 'power.' We think that power is dangerous, that it is not good. But no! Power is only power. It is the difference between being able to do something and not being able to do it. If you want you can do good things. If you want you can do bad things, because for that you also need power. But if you want to do good things in your life and in the lives of those around you, you must have power. You need power.

"But power is only power," he stresses. "You must decide how to use it not based on your ability to use it, but based on your moral rule. Sometimes you will *not* do something not because you do not have the power to do it but because you follow a moral rule that tells you not to do it. On the other hand, there are people who are prevented from acting not because of their moral rule but because they do not have the power to do it. They have no choice. Understand? The thing is to have the power to do everything! Then the next thing is to have the personal morals to know how to use or not use your power. But do not be mistaken—we are looking for power when we try to establish a connection with the living energy."

LIGHT AND HEAVY ENERGY

Power in the Andean tradition is the ability to "push the kawsay," that is, to be in conscious interchange with the *kawsay pacha*, the cosmos of living energy. To an Andean, the consciousness of this energy world dawns at birth and intensifies throughout a life so intimately aligned and interconnected with the spirit realm that to deny its existence is not to exist at all. The kawsay pacha, however, is not a difficult or complex world. It is, in fact, quite simple, for it is comprised of only two basic energies: *sami*, which is light or refined energy, and *hucha*, which is heavy or dense energy. Sami suffuses the natural world, animating all living beings and imparting "power" to natural objects and places where it accumulates. The more sami we incorporate into our energy body, the more effortlessly and fully we live in harmony and well-being with others and the natural world. It is by lightening our energy body by incorporating this vital, refined energy that we are able to raise our level of consciousness.

Hucha, in contrast, is heavy energy, and it is created only by human beings. Hucha manifests because we do not live in perfect *ayni*—reciprocity—with the kawsay pacha; it results from the flux of our interrelations with one another, from the very activity of being and living in the *kay pacha*, the very human, physical world. It is an emergent energetic property of our interrelations with each other and with the natural world, generated by the power of our emotions, thoughts, and actions. At our current level of consciousness, hucha cannot be avoided. Thus, any space humans have occupied, in which they have lived their humanness, accumulates hucha. We can attract hucha walking through a congested city or through a field of flowers. Most often, however, we accumulate hucha through our emotional interactions with others. It is generated as we weave our energies among those whom we love, hate, envy, nurture; it is an energetic byproduct of our pains and sorrows, our fears, our hopes, of the range of feelings that drive our thoughts and actions. Although hucha is a type of energy we cannot help attracting if we are living fully in the current human world, it is a density of energy we do not want to accumulate, for it turns the lightness of our energy body heavy like itself. It keeps us from functioning optimally, and it prevents us from engaging the kawsay pacha as fully as we can. Yet, hucha in and of itself is not "negative" or "bad" energy. It is simply heavy. "Hucha does not have a moral category," Américo Yábar explains. "You can think of it as ordered energy that becomes disordered. We feed that disordered energy to Pachamama . . . but it has no moral reflection."

That hucha is *heavy energy*, and not negative or bad energy, is perhaps one of the most difficult concepts for newcomers to the Andean path to grasp. Juan Núñez del Prado says, "In the West we are always trying to reduce everything to dualities, to positive or negative, to good or bad, to right or wrong. But heaviness is a relative thing. Density or vibration or color may be a better way or metaphor to understand hucha. For example, something may be a violet color, or it may be red. The energetic vibration of the color red is lower than the vibration of violet, so you could say, then, that heaviness is red. Violet is more refined, but it is also cold. Red is warm. Radiators are red, they give warmth, but ultraviolet rays are violet and cold. Which is better, the violet or the red thing? It depends."

It is the *symptoms* of our accumulation of heavy energy that manifest in ways we tend to think of as negative. When we are not in peak energetic form, then we tend to not experience full physical, mental, or emotional well-being either. Too much hucha in our *poq'po*—that energy bubble that surrounds and suffuses our physical body—may also reflect an imbalance in our relationship with the natural world of living energy, that we are isolated from the free flow of nature energies and our place in the Great Web of Being. From a psychological perspective, hucha can be seen as the accumulation in our energy body of all that does not serve us: negative attitudes, untruthfulness, inability to love, self-destructive or hurtful behaviors, a poor self-image, and the like. If you are experiencing these conditions then you are probably in contact with an energy that is heavy. Heaviness, however, is relative to individuals and the condition of their poq'pos, and to the energetic power they have at their disposal, to how well they can push the kawsay. Heaviness indicates an *incompatibility* between personal energy and an external energy. "Fear or pain—the emotions—from the Andean point of view," says Juan, "are only symptoms of being in contact with hucha. Fear, for example, is an indication that you are in contact with something that is heavy for you. Incompatible types of energy feel heavy. But heaviness is a relative thing. What is heavy for you may not be heavy for me."

From the Andean perspective, understanding energy as

"heavy" and not as "negative" is crucial, because this perceptual shift is imperative to living fully and consciously, open and receptive to the energies of others and the natural world. As Juan explains, if you meet an energy you conceive of as negative, your only course of action, or probable course of action, is to protect yourself. In the posture of protection, you close yourself off and risk turning your energy body into "an energetic jail." According to the Andean view, it is rarely beneficial to withdraw from an interchange with the kawsay pacha. But when you conceive of energy as heavy, there is nothing to protect yourself from; you are simply recognizing an energy as incompatible with you. Your awareness of this incompatibility allows you to then act to transform the energy, to in effect lighten it so that it either becomes compatible for you or simply does not affect you. Even if you cannot deal with the hucha, if it is too much for you to handle all at once, it presents no danger to you and there is no need to close off your energy body in the impulse toward protection. Juan likens hucha to a stone in a garden that you are trying to move. If the stone is too heavy for you to lift, you will simply have to let it lie until you become stronger. But the stone itself has no capacity to harm you.

THE ENERGY BODY

As explained briefly earlier, we engage the world of sami and hucha through our poq'po, our energy body. This body is a bubble of energy that surrounds and suffuses our physical body. It has an outer layer, like a skin, that prevents heavy energy from easily infiltrating deep into our energy body. However, if we do not cleanse the heavy energy from the surface of our poq'po, then hucha can accumulate, building up and seeping deeper and deeper into our poq'po. As hucha builds and penetrates, it affects our physical, emotional, mental, and spiritual states. The deeper it goes into our energy body, the more pronounced its symptoms—the loss of well-being—may be.

In the Andes, a paqo's first lessons as an apprentice are often those dealing with cleansing hucha from and drawing sami into his poq'po. He must first becoming conscious of how he is in ceaseless energetic interchange with others and with the natural world. I remember one of my first experiences of the flow of energy, a flow that physically knocked me back from where I was sitting on a rock. I was at Machu Picchu with a group of fellow paqos, and we had split into two groups. One group had climbed Huayna Picchu; the other had stayed behind to meditate in the ruins. I chose a large, flat rock on the eastern edge of the ruins, a short distance from the rest of the group. Our instructions had been to exchange our energy filaments with the group up on the mountain. We were to "throw" our energy filaments up to those on the mountaintop, and they would cast their filaments down to us. At the appointed hour I was in deep meditation, sitting in the lotus position atop the large, flat rock. As I felt my energy building, I opened my qosqo—the primary energy center that is located around the navel—and cast my energy up to my friends on the mountain. I can't say I felt a tangible flow of energy traveling upward, but my intentions were clear and directed so I trusted that I was making an exchange. What happened next dispelled any doubts. I was suddenly struck by a whooshing blast of blue air (I could see the brilliant color blue even though my eyes were closed) that came rushing down from the mountaintop. It felt like a giant blue bird had winged its way through me. I was physically propelled backward, and I had to throw my arms back to stop myself from being toppled off the rock. Later, I polled a few of my friends who had been on Huayna Picchu.

They told me that they had agreed, as an aid to the energy transfer, to visualize themselves as giant condors of energy flying down the mountain toward our group below.

As paqos, our fundamental task is to always "maintain the ecology of our energy environment."[1] That environment should be light, replete with sami, which is empowering and helps us acquire the personal power to push the kawsay in service to others. If our environment is not light, then it must be cleansed. The cleansing task begins with the self, and then moves outward to encompass larger and larger energy fields, in a widening series of concentric energy circles. After we cleanse our own poq'pos, for instance, we can then begin to cleanse our immediate environment and the people with whom we are in close contact, such as family members, friends, and colleagues. Cleansing can then be directed further outward, toward those with whom we have difficult relationships or toward whom we feel discomfort or animosity. We can even cleanse hucha from groups, communities, and entire populations. Finally, we can cleanse physical localities, such as a house where dense energy has accumulated or a landscape energetically suffering from the effects of violence, desecration, or pollution.

There are various methods of cleansing hucha. Paqos may work with specific tools, such as their *mesas*—the ritual bundle of power objects—or a particular object from the mesa, perhaps a *khuya*, a stone of power. Coca leaves or other herbs may be passed over the body, energetically trapping the hucha and drawing it from the person. The two main hucha cleansing techniques, however, are entirely energetic and require no accoutrements: the simplest is the *release* of hucha from the poq'po; the more intensive technique involves *digesting* the heavy energy. These techniques are discussed in detail in the exercises of Part III, but, basically, the release technique is a simple practice whereby through intention the hucha is drawn down the body and released to Pachamama. As the release occurs, you simultaneously draw in sami, refined energy, through the crown chakra to complete the circuit of ayni. Sami is usually drawn down from the *hanaq pacha*, the upper world of Andean cosmology, a world composed entirely of sami because the hanaq pacha beings always act with perfect ayni. However, sami is also the elemental energy of the natural world and so can be drawn from just about any natural source. The digestion technique, called *hucha mikhuy*, literally "eating hucha," is more elaborate but is still a technique of intention. In this process, you open your *qosqo*, your spiritual stomach, and command it to "eat" the hucha, either your own or someone else's. As you feed this energy through your spiritual stomach, the flow of hucha is split into two streams, the hucha going down into Pachamama and the sami moving upward through your body to your head or crown chakra. You actually extract sami from the hucha just as your physical stomach is able to extract nutrients from food.

No matter which technique you use, you always feed hucha to Pachamama, who loves hucha almost as much as, if not more than, she loves the sweets and candies in *despacho* offerings. Hucha empowers Pachamama; to her it is food, not waste. In return for her energetic meal, she returns sami, refined energy, to the person doing the cleansing. "When we give hucha to Pachamama, we are giving her food," Juan says. "When we are working with heavy energy, we are working with real, living energy, and this real, living energy empowers Mother Earth. She needs living energy, and if you release hucha to her you are empowering her. Also you are empowering yourself."

You can perform mikhuy on hucha you accumulated very

recently or that you acquired long ago, such as from the traumas or relationships of childhood. You can perform it on yourself or on others, and others may perform it on your behalf. It is not necessary for a person to know the technique is being carried out on his or her behalf for it to be useful. Neither is physical proximity required. Hucha mikhuy is fundamentally an act of intention, and so its efficacy is not dependent in any way on time or space. Américo Yábar tells a story about the art of hucha mikhuy and his teacher of six years, the famed kuraq don Benito Qoriwaman, that illustrates the flexibility and practicality of the process. Américo was visiting don Benito one day when a group of tourists came to his house. "He was very famous," Américo said of don Benito, "and people from all over came to consult with him." On this day, when these tourists came, Américo felt that don Benito was being imposed upon and so he tried to steer the tourists away. But don Benito stopped him and said, "'Look at all the heavy energy they have.'" After a half hour or so of conversation, Américo reported, the kuraq excused himself and left the hut. Américo followed him, and found him doubled over, vomiting. When Américo asked him what was the matter, the kuraq replied: "'Don't worry. I just ate all their hucha, and I'm getting rid of it.'" This story is typical and atypical: it is typical in that kuraqs and other paqos can be working on you or another person energetically without your even knowing it; it is atypical in that performing mikhuy rarely affects you physically. Usually, you can feed the heavy energy through your qosqo to Pachamama without ill effect.

The cycle of cleansing hucha and of digesting it is completed by drawing sami into your poq'po and into the poq'po of the person being cleansed. As you release heaviness, you increase your lightness. But we don't have to do this only during a mikhuy session. We should always be cognizant of empowering ourselves by drawing sami whenever we need it or whenever an especially powerful source is available to us. Other people may be potential sources of sami. For example, when a person, particularly an apprentice on the sacred path, is in the presence of a master paqo, than that person has the right to draw sami from the master. There is no need to ask permission to do this, as it is a given that a great paqo, a kuraq akulleq for instance, is an open conduit to the most refined energies and that anyone is free to drink from this stream. In the Andean tradition, according to Juan, "if someone comes to me and tells me that he is more powerful or more enlightened than I am on the sacred path, then immediately I have the right to share that person's refined energy. But if someone is my equal, then I have no right to his finest energy. I can only eat his heavy energy, to cleanse him of his hucha. But from the more powerful I can take sami. And from the mountains, who are our older brothers, we may take sami. And from Pachamama, we have the right to absorb the finest energy. But with an equal, no. We have only the right to digest his heavy energy, and to give it to Pachamama."

I remembered Juan's counsel when I was in Q'ero, at don Manuel Q'espi's house at Chua Chua. Don Manuel is the eldest kuraq in Q'ero and one of the most respected elders in the region. I was part of a small group undergoing the *Karpay Ayni*, an initiation during which there is a transmission of energy from master to apprentice. As I sat in the small circle in the darkness of the small hut waiting for the ceremony to begin, I opened my qosqo, connected energies with don Manuel, and drank and drank and drank in his sami. I saw no indication that don Manuel was aware of what I was doing, but I felt energetically empowered and physically lighter as a result of sharing his sami.

BELTS OF POWER

We mediate the heavy energy of hucha and the refined energy of sami through our poq'po via our primary energy center, the qosqo. Located at the navel area, the qosqo is our spiritual and energetic stomach. In order to sense energies or interchange energy with the kawsay pacha or another person, you open a point in this spiritual stomach just as if you were opening your mouth to take in food. As you open this center, you can also expand it or extend it outward. Although the qosqo is the primary energy center, it is only one of four major and three minor energy centers in the poq'po. These seven centers comprise an energy system analogous to the Eastern chakra system. The four primary energy centers are called *chunpis* in Quechua, which means "belts." These "belts of power" extend around the body and each has a point, or an "eye," called a *ñawi*, as an opening. Each chunpi is also associated with a color and an element.

At the base of the spine is the *siki ñawi*, the "eye" of a black belt (*yana chunpi*) that surrounds the body. This belt is associated with the element of water and with the Black Light, the most powerful energy of the Andean tradition. Next is the *qosqo ñawi*, the primary energy center at the stomach/navel area that is part of a red belt (*puka chunpi*), which is associated with earth, with Pachamama. At the heart center is the *sonqo ñawi*, the eye of the gold belt (*qori chunpi*) that is associated with love, empathy, and with fire and the power of the sun. Finally, there is the throat center, the *kunka ñawi*, which is the "eye" of the silver belt (*qolqe chunpi*) and is associated with creativity, communication, the wind, and the moon. The two physical eyes are the fifth and sixth centers, or points. The third eye is the final, seventh, point; it is called the *qanchis ñawi*. Sometimes a fifth belt is recognized as forming a band around the head encompassing these final three points, and this is the *kulli chunpi*, or violet belt. A paqo who has been trained to transmit the power of the belts, to in effect open the energy centers of another person's energy body, is called a *chunpi paqo*. He uses a special set of five khuyas in an elaborate and systemized ritual in order to perform the chunpi initiation.

TRADITION AND RITUAL IN TRANSITION

Alarmingly, knowledge of these energy belts seems to be on the decline in the south-central Andes, as are the number of paqos able to perform the chunpi ceremony. As far as I or Juan Núñez del Prado knows, there are no chunpi paqos in Q'ero; nor, surprisingly, are there any current Q'ero paqos trained in the hucha mikhuy technique. The late don Benito Qoriwaman and Q'ero master don Andreas Espinosa, teachers to Juan and Américo, both held the chunpi rites and the hucha mikhuy teaching, and they taught both techniques to Juan and Américo. But they did not pass these technique on to any of the Q'ero I interviewed in Urubamba or any other Q'ero I have worked with over the years. During the interviews, for example, when I queried the Q'ero specifically about the hucha mikhuy technique, they claimed they knew of no such digesting technique. For them hucha can only be cleansed using a mesa, khuya, despacho, or coca leaves. "We do not eat or digest it," they said through don Mariano Apasa, "we just capture it, cleanse it from a person, and offer it to the Apus. First, we take the hucha and after that we offer it up to the Apus. Then the Apus offer it to the *Taytacha* [supernatural being, equivalent to the Christ energy], and the Taytacha decides how to get rid of it."

When Juan explained the hucha mikhuy technique to them, the Q'ero were amazed. They talked excitedly among themselves for a while and then said, "We think this is a good tool. We think that if you do this with another person, that person will become totally clean. We have shared with you the things we learned with our teachers. Because you have learned that practice, you must tell us how to do it! If you are able to share that technique with us, we will be very happy!" Juan has promised to teach them.

Surprisingly, the Q'ero, although they are the most respected mystics of the Andes, have not managed to preserve all of the energetic techniques or shamanic traditions of their forebears. The reasons for this disruption in the sacred lineage are complex, and the explanation only begins with the reality that for the current generation of indigenous Andeans the pressure is to become less Indian and more Peruvian. It was only about twenty-five years ago that Peruvian Indians were allowed to become citizens. Since then, the pressures to abandon the indigenous practices have only became more intense, perhaps more so than at any time since the Spanish conquest. Juan Núñez del Prado reports that, throughout the Andes, elderly paqos have become the object of ridicule as the rest of the village acculturates into mainstream Peruvian society. "I know of one paqo, don Jésus, who lives in a village near Pisac, who is totally isolated, because nobody believes him," Juan says. "He performs the ancient ceremonies only for himself. Everybody laughs at him, at his ceremonies and techniques."

When, after diligent searching, I found and purchased an authentic set of chunpi khuyas in Cuzco, I asked Juan where the set could have come from. His reply was telling, and rather depressing. He explained that as the elders age and pass on, there are no family members with sufficient interest to learn the ancient ways or heed the call of an estrella, so the families sell off the deceased paqos' most cherished shamanic possessions, like the chunpi khuyas.

In addition to the pressure to acculturate as Peruvian citizens, the indigenous populations are feeling the effects of years of Marxist political and social practice. "Almost all the school teachers in Peru," says Juan, "took Marxists positions over the last twenty or more years. They saw the indigenous mystical tradition and customs as lies, deceptions, and outright foolishness. The young people in don Jésus's community laugh at him because they have been taught by their teachers that his knowledge is a foolish thing, nothing more than superstition."

While the situation is not so dire in Q'ero, still, the current impulse is to question, if not to abandon, the old ways. "Q'ero is the place where the impulse to preserve the ancient ways is the strongest," Juan says. "Yet in Q'ero there is an evangelical group, and for them the ancient ways are the ways of the devil. Two sons of don Manuel Q'espi, the highest paqo in Q'ero, belong to it. They see the mystical tradition as evil. Don Manuel himself was pulled into this new church. He became a member, but only for two or three months. Finally he decided to abandon that church and to reincorporate the ancient ways. And his sons are angry with him because of this. Now he is passing on his knowledge not to his sons but to other relatives, in particular to a nephew, who was just given the third-level initiation at Q'ollorit'i this year [1996]."

Sometimes human nature accounts for the difficulties. For instance, don Manuel Q'espi had a falling out with his colleague don Andreas Espinosa, who is now deceased but was one of the greatest modern paqos of Q'ero. As a result of their disagreement, don Andreas denied don Manuel the chunpi teaching. Juan Núñez del Prado, however, was shown the technique by don Andreas after only their second meeting as teacher and apprentice.

This state of affairs, while troubling, also is not unusual within a living mystical tradition. Such traditions are by nature fluid, and this malleability is even more pronounced in the Andes, where mysticism is grounded in practicality. Techniques change as the lives and the needs of the people change. Because a paqo does not share the same technique as his brother or sister on the sacred path, or as his ancestors, he is not any less powerful or accomplished a paqo. Andean paqos generally do not work from a stance of competition or domination. Although there is a clear hierarchy within the mystical priesthood, cooperation is usually the operating principle to its practice. There is a psychological principle in Andean culture that beautifully illustrates the non-competitive nature of the Andean mindset and the openness and availability of the mystical teachings. According to this principle, which is at heart an energetic teaching as powerful as any other, there are three levels of relationship: *tinkuy, tupay,* and *taqe*.

Tinkuy is the encounter, when two entities (two people, two animals, even two nations) first meet and their energy bubbles touch. Tupay is the next stage of the relationship, the sizing up or the confrontation between the two entities. In the Western world, the final stage of the relationship would be the outcome of that comparison, undoubtedly one person would be proven superior to the other. But in the Andes, the final stage of the relationship is taqe, the joining of energies. In a classic example, which clarifies the important distinction between the Andean and Western notions of relationship, suppose two Indians are racing up a mountain. The third level, according to the Western mindset, would be reached when a winner is identified—whoever reaches the mountaintop first. But in the Andean tradition, the third level of relationship, taqe, is not a domination of one person over another, but a joining of energies, a union, a communion. So when one racer is declared the winner, it becomes the winner's duty—his or her highest honor—to teach the loser how to become a winner like himself. Américo says that taqe is the "complement of differences," where the gifted person shares his or her gift with the less gifted to create two equally gifted persons. We in the West are brought up thinking it is impossible that we can all reach the mountaintop simultaneously, but in the Andes, such an accomplishment is not only possible but preferable. The perceptual shift, basically, involves moving from the stance of competition to that of cooperation. Thus, although it may seem odd, and indeed unfortunate, that the most respected paqos in the Andes have not preserved all of the ancient knowledge and energetic techniques, we must beware of imposing our own Western values and expectations on a culture where taqe, not power or competition, is the guiding principle.

HARMONIZING SIMILAR AND DISSIMILAR ENERGIES

The "complement of differences" is an important concept in the Andes and underlies all energy work. Like the two kinds of energy, sami and hucha, there are two "stances" within the tripartite field of relationship: *yanantin* and *masintin*. Yanantin is the alliance between or harmonizing of two different entities or energies. Masintin is the alliance between two similar entities or energies. It is important to note that being in "harmony" does not mean being in "balance." Balance is a dualistic term—we seek to equalize two things or, alternately, to make them the same. Andeans, however, prefer to recognize inherent differences and to preserve the individuality of the two entities.

Within the kawsay pacha, for example, male energy is a quality of energy distinct from female energy. Each energy may be said to be a "flavor" or "distinct vibration" of the energy world. One is not better or more powerful or purer than the other; they are just two expressions of the infinitely creative kawsay pacha. Remember, there are only two basic kinds of energy, sami and hucha; however, there are many expressions of these kinds of energy, what Juan Núñez del Prado calls "flavors" of energy, including male and female, or that of a rock, a tree, a cloud. Therefore, in the Andean tradition, as we encounter different flavors of energy, we strive to recognize the distinctions and to harmonize any differences, so that these energetic differences aren't obliterated, but celebrated.

We are all immersed in countless yanantin and masintin energy exchanges every moment of our lives, and to be fully conscious we have to be aware of how our energies are forming or transforming the alliances between similar and dissimilar relations in our life. For example, male and female are fundamentally dissimilar energies, so they are yanantin, we could say, based on physical gender. *Inti*, the masculine sun, and *Mama Killa*, the feminine moon, are yanantin based on energetic "gender." Yet both of these energies, the male and the female, although different, can align to complement each other. When a perfect yanantin relationship is achieved—when the two energies are in harmony—the union is called a *japu*.

Other yanantin relationships may not be so clear cut; they may appear to be more perceptual than energetic. A North American and a South American can be yanantin based on culture and ethnicity. A baker and candlestick maker are yanantin based on occupation. Labor and management may be yanantin based on a hierarchical power structure. All of these interrelations have the potential to become defined by their

differences. But when we evaluate our relations from the mystical or energetic point of view, we are moved to always seek
alliance, to discover points of contact and similarity while still
acknowledging and honoring the fundamental differences. This
is the "complement of differences" of which Américo speaks,
and it is the doorway through which we can easily access the
third level of Andean relationship, that of taqe, or joiner of energies, and operate from cooperation rather than competition.

We can do the same with our masintin relations. Masintin
relations can be found in relationships of sameness: two males
are in masintin relation, as are two females. *Inti*, the sun, and an
Apu, a lord of a mountain, are both male and thus are in masintin relation. *Mama Killa*, the moon, is in masintin relationship
with *Mama Qocha*, the mother of the waters. Two accountants,
three surgeons, four salesclerks are all in masintin relation
according to occupation. Two mothers can be in masintin relation according to their nurturing role. When we acknowledge
points of similarity, then we can more easily form alliances.
When a perfectly harmonized masintin relationship is achieved,
the alliance is called *ranti*.

Thus, each of us shares many simultaneous yanantin and
masintin relations with every individual in our lives. If we are
aware of the yanantin and masintin aspects of the relationship
and strive to harmonize these energetic interchanges, we can
improve our interactions with the other person and avoid accumulating hucha. By noting the similar energies and dissimilar, or
incompatible, energies that we are in contact with, we can
almost immediately assess the potential for creating or attracting hucha. We can't turn a yanantin relation into a masintin
relation—what is different is different, what is similar is similar—but we can seek points of alliance, work to harmonize the
energies, and thus lessen the chance for the creation of hucha.

New perspectives, new possibilities, new ideas, new alliances are created fluidly when we are conscious of the yanantin and masintin energies in our personal lives and in our interactions with the energies of the natural world.

PROPHECY OF A GOLDEN AGE

All of these energy concepts coalesce into a philosophic whole within the framework of Andean cosmology and prophecy. As outlined in chapter 1, the Andean cosmos is comprised of three worlds: *the hanaq pacha, kay pacha,* and *ukhu pacha.* To briefly review, the hanaq pacha is the upper world of the most refined energy; it is composed entirely and solely of sami because the upper-world beings always act from perfect ayni. The kay pacha, our mundane, physical world, is comprised of both sami and hucha. This world is a constant flux of these two vital energies, because we humans are energetically and spiritually immature; we sometimes act with ayni and sometimes do not. The ukhu pacha, the lower world, contains only hucha, because the beings of this world do not yet practice the law of ayni. Thus, the lower world is one of heaviness.

However, we beings of the kay pacha have the capacity to interchange energies between the three worlds. In this way, when we feed hucha to Pachamama, in the kay pacha, we are able to draw sami down from the hanaq pacha in an act of ayni. As part of our work on the Andean spiritual path, we also work to bring sami to the beings of the lower world. It is part of Andean prophecy that these beings must be taught ayni, and that when they do, the three worlds will coalesce into one, ushering in a golden age during which humankind will have the capacity to consciously evolve.

The historical framework within which this prophecy fits

concerns the two rival Inkas, the half-brothers Atawallpa and Waskar.[2] Their power struggle for control of the Inka empire occurred concurrently with the Spanish conquest, and the civil war that resulted from their rivalry weakened the empire and no doubt made it especially vulnerable to the Spaniards. According to Juan Núñez del Prado, "because these two brother-kings did not have the capacity to collaborate, to act with ayni, they lost the empire." They were not able to pass on their inheritance of a stable Tawantinsuyu to their children, and because they could not act with ayni they generated a lot of heavy energy. When they died—Waskar during the civil war and Atawallpa at the hands of the Conquistadors—they descended into the ukhu pacha. "All that heavy energy they generated captured the two Inkas," Juan explains, "and pulled them into the lower world." The two Inkas now live there, and their task, their ayni, is to teach the lower-world beings how to perform ayni. "Our work in the kay pacha," says Juan, "is to digest heavy energy, to cleanse our environment. The work of the Inkas in the lower world is to teach ayni." When they have succeeded, then the lower world will rise into the kay pacha and the upper world will descend to the kay pacha, forming one cohesive and paradisiacal world. We in this world can contribute to the realization of this golden era not only by cleansing the kay pacha of hucha, but by creating *saiwas*, columns of energy that connect the three worlds, thereby acting ourselves with ayni to empower the two Inkas in their task in the ukhu pacha. "We have the capacity to practice ayni with the Inkas," Juan says. "They miss their contact with the upper world. We can establish that contact for them and pull cords of light, of living energy, down to empower them in their job in the lower world. Then, because of ayni, the Inkas must give us their qualities, so that we can become something like Inkas in this world." To become like an Inka is to raise your level of consciousness, to become a Child of the Sun, to step fully and consciously into your energy body.

In the next chapter we enter more fully into the world of Andean prophecy, a world where the Inkas—the sons and daughters of the Sun—live and are awaiting a propitious time to return. This prophecy is a living prophecy; it is not so much a shared conceptual or mythic ideology as it is a flow of energy between and among us and the three worlds. We are living in the time of the prophecy, of the *Taripay Pacha*—the Age of Meeting Ourselves Again. This is a time during which we can transform our relationship to the kawsay pacha, consciously evolving, stepping more fully into our energy bodies and generating heightened modes of awareness. Although we are not Andeans, we can utilize the energy techniques they can teach us so that we too can become Children of the Sun.

Chapter 3

Andean Prophecy: The Age of Meeting Ourselves Again

As a paqo on the Andean path I am acutely aware of Andean prophecy, of the promise of a golden age during which we can step more fully into our energy bodies and manifest fantastic new levels of awareness on Earth. Therefore, one of my intentions as I interviewed the Q'ero for this book was to discuss the *Taripay Pacha*, the Age of Meeting Ourselves Again. We are living in the midst of this nineteen-year period during which humanity has the potential to establish the energetic vibrations to foster our own spiritual evolution. But when I asked the Q'ero assembled before me in Urubamba about the prophecy, I was met with blank stares and confused looks. After much discussion I realized that the prophecy, which Juan Núñez del Prado had carefully pieced together from various sources, including the great Q'ero kuraq akulleq Andreas Espinosa, had not been passed on to these paqos, except in the most generalized way and in small concrete bits to don Mariano Apasa. In fact, the Q'ero insisted they have no capacity to foresee the collective future, and thus such prophecy is not possible.

I discussed this turn of events with Juan Núñez del Prado at the time of these interviews. Could it be possible, I asked him, that the Q'ero just do not want to reveal this knowledge? Perhaps, I suggested, they know about the prophecy but they simply to do not want to discuss it with me. Juan insisted this was not the case. "You heard don Mariano," he reminded me, "urging everyone to share their knowledge about such things. No, I'm afraid, like the process of *mikhuy* [digesting hucha], this knowledge was not passed on to these paqos." To learn more about this exchange with the Q'ero about the prophecy, refer to appendix II.

Later, in the United States, I asked Juan once again about the Q'eros' lack of knowledge of the prophecy. He replied, "I think that in the last generation you could find almost all the paqos of Q'ero carried the prophecy. But all these people have died. The next generation are for the most part focused on other things, not on preserving the knowledge, techniques, or prophecy."

Juan then offered an illustrative story that helped explain the additional challenge of discussing such philosophic subjects with the paqos, a challenge that had frustrated me to no end during the interviews. "Let me tell you something," he said. "One day I went with don Manuel Q'espi to Moray. In Moray, there was a group of workers from the National Institute of Culture. They were fixing the ruins of Moray. I asked don Manuel what he thought about the work of these men. He told me, 'They are fixing this place for the return of the Inka.' For don Manuel, these were Inka houses, and they were working to restore them so the Inka could return. This is the way you find new information. The thing that is very interesting is that the workers did not have any interpretation about this. They were simply doing their jobs because they received pay. But for an alto mesayoq, they were preparing the way for the Inka. So the alto mesayoq is coming from a totally different perspective. But with only this piece of information, you have the right to affirm the prophecy. It is real for this man [don Manuel]. The Inka is alive and going to return! You know, in your records [from the Urubamba interviews] you have a part where the Q'ero say,

'The Inka is alive. The Inka is alive, living in Paytiti.' They never say, 'We have a messianic prophecy that says the Inka is going to return. We are waiting. The Inka is alive, and we'll restore his houses so he can come. . . .' In only a few cases will you get that type of information. But mostly with them, someone will tell you, 'The Inka lives in Paytiti and sees in the river what is happening with the trash we are putting in the river. The llama dung. We are his children . . . and so on.' You need to interpret and infer from that." Such was the challenge I faced while interviewing the Q'ero about the prophecy, and no doubt it is the same challenge Juan faced while gathering the prophecy from many paqos over several decades.

Despite the lack of knowledge about the prophecy from the six Q'ero I interviewed in Urubamba, there is an ancient and wide-ranging prophetic tradition in Peru. The prophecy of the Taripay Pacha as recounted below was gathered by Juan Núñez del Prado during his nearly thirty years of inquiry as an anthropologist and nearly twenty as a paqo on the sacred path. His two primary informants, to use the anthropological term, were don Benito Qoriwaman, a kuraq akulleq of the Waskar lineage from the Cuzco area, and the Q'ero master Andreas Espinosa. The specifics of the prophecy are retold here with the kind permission of Juan, and it is reproduced in large part from my discussions with him, with additional information from his Spanish-language scholarly articles, which were published in Peru. This prophecy, while not intimately familiar to the Q'ero I interviewed, is a living message and unfolding promise that many Andean paqo are working to manifest during our lifetime. Even the Q'ero contribute, for like those of us working to cleanse our own energy environments and to raise the energetic level of the kay pacha, we all contribute to the manifestation of this golden age.

ANDEAN PROPHECY OF SPIRITUAL EVOLUTION

Juan Núñez del Prado is keenly interested in Andean prophecy, because as a paqo in service to others, he is always looking for ways to help others empower themselves. What better way to serve than to contribute to the spiritual evolution of humankind! Juan, like most of us, is familiar with other prophecies, especially those of the Hopi and Maya. Interestingly, the Andean dates correspond with the famous A.D. 2012 date of the Maya. One day, sometime in the mid-1980s, while talking with kuraq don Benito Qoriwaman, Juan asked if the time of conscious evolution was upon us. Don Benito walked outside and gazed out over the Sacred Valley of Cuzco and at an Apu that overlooks the area. "No," he said. "It is not yet time." When Juan asked how he knew this, don Benito pointed toward the Sacred Valley and said, "It's poq'po [energy bubble] is only halfway up the Apu. That time will not come until the bubble of Cuzco has reached the top of the Apu." We have no report of how high the bubble of Cuzco has risen since then, but we do know a series of specific occurrences and dates by which we can gauge the progress of the prophecy.

What follows is an overview of Andean prophecy. The opening theoretical discussion is my own understanding, based on conversations with Juan Núñez del Prado and others, but the specific details of the prophecy are those Juan has gathered during decades of talking with paqos throughout the Andes. The reader should understand that this is *Andean*, not specifically Q'ero, prophecy, although some Q'eros, such as don Manuel Q'espi,[1] are keepers of portions of it.

As has been explained, generally, there are two paths in the Andean mystical tradition, the path of the pampa mesayoq and the path of the alto mesayoq. I have elsewhere described the four levels of the alto mesayoq path: the ayllu alto mesayoq, llaqta alto mesayoq, suyu alto mesayoq, and kuraq akulleq. However, there are three additional levels to the mystical priesthood, although there are currently no paqos working at these levels. They are levels that are part of the unfolding of the prophecy, and they represent the potential evolutionary path of human consciousness.

AN OVERTURNING OF SPACE-TIME

From approximately August 1, 1990, to August 1, 1993, according to Andean prophecy, the world experienced a *pachakuti*, an "overturning of space-time."[2] The word *pachakuti* comes from the name of the ninth Inka, Pachakuteq, who was largely responsible for building the great Inka Empire, expanding the empire by conquest from present day southern Colombia to northernmost Chile. Inka Pachakuteq is also credited with codifying moral law into civil law and with masterminding a great building campaign—from the storehouses that dot the thousands of miles of roadways to the magnificently designed city of Cuzco to that famed citadel in the clouds, Machu Picchu. Through Pachakuteq's vision and will, the relatively small Inka state was transformed into one of the most astonishing empires in the world. Accordingly, whenever society underwent a momentous change, the upheaval or reordering was referred to as a *pachakuti*.

Within the prophetic tradition, the term pachakuti is applied to any cosmic transformation. Such a movement of energy, of consciousness, ripples through space-time, affecting every aspect of our sense of selfhood in time and space and of our sense of interconnectedness with the Great Web of Being. A pachakuti signals a dynamic point of intersection in space-time between human consciousness and kawsay, the multidimensional creative principle and the animating energy of the cosmos, an intersection from which the arrow of time for each possible future is nudged in one direction or the other.

According to Andean prophecy, such a cosmic reordering took place in the early 1990s, ushering in the formative years of the fabled Taripay Pacha, the Age of Meeting Ourselves Again. This initial period will last seven years, through the millennial year 2000, and during this period the choices humankind make will affect which possible future will likely manifest. The great pull of our interconnected consciousness, our collective mind, will collapse the wave function, to use the terminology of quantum physics, to make one probability, one possible future, measurable in space-time—that is, reality. During this period, human consciousness has the opportunity to evolve, resulting in our harnessing incredible healing powers, as detailed below in the discussion of the *Inka Mallkus*. This infallible healing capacity signals the "fifth level" of the sacred priesthood, or the fifth level of human consciousness manifest on Earth. The fifth level of the mystical priesthood will be heralded by the deliverance of a new *karpay*, or rite of initiation, called the *Mosoq Karpay*. It does not yet exist, and all Andean paqos are awaiting it. (At least one North American teacher of Inka shamanism has claimed that the Q'ero are giving the Mosoq Karpay initiation. This is either a misunderstanding or misinterpretation on his part, for this karpay is part of the prophecy and has not yet been given to any Andean paqo.) One can think of the fifth level in terms similar to the concept of the fifth world of the Hopi or Maya, as a new epochal cycle that initiates the formation of a new kind of human being. During this period, when our healing capacities are fully harnessed, we can begin to move out of the deterministic stream of physical evolution and into the more creative stream of conscious evolution. That is, the emphasis of life begins to shift from a physical expression to an energetic one. We will move closer to becoming true light beings, literal Children of the Sun.

Following this seven-year period is a twelve-year period during which humankind, if it has the energetic capacity and the spiritual will, can mature and evolve still further in order to manifest a new era of peace, harmony, spiritual renewal, and reconnection to the realm of nature. During this period the *Sapa Inka* and *Qoya*, enlightened political leaders who will be known by their visible glow, or aura, will govern the reunited Tawantinsuyu and become models for other world leaders. The word Tawantinsuyu, the Quechua name for the Inka Empire, means "four quarters." Anyone familiar with Native American concepts, or, for that matter, with the terminology of most mystical cosmologies, will recognize the correlation between the four quarters and the Four Sacred Directions, a concept which stands for the Whole, the Collective, the Cosmic. The reunification of the Inka Empire will be a physical reality according to the prophecies, but metaphorically it signals an end to the boundaries of all kinds that separate us; it signals the possibility of a harmonious world culture and of a refined human consciousness that is receptive to and in harmony with consciousnesses of all kinds, those of nature and those we cannot yet imagine.

Paqos—or spiritual seekers of any kind—are integral to this maturation process. In fact, it is Juan Núñez del Prado's belief that within the Andean vision for the Taripay Pacha, anyone of sufficient spiritual awareness, of any ethnic heritage or cultural or religious background, can contribute to raising the vibrational energy and the spiritual consciousness to the level needed to complete the transformation and fully manifest this "plentipotencia."

THE MANIFESTATION OF HEALING POWERS

Andean prophecy as gathered by Juan over the past two decades details specific occurrences that will signal the unfolding of this new era. The first is the rise of twelve *Inka Mallkus*, or supreme healers called *tukuy hampeqs*. All paqos are healers, although they recognize that their abilities are often sporadic and inconsistent. Sometime they can heal and sometimes they cannot. They can heal some disease better than others. The Inka Mallkus, however, will be infallible healers, able to heal any ailment every time by the simple laying on of hands. This miraculous healing capacity, according to Juan Núñez del Prado, means that there can be no impostors to this, the fifth level of the Andean alto mesayoq path and the fifth level of consciousness. These twelve fifth-level paqos will manifest in very specific places and times. The first is to reveal himself—and it will be a male—at Q'ollorit'i, a sacred annual festival held at the base of a glacial mountain more than 16,500 feet above sea level. His manifestation is imminent, and he will travel from Q'ollorit'i along the ancient *seques*, or geographic and energetic lines that connect the sacred sites and *wakas*,[3] toward Cuzco.

Simultaneously, the second Inka Mallku will manifest somewhere in the vicinity of the ancient temple of Wiraqocha at Raqchi. He too will travel the seques to Cuzco, where these two Inka Mallkus will recognize each other during the feast of Corpus Christi. At that time the third Inka Mallku will reveal himself at the shrine of the *Taytacha Temblores*, the

Earthquake Lord, in Cuzco, and there the three Inka Mallkus will unite.

Together this group of three will travel to Lima, where at either the sanctuary of Nazarenas or the sanctuary of Pachakamilla, the center of the cult of the *Taytacha Milagros,* the Lord of Miracles, they will recognize the fourth Inka Mallku and the first *Ñust'a,* or female Inka Mallku, who will reveal themselves simultaneously.

This group of fifth-level paqos will then travel by boat to southern Peru, to the sanctuary of the Virgin of Chapi in the city of Arequipa, where the second Ñust'a will reveal herself. They will travel on to Bolivia, where the third Ñust'a will make herself known at the sanctuary of the Virgin of Copacabana. From there the group of seven will travel to Puno, where they will recognize the fourth Ñust'a at the sanctuary of the Virgin of Candelaria.

After returning as a group to the Wiraqocha Temple, the most sacred temple in Peru and the site of the ancient ceremony to elect the Inka, these Inka Mallkus and Ñust'as must await the arrival of the final four fifth-level paqos—two Inka Mallkus and two Ñust'as—who will come from the north. Once all twelve fifth-level paqos are united at the Wiraqocha Temple, they will re-enact the ancient ritual of the crowning of the Inka, thereby preparing the way for the manifestation of the Sapa Inka and Qoya.

THE MANIFESTATION OF ENLIGHTENED RULERS

The Sapa Inka, which means Sole Lord or Supreme Ruler, and the Qoya, who is the Sapa Inka's female equivalent, are a spiritually enlightened couple of the sixth level. They are recognized by the bright white or golden aura that surrounds their physical bodies. It is unclear if they will arise from among the twelve fifth-level paqos or from elsewhere, but together they will enter Cuzco, the ancient Inka capital, and reunite and extend the ancient Inka Empire, the Tawantinsuyu. From there, they will serve as role models, teaching political leaders how to govern with love and respect, and teaching all humankind how to live in harmony with nature. They will be capable of such teachings because they will be masters at pushing the kawsay and will be supreme *taqes*, joiners of energy, with expert capacity to unite *munay* (love), *yachay* (wisdom), and *llank'ay* (will). Thus they will be initiators of the culminating process of reinfusing the world with sami and of joining the three worlds—the hanaq pacha, kay pacha, and ukhu pacha—into one cohesive world.

As I have already explained, the Inka Mallkus and Ñust'as do not work alone in preparing the way for the emergence of the sixth level of human development. The prophecy suggests that all of humanity must help, that it is the collective consciousness that is important to this cosmic transformation. Therefore, any time an individual, anywhere and through any spiritual tradition, raises his or her own spiritual awareness, cleanses him- or herself of hucha, and acts from love rather than from self-interest, the energetic vibration is raised and the likelihood of a collective spiritual evolution is heightened. Consequently, each of us bears responsibility for the prophecy, and each of us has the ability to further its fulfillment. The prophecy suggests that persons of the fifth and sixth levels—the Inka Mallkus and Ñust'as, and the Sapa Inka and Qoya—do not have to be blood descendants of the Inkas. In fact, they do not have to be Andeans at all. They can come from any ethnic, racial, religious, or cultural background. It requires only that they be beings evolved to the fifth and sixth levels of consciousness.

Once the sixth level has been manifested on Earth, then the

"golden age" of the Taripay Pacha will unfold and the meta-physical city of Paytiti, where Inkarí, the mythical first Inka, has been waiting, will manifest itself. The seventh level, the level of the Godhead or the Supreme Creative Principle, is then possible. The prophecy does not outline the way that the seventh level will manifest itself on the physical plane, nor does it describe the abilities associated with this culminating level of human consciousness. However, the manifestation of the seventh level on Earth is not achieved by humans alone but through our collective, collaborative interchanges with Nature. During the Taripay Pacha, an intricate web of interaction will be rewoven between the human and non-human, the physical and metaphysical, and the natural and supernatural, an interaction that was once the ordinary state of being in the dim recesses of history. Thus, the Taripay Pacha is not so much the creation of a new form as the remembering of an ancient form, when we lived in sync with the pulse of the cosmos instead of, as we do now, with the artificial rhythms of manmade time.

For these reasons, Juan has been working with certain Q'ero paqos to push the kawsay, or lay down the energy filaments, connecting the most sacred ancient sites of South America and Peru. They are, in effect, cleansing and reinvigorating ancient power places on the light body of Pachamama that have become encrusted or dimmed from disuse or desecration. They are spinning the chakras, the *chunpis* or energy belts, of the Mother. In early 1996 they completed connecting the energy belts of South America at a site in Bolivia. In October 1996, I was fortunate to be part of a small group, under the auspices of The Wiraqocha Foundation, which was founded by Andean paqo Elizabeth Jenkins, that accompanied two Q'ero paqos to Hopiland. Before the meeting with the Hopi elders, we took the Q'ero to the San Francisco Peaks, where the Q'ero connected the seques of South America to North America. In a moving ceremony, they joined the "spine of the Mother" via the sacred mountains of the San Francisco Peaks, and with that act the prophecy began to flow through the "nervous system" of the North. Over the next two days, during auspicious meetings between the Q'ero and their "brothers," the Hopi, these two lineages renewed ancient spiritual ties, reuniting the energies of the keepers of the ancient knowledge of north and south.[4]

And so the prophecy of the Andes filters down to you from the isolated heights of the Peruvian mountains, where it has existed for centuries, perhaps millennia, in a state as enduring and pristine as the snows that blanket the Apus. The prophecy and the Nature wisdom contained in these pages are more than the beliefs of one culture, they are the living tradition of a people who know that the lifeblood of the cosmos is *ayni*, reciprocity. Every breath they inhale is preceded by the exhalation of Pachamama; every dream they dream influences the movement of the stars; every action they perform reverberates throughout the Great Web of Being. "Sharing with strangers is the power of kawsay," don Agustín says. But he knows, and you know, that in the Great Web of Being there are no strangers. The gift bequeathed to you by the Q'ero paqos and their students who reach out to you through this book is not intellectual, nor conceptual, nor material—because it lives. It is a way of being. It *is* being. Because this consciousness lives in and through the Q'ero, their students, and other Andean paqos, it lives in and through you. And through you it will live in someone else—until, finally, as brothers and sisters, we recognize, as the Q'ero do, that "we are human beings. The only difference is our clothing. But we are all human beings, with love for each other."

Part II

Walking the Sacred Path: Interviews with Q'ero Mystics

I WAS HERE AT LAST—Machu Picchu, the lost city of the Inkas, the city in the clouds, the sacred citadel of the ancient paqos. I sat in the main courtyard under the single tree, called the Tree of Peace, in a circle of friends who had only the day before completed the arduous Inca Trail trek. We had walked in our Medicine Bodies, dying to our old selves and calling to us our new, shamanic selves. We had performed ceremony along the Trail and practiced working with our energy bodies. This work was new to me. I had only been on the Andean Path for little more than a year, and I had a long way to go before I could even sense my energy body never mind control it. Little did I know I would momentarily be put to the test.

One of my teachers, Américo Yábar, was seated among us, and he began to talk, in his usual poetic way, about energy. He spoke only Spanish, so his words were translated, but still they retained their beauty. "We are not only flesh and blood," he began, tapping his fist against his chest. "We only think we are. We delude ourselves, and our delusions construct our reality. They are the screen between what is and what we think there is. What are we really? Ahhh! There is a question!" Américo's notoriously charming smile made his eyes sparkle.

Then his expression changed almost instantaneously. He became serious, and he thoughtfully stroked his thick, black mustache. "Ah, such an impossible question. But then we shamans love the impossible, don't we? We court the impossible as if it were a lover. Beautiful, no? Seductive, no?

"We are energy beings. Luminous beings. And when we gain control of our filaments, we gain control of everything! I will show you, no? You will see, okay?"

I'm not sure most of us understood much of what Américo had said, but I was about to be put on the spot in his little demonstration. I was sitting opposite him in the circle, and he pointed toward me.

"Joan," he declared, smiling his mischievous smile, "you throw your energy filaments to me." He cocked one dark eyebrow, signaling a challenge.

I squirmed uncomfortably and shrugged my shoulders. "Whatever you say," I replied, attempting to mask my nervousness with nonchalance. In fact, just the night before I had had a sublime energy experience while meditating in the sacred baths at Aguas Calientes. I had become lost in the magic of the moon, merging with her, losing all sense of self and becoming one with the enigmatic energy of the cosmos. But now, in the harsh glare of daylight, I was undeniably flesh and blood. My skepticism quickly dimmed the reality of the previous night's luminous experience.

Américo said nothing. He stared at me, stroking his mustache, his face a blank slate. He nodded his head once, that arched black eyebrow relaxing. The experiment was about to begin.

I sat cross-legged, my hands resting on my lap. I closed my eyes and breathed deeply. I focused my intention on my qosqo, the area just below my navel that is our primary energy center. I visualized a ball of energy, a brilliant sun composed of intertwined strands of light, and I imaginatively unfurled these luminous filaments and cast them out toward Américo. Or I should say I tried. I could feel myself straining, physically pushing the muscles of my belly outward. Soon I gave up. I knew within moments that I was going about this all wrong. I was trying too hard. I should have been "non-doing," using not my physical will but my shamanic intent. I was simply exercising my imagination, not my energy body. I felt defeated and embarrassed. I was sure Américo was aware of my failure, although he exercised Latin graciousness and talked around my failure, instead enrapturing us with a description of how he cast out his own energy filaments.

This had not been my first failure at gaining control of my energy body; it wouldn't be my last. In fact, in a few days I would be called before a Q'ero *kuraq akulleq*, who would tell me, point-blank, that I had a lot of work to do before I could even hope to gain control of my energy bubble. Little did I know that within two years I would achieve a measure of such control, and I would be sitting in front of six Q'ero *paqos*, interviewing them about their knowledge of the world of living energy. It is a very real world, one in which we all live as energy beings. But all that lay in the future. Now, I was simply content to experience Peru for the first time, to begin that series of teachings that would begin to peel away my illusions of material realism. My teachers had warned me that this work would be like walking through a doorway to a new, perhaps unrecognizable world. They weren't incorrect; they were just too kind. In reality, the next few years were more like falling down the rabbit hole. Like Alice, I would be reeducated in a language beyond the scope of words and logic.

Chapter 4

Ancient Tradition,
Modern Practice

The conquest of Peru by the Spanish, following the pattern of most other colonialist enterprises, had a devastating effect upon the local populations. Between 1532 and 1572, the conquest and colonizing period, the indigenous population of Peru was reduced by eighty percent, from a high of between nine and sixteen million people to about three million.[1] Like most other indigenous Peruvians, the Q'ero lost their land and, for all intents and purposes, their freedom under the Spanish. Land was carved up into huge estates upon which the indigenous peoples were obligated to work. In effect, they became serfs. To understand the Q'ero, one must understand their life since the Conquest, which was a life of serfdom that continued unabated into the twentieth century. It was only in the late 1950s that the Q'ero, with the help of a group of visionary anthropologists and journalists, were released from the shackles of the hacienda system. The Q'ero were one of the first communities to overcome this colonial system, ten years before the landmark 1968 Agrarian Reform Law, which started Peru onto the path of real land reform. To read more about Q'ero existence under the hand of the *hacendado*, refer to appendix III.

Despite their more than four hundred years of physical bondage, the Q'ero retained their sense of community and their historical identity as the grandsons of Inkarí, the mythical first

Inka. Their mystical system, however, had undergone an inevitable syncretization with the Catholicism introduced by the Spaniards. As the story of their recent history, some of which is recounted below, makes clear, the Q'ero feel no contradiction calling themselves Catholic even as they perform ancient ceremonies to establish their connections with the Apus and Pachamama, make ritual offerings to supernatural beings, and interact with a natural world that is alive and responsive.

The Q'eros' willingness to embrace the best of both their ancient, animistic traditions and Catholic ceremony and doctrine is a testament to their adaptability, an instinct, perhaps, that allowed them to survive and to retain, as few other communities in Peru have, their ethnic, cultural, and mythic ancestral memory. The Q'eros' reputation as the "keepers of the ancient knowledge" comes not only from among local populations in the southern highlands of Peru, but even from such an unlikely source as the U.S. Library of Congress, which in their encyclopedic tome on Peru, one of a series of statistical books about the countries of the world, singles out the Q'ero as one of the few peoples to "preserve many ancient practices and lifeways."[2]

The Catholic Church waged a bitter campaign to suppress indigenous beliefs and practices, destroying mummies and ancient deities, which they replaced with saints, and building Catholic churches over the sites of Inka temples. In one year alone (1617–1618) it was reported that in a single coastal region of Peru, 603 wakas and 617 mummies were destroyed.[3] By the end of the seventeenth century, Catholicism had been successfully integrated throughout Peru.

One issue that had not come up in my earlier discussions with the Q'ero about their life under the hacienda system (see appendix III) was the issue of religion and ceremony. I was curious to know if the hacendados, the feudal landowners, who were mostly mestizos and Catholics, had forced Catholicism upon the Q'ero and suppressed their indigenous beliefs and practices. The hacendados seemed to control every aspect of the indigenous populations' lives, so I thought it likely that their ceremonial life—practices such as making despachos, performing coca divinations, making pilgrimages to important sites of initiation such as Q'ollorit'i—may have been eradicated, or at least forced underground. It was obvious that somehow the Andean people had managed to preserve their ancient traditions. I wanted to spend at least part of our interview time, precious though it was, to open this line of questioning and find out how the imposition of a foreign religious system had affected the communities of Q'ero. I began by asking the five male Q'ero paqos assembled before me in Urubamba if the hacendado had forced Catholicism upon them.

There was a long discussion among the Q'ero as they considered this broad query. Then don Juan Pauqar Flores, the eldest paqo among them, answered on behalf of the group. "In the old times, we remember hearing stories about this, but none of us witnessed this. In the time of our grandfathers, the hacendado brought a priest to the hacienda. He paid the priest to come to supervise the religious festivals and then to return to his own town, Paucartambo. Our grandfather told us [he and his younger brother, don Julian] that once the hacendado invited the priest to come to Q'ero, to be like a missionary there. When he came to live in Q'ero, the people offered him part of their crops and livestock in return for his services. The missionary stayed in Q'ero, and the people supported him freely, of their own decision. But when the hacendado saw that they were supporting the priest, he was angry. He saw that this went against his own interest. He said that the people could only give things to him, not to anyone else, not even the priest. He forbade them to support the priest. So the priest returned crying to Paucartambo because he could not stay with us in Q'ero. This thing happened in the time of our grandfather.

"That was the only occasion when a priest was in Q'ero, when the hacendado invited him. After he left, we did the Catholic religious ceremonies and festivals on our own, because we wanted to continue them."

I was unconvinced that the Q'ero had so willingly embraced Christianity. "Did the hacendado suppress your own beliefs and ceremonies?" I asked again.

The group again discussed my question among themselves, often heatedly, and then don Juan recapped their discussion. Their answer was directed at being force-fed Christianity and why they continue its practice today, not at how their ceremonies may have been suppressed. "We were not obligated to do this [Catholic ceremony]," don Juan explained. "The obligation arose from the community itself. In the community there are elders who perform the ceremonies of the Church, and they say this is our [the younger people's] time to assume these responsibilities. It is our turn to step into, to take over, these obligations. If we do this it increases our social standing; we can further ourselves. But these elders say, 'Do this only if you have the qualities to do it.' However, it is an obligation to the community."

I was about to ask a follow-up question to the group when don Juan decided he wanted to talk about Catholic observances and Q'ero ceremony. We gave him free rein.

"Today in Q'ero, during Holy Week, we observe the religious festival of Santiago [St. James], which is the most important religious fiesta in Q'ero. In addition to the fiesta of Santiago, we observe another ceremony, the ceremony of the 'Breast of the

Virgin.' [This ceremony, I discovered, is one in which the people give homage to the Virgin for the spiritual sustenance she gives them and during which they pray for physical sustenance, as in abundant crops and healthy children.] At the same time we also have another ceremony that is only for single people, for the unmarried men and women. In this ceremony there is a banner that is paraded around. These three ceremonies—Santiago, the Breast of the Virgin, and the Banner of the Single People—all happen during Holy Week.

"In the time of our grandfathers, there were other ceremonies, for example, the feast of Santo Domingo and the ceremony of *Qollena* [a festival honoring people who excel in their work or in other endeavors]. Now we don't do these ceremonies.

"The other ceremony that we do continue is the pilgrimage to the sanctuary of Q'ollorit'i. In this pilgrimage we carry two different types of dancers: the *Qolla*, who represent the people of the high plains, and *Ch'unchu*, who represent the people of the jungle."[4]

The way don Juan talked of "continuing" the pilgrimage to Q'ollorit'i, I could only assume that even the authority of the hacendado had not prevented this most important of sacred duties. I had been to Q'ollorit'i, in June 1995, and been overwhelmed with the energetic intensity of this most sacred of sites.[5] I had also been surprised at the obvious overlay of indigenous and Catholic practices at Q'ollorit'i, which are evident even to the untrained eye. It may be beneficial to take a brief pause here in order to review the history and significance of the Q'ollorit'i festival, because the Q'ero hold a special status in relation to it.

Q'ollorit'i[6] is one of the most important sanctuaries for an Andean paqo. Nestled at the base of a glacial range called Sinak'ara, which is near the holy mountain of Ausangate,

Q'olloriti'i is where most paqos go to receive their initiations. There they cleanse themselves in sacred lagoons and make despacho offerings to the Lord of Q'ollorit'i himself. There are four principal *wakas*, or sacred sites, in the area beneath the glacier, the most important of which is a large stone upon which an image of Christ is visible. The myth of the origin of this waka describes a mysterious shepherd boy who, in a flash of brilliant light, disappeared into this rock, leaving only the image of Christ behind on the rock's surface. Although the site is ancient, the Catholic authorities seized the opportunity to control the indigenous practices by building a sanctuary building over the site. Today, the rock, upon which the image of Christ as been enhanced with paint, is kept enclosed in glass behind a simple altar within the sanctuary building. Even today, most paqos make a yearly pilgrimage to Q'ollorit'i, as do thousands of villagers and a few hundred tourists. There, the paqos perform their ancient initiation and cleansing ceremonies and also call upon the Lord of Q'ollorit'i and Jesus Christ to bless them and their communities.

The Q'ero, because of their reputation as "keepers of the ancient knowledge," are considered by the Q'ollorit'i pilgrims as the link to the ancient lineage of the Inkas and to Inkarí, the legendary first Inka. As such, they occupy a special, reserved area on the outskirts of the sanctuary grounds, where a waka, called the Q'ero Stone, is located. Because of their special status as paqos, as don Juan Pauqar Flores explained, "the Q'ero are the last to arrive at Q'ollorit'i and the last to leave." With their arrival comes the "spirit of the Inka," and before their departure, but after all the other pilgrims have left, they perform private ceremonies at the wakas and upon Qolqe Punku, an Apu in the sacred glacial range. "This has always been," don Juan declared. "This is forever—from the time before our grandfathers, and it is how we do things now.

"But," he continued, getting us back to the subject of the Q'eros' observance of Catholic ceremony, "we never go to Paucartambo for the feast of Mamacha Carmen [a feast in honor of a Catholic saint, whose shrine is in Paucartambo]. This is a feast that belongs to the *mistis* [a term indigenous people use for "mestizo," a Peruvian of mixed Spanish descent]. We only go to Paucartambo to have our new president recognized, to receive the authority of Paucartambo [so their community president will be officially recognized]."

Here don Juan seemed to veer off into a narrative of the political structure of Q'ero, but it soon became apparent that his real subject was how the Q'ero blend Colonial social structures with indigenous ceremonies.

"The person who becomes our president," he explained, "invites the entire community—even the women and children—to eat and drink. He extends an invitation to the community to acknowledge his authority. The invitation is given twice: once when he assumes his charge and once at the end of the Carnaval [a fiesta celebrated as part of Holy Week]. This invitation is not only the responsibility of the president, but of his two helpers also. They must invite all the people to a fiesta twice.[7] We eat, drink, and dance.

"Another part of the president's invitation is very important. He must perform a set of rituals to the Apus and to Pachamama. These rituals are for the spirits, asking for bountiful crops, for rain, for health for us and our animals, for a good year during the time of the president's service, which is one year."

As interesting as don Juan's exposition was, it was still unclear whether these Q'ero paqos considered themselves Catholic. Juan decided to simply and unabashedly ask that question. "Do you consider yourselves Catholic?"

All five Q'ero immediately responded, nodding their heads emphatically. "Yes, we are Catholic. Totally Catholic."

Despite my having witnessed the Andeans' curious blend of Catholicism and indigenous ceremony at sacred sites such as Q'ollorit'i, I was still struck by the Q'eros' emphatic response. After all, the Q'ero are considered the most respected paqos in the Cuzco region. How could they be master practitioners of nature mysticism and still so ardently believe themselves to be Catholic, especially since there was no longer a hacendado forcing a religious system upon them?

Ricardo Valderrama, an anthropology professor who was serving as my Quechua interpreter and who has for more than twenty years studied and recorded the stories of indigenous peoples throughout Peru, explained that there really is no conflict. "In Peru, to be Catholic is a very special thing, even for mestizos like myself. We are Catholic with the Apus, with Pachamama. We go to Mass but there is no contradiction when we then do a despacho and invoke the Apus."

Juan Núñez del Prado, sounding suddenly more like an anthropologist than an alto mesayoq, explained that the Catholicism of the Q'ero, and of other indigenous peoples in Peru, is not the modern, "official" doctrine espoused by Rome. It is instead the Catholicism of the sixteenth century, when many heretical beliefs flourished asserting the possibility of personal revelation and an individual's capacity for direct communion with God. It borrows from the doctrine of St. Francis, professing that God can be revealed in the hills, the trees, the animals, in all of nature. Many of these doctrines infiltrated the countryside at the time of the Conquest, and they are still alive today, inextricably wedded with the ancient indigenous mystical beliefs.

It was clear to me now that the Q'ero paqos sitting before me, and certainly their ancestors, had learned not only to survive in the often strange, usually confusing, and always threatening world of the Conquistadors and of Spanish colonial rule. They had borrowed from their oppressors certain spiritual concepts and ceremonies that they made their own and that have enriched their lives. Because of my new understanding, despite its still limited scope, I would not find it strange in the days ahead to hear the Q'ero equate an Apu with Jesus Christ or to hear them use the terms "Lord of Q'ollorit'i" and "God" interchangeably.

Moreover, it seemed only natural that our next topic of discussion would take us deeper into the collective memory of the Q'ero Indians, back to times far distant from their bondage under the hand of the hacendado, back to the very founding of Q'ero and to the bestowal of the mystical knowledge upon the Q'ero by the mythical first Inka, Inkarí.

Chapter 5

The Grandsons of Inkarí

For the Q'ero, as for many other indigenous peoples in Peru, the Inka lives. He not only lives, but he is patiently awaiting the day when he can triumphantly return to rule once again, restoring Peru to its ancient glory, liberating its people from their centuries of oppression, and cleansing the contamination spread by the foreign cultures who have remade Peru in their own images.

The Q'ero call themselves the "grandsons of Inkarí," the mythical first Inka who founded the Inka Empire, and they patiently await Inkarí's return, as had became clear to me from Juan's story, recounted in chapter 3, about his walk with don Manuel Q'espi through the ruins of Moray. There, Juan saw only workmen restoring the ruins. Don Manuel, however, saw the Inka's houses being repaired in preparation for his return. I also had heard Juan extensively explain his understanding of Andean prophecy: the rise of infallible healers; the return of the Sapa Inka and Qoya, who would serve as role models for a new kind of political leadership; the potential spiritual evolution of humankind that would flower into new levels of consciousness and fertilize the manifestation of new human abilities that depend upon our accessing our energy bodies more than our physical bodies. But for all my work in Peru and conversations with my teachers, I had heard little about the Q'eros' mythical forebear, Inkarí. These interviews were my chance to fill this gap in my understanding of Q'ero mythical history and mystical belief.

The Inkarí myth was first heard in Q'ero by Juan's father, anthropologist Oscar Núñez del Prado, and his colleagues during their 1955 expedition to Q'ero. Until then, the origin myth of the Inkas was largely restricted to the Manco Qhapaq legend.[1] According to this legend, which has many, more detailed, variations,[2] at the dawn of time Manco Qhapaq, the son of the Sun, emerged from a cave on an island in Lake Titicaca carrying a golden staff and accompanied by his sister-wife, Mama Oqllu,[3] the daughter of the Moon. The two Royals gathered the people of the region, who had been living as savages, together into ten groups, or *ayllus*, and taught them the ways of civilization— weaving and farming. Then Manco Qhapaq and Mama Oqllu went in search of a suitable place to build their imperial city. Manco Qhapaq had been instructed by Father Sun to throw a golden staff from the top of a mountain; where it landed upright would be deemed the "navel," or center, of the empire. Many times Manco Qhapaq threw the golden staff, and each time it landed askew. Finally, however, it sank upright into the rich soil of a fertile valley, and there Cuzco was founded. Once the city was built, including the magnificent Qoricancha, the Temple of the Sun, Manco Qhapaq and Mama Oqllu set out across the empire to gather together all the people. Manco Qhapaq journeyed north and Mama Oqllu ventured south, proclaiming to all that Father Sun had bestowed his gifts upon this land for the good of the people. Gathering people from the four corners of the empire, they formed the Tawantinsuyu,[4] the Inka empire, where they began the divine dynasty of the Inkas.

Oscar Núñez del Prado no doubt noted the Inkarí myth's striking similarities to the Manco Qhapaq legend, except for one crucial difference—the Inkarí myth suggests the Inka still lives and is awaiting the proper time for his return. Núñez del Prado and other anthropologists, cognizant of the messianic quality of this new legend, began to search in other geographic regions for this myth. To their surprise, once they began looking for it, they found versions of the Inkarí myth not only throughout the central Andes, but throughout Peru and even in neighboring countries, such as Colombia, Ecuador and, especially, northern Bolivia.⁵ The creation myth of the indigenous peoples of the Andes was no longer a sterile artifact recorded in sixteenth-century journals; it was a vital, living legacy, a hope that still stirred the hearts of the indigenous peoples.

Explicit in the Q'ero version of the myth recounted below is the Q'eros' claim that they are descendants of this first Inka—they are Inkarí's grandsons. What is not explicit is their belief that Inkarí bestowed upon the Q'ero a unique and precious gift. According to Juan and Américo, the Q'ero claim that Inkarí bequeathed them the mystical knowledge, designating them keepers of the ancient knowledge, a reputation they retain to this day among Andean paqos. In contrast to the Q'ero, who were bequeathed the sacred knowledge, were the people of Cuzco, the imperial capital, to whom Inkarí bequeathed the administrative and political knowledge that allowed them to build one of the greatest empires of the Southern Hemisphere.

Julian Pauqar Flores was the bearer of the Inkarí myth for the Q'ero assembled in Urubamba. He told me the tale of Q'ero's founding with reverence and solemnity. After the telling of the tale, other Q'eros added variations they had heard from their relatives and ancestors, or added details that don Julian had missed. For the sake of narrative flow I have merged these details into the tale proper. What follows is the story, passed down generation to generation, of the Q'eros' royal lineage and of the origin of their identity as master paqos and as the bearers of the spirit of the Inka to such sacred festivals as Q'ollorit'i.

• • •

"My grandfather told me that Inkarí had a golden staff," began don Julian, "and he threw the golden staff from Raya Qasa [a border town between the high plains and the mountainous regions of south-central Peru]. As Inkarí was trying to throw the golden staff, Qollari, the wife of Inkarí, tickled him in his right armpit. Because she tickled him, the throw missed Q'ero. If the staff had hit the land of Q'ero, Q'ero would have been the qosqo [literally the "navel"—the center or capital city] of the Tawantinsuyu. But the staff missed Q'ero and landed in Cuzco, which became the capital of the Tawantinsuyu. And so Cuzco was founded. If this golden staff had landed in Q'ero, Q'ero would have been a valley, rather than in such high mountains.

"In Cuzco, Inkarí built a huge temple. He also built many houses, grand houses such as Saqsawaman. He built a solar clock[6] in order to measure the towns. He went to Machu Picchu, and there he built more grand houses. Returning from Machu Picchu, he built Ollantaytambo [a monumental fortress near Pisac that is the temple of the wind gods and of the moon]. Then he remembered Q'ero. He said, 'I will return to Q'ero to see my children.' The proof of Inkarí's visit to Q'ero is two footprints in stone, which are still there in Upispata [a hot springs near Q'ero].

"After that, Inkarí descended to the *quebradas* [the canyons], where he worked with gold. Qollari, the wife of the Inka Inkarí, was weaving, just as the woman today weave. On their way to the canyons where Inkarí was working were a man and a woman *arriero* [hired porters who haul goods with their mules]. The woman arriero appeared from the right side of the river. The male arriero appeared from the hills. The woman said, 'If God permits it, I will camp at Maratuni.' Then she said, 'If God permits it, I will camp at Kinsapampa.' Then the woman said, 'If God permits it, I will camp at Castilla Uno.'[7] Then the male arriero came with his animals and with his assistant, who was riding a mule. Following them was a *tunki* [a brilliantly colored bird], who alighted near a lagoon and began to sing. The male arriero killed the tunki. When this happened, his assistant became enchanted and wandered to the lagoon, which consumed him. He remains enchanted in this lagoon to this day. And so only the mule arrived at the canyon where Inkarí was working the gold.

"The Inka did not live very long in Q'ero. He was there only for a short time. Maybe he stayed only about a week. If he had stayed, he would have had to build a town. He was waiting for the arrieros, and when they did not arrive, he left. He went to Ollantaytambo, and as he was building his house there, our God arrived.[8] God appeared as a man to Inkarí and told him, 'Inkarí, I will give you more *munay* [capacity to love].' But Inkarí said, 'What munay? I have my own munay.'

"God saw out of the corner of his eye that Inkarí was herding rocks with a crop, like we would herd llamas. Inkarí built houses this way, not doing useful work but saying to the stones, 'You must become a wall!' and the stones became a wall. But over time, the stones began to disobey Inkarí. Seeing this and wanting to restore the stones' abilities, Inkarí remembered the person who had offered him more munay. Inkarí now looked for this person, but the person had disappeared. And because of that, now men must carry stones only by the power of their own arms. We can no longer make the stones obey our will. If Inkarí had received that additional munay, we could today build houses by commanding the stones to move.

"Inkarí left Ollantaytambo and went to Paytiti [a metaphysical "male" city where Inkarí resides; its "female" counterpart is Miscayani]. That is where Inkarí now lives. Because of the will of Inkarí, now the Vilcanota [a sacred river] carries the excrement of the llamas.[9] When Inkarí sees the excrement of the llamas, he cries.[10] Because of all these things, we in Q'ero are known to this day as Inkas.

"My grandfather said that Inkarí posted a paper on the door of the temple at Cuzco saying that he will return one day to Cuzco. If he returns to Cuzco, surely he will build houses like he did in the past [by commanding stones to move instead of through manual labor]. We will return to times past, to the days of the Inkas.

"We are the grandsons of Inkarí."

When don Julian's story was translated from Quechua to English, I was mesmerized. The story's simplicity, beauty, and austere reverence moved me deeply. For me the story was enough; I had no questions to ask, no curiosity for more details. But the anthropologists with me were not so sentimental. We had only a short time left with the Q'ero, and there were aspects of this version of the myth that Ricardo in particular wanted don Julian to elaborate. So after initiating a round of pisco, a strong alcohol that refreshed us all, I sat back, content to let Juan and Ricardo lead the questioning. Ricardo began by asking don Julian about the notice Inkarí posted on the cathedral door. The Inkas had no written language, so a myth detailing an Inka conveying a written decree was intriguing. Ricardo was wondering if this was an anachronism. Don Julian's answer surprised us all.

"It is possible that he now knows how to write," don Julian began, "because our Inka is not dead. He is the person who does not die; he is immortal."

When we asked about Inkarí's immortality, don Juan Pauqar

Flores, don Julian's brother, broke in to offer us a variation on the myth. His variation revealed further correspondences to the Manco Qhapaq myth and to sixteenth-century historical events surrounding the execution of Inka Waskar by his half-brother, Atawallpa, during the Spanish conquest. At about the same time that Pizarro's army was pushing into Peru, the half-brothers Atawallpa and Waskar were battling for control of the Inka empire. Waskar was killed while being brought as a captive back to Cuzco, where Atawallpa was pushing his own claim as Inka to Pizarro.[11] A messianic legend grew up surrounding Waskar's death, relating how Waskar's head became separated from his body and rolled through a grate in the street into the *ukhu pacha*, the lower world. Waskar's head still lives there, awaiting the propitious day when it can be reunited with its body.[12] When that occurs, the city-states of the ancient Tawantinsuyu will also be reunited, restoring the Inka Empire to its former glory. This Waskar legend was almost certainly a subtext for don Juan's variation on the Inkarí myth.

"My grandfather told me that Inkarí was in Miscayani, where he worked with the gold. The Spaniards came and found him. They asked why Inkarí had the right to work with gold. Inkarí escaped to Lima, but the Spaniards followed him. In Lima he was called Rey Ulanita [King Ulanita], and he was captured there and killed by the Spaniards. In that way, Inkarí was killed in Lima because he was working in fields of gold. In Lima the Spaniards also killed Qollari.

"Now, the only thing I know is that the Inka is waiting in Paytiti, working the gold there. And Inkarí, in Paytiti, is crying, telling himself, 'I don't know how my grandsons are faring.' So he cries, in Paytiti. This city is very far away, deep in the jungle."

Ricardo asked where the city is in the jungle, and don Julian answered, demonstrating with his answer not only how

pragmatic the Q'ero are but also how deeply held is their long-
ing for the past and to be reunited with their beloved Inkarí.
"The city exists. This city *must* exist. Because of Inkarí, the
Vilcanota carries llama dung to this city. It must be lower than
Q'ero, because a river does not carry things upwards. And
Inkarí is down there crying, because he sees the llama dung in
the water and longs for us, his grandsons."

Now don Mariano leaned forward, ready to offer his version
of the myth, or so we thought. Instead, his ironic commentary
left us all laughing, perfectly lightening what was becoming an
overly intense interview. His commentary was all the more
amusing because it was coming from a kuraq akulleq, a respected master paqo and leader of the community.

"If I had known when I was a child that I was going to have
the opportunity to talk about these things," don Mariano said,
"then I would have listened better. But I was a child who listened to these things and they went in one ear and out the
other! If I had known then that I was going to have this opportunity to speak with you, maybe I would have spent even a day
learning these stories. I would have asked for these stories, even
offering the elders a drink to tell me these stories!"

Don Juan shook his head in agreement and said, rather
wearily, "The young people today do not want to hear these stories; they do not listen. I heard these stories when I was nine
years old. Then my grandfather died. If my grandfather had lived,
I would have had the opportunity to learn more of these stories."

Suddenly the group became animated, one Q'ero talking
over another. As translators, Ricardo and Anamaria straightened
out the cross comments and reported that the younger Q'ero
were saying of don Juan, "Of course, he knew his grandfather.
But we did not know our grandfathers. We did not have the
opportunity to speak with our elders."

Ricardo surveyed the group of five male paqos and quietly asked, "If you are paqos and you don't know these things, what will happen with your children?"

The Q'ero were silent for a moment, then don Julian spoke, soberly, ending the interview on a typically pragmatic Q'ero note and highlighting the fact that despite this being the close of the twentieth century, the Q'ero culture remains largely an oral culture: "I am teaching my grandchildren about these things. Whether each remembers depends of each person's capacity. But they must have interest in order to remember. If they have no interest, they will not remember."

Don Julian's comment brought home to me the import of our project, of recording at least part of Q'ero mystical knowledge before it was lost. I was grateful for the opportunity to hear this primordial myth of the Q'eros' mystical history from the Q'ero paqos themselves, especially after having heard their version of their recent historical and political past. Both perspectives helped me more deeply appreciate the initiation stories I had already recorded, for I now better understood how the Q'ero could so easily and seamlessly synthesize the best from both lineages—the Western, Christianized tradition of their conquerors and the animistic and magical tradition of their mythic forebears. The Spaniards may have founded Lima and birthed a nation, but Inkarí had founded Q'ero and birthed a lineage of mystics. Each of the Q'ero priests who sat before me now had struggled to find his or her rightful place in both of these worlds, and their personal initiation stories, which follow in the next two chapters, reveal their individual journeys along the sacred path and into the heart of the mystery.

Chapter 6

Pampa Mesayoq:
Master of the Earth Rituals

A pampa mesayoq is a master of the nature energies, particularly of the feminine energies, those of Pachamama or, as Américo Yábar would characterize it, the energy of the "cosmic Mother." He or she is initiated into the ways of the nature spirits and is responsible for giving them ritual acknowledgment. "The rivers, the trees, the rocks, the plants, the animals are all the province of the pampa mesayoq," Américo claims. But the pampa mesayoq is in service to the community as well as to Nature. Expert in despachos, coca divination, and herbal and energy healing, the pampa mesayoq serves as intermediary between villagers and the supernatural forces that affect every aspect of their lives. The pampa mesayoq can treat a physical disease, diagnose a psychological or spiritual illness, propitiate the spirits to increase your good luck and fortune, or cleanse your house or your energy field of heavy energy.

Although the pampa mesayoq does not wield the same intensity of power nor the same range of influence with the spirits as does an alto mesayoq, his or her initiation is no less rigorous. The same irreversible decisions, initiation perils, spiritual challenges, and personal self-scrutiny face them both. As the two initiation stories told below make clear, the pampa mesayoq's power is awesome in its beauty and in its capacity to penetrate to the heart of the mystical universe, where by taking the pulse of the metaphysical, the paqo learns to reveal the condition of the physical.

Don Agustín Pauqar Qapa

Agustín Pauqar Qapa, age 32, is the youngest of the five male Q'ero paqos I interviewed in July 1996. A thin, boyish-looking father of five, Agustín quickly became identified in my mind as the paqo with *"the* hat." Anamaria and Sandy laughingly agreed with my assessment that with his unadorned, floppy brown hat and pointed chin, Agustín looked rather like Ray Bolger in his role as the scarecrow in *The Wizard of Oz*. Like that character, Agustín was one minute the thoughtful, soft-spoken man and the next the merry prankster. A characteristic Agustín moment, and this was only one of many, occurred one evening after dinner, when Ricardo began teaching me, Anamaria, and Sandy the Quechua terms for various parts of the human body. Eye, *ñawi*; nose, *senqa*; mouth, *simi*. Before long all the Q'ero were joining in. Head, *uma*; hand, *maki*; foot, *chaki*; shoulder, *rikra*. Then Agustín offered *ñuñu*. Like the attentive students that we were, we three repeated the new word several times before we realized that Agustín had not pointed to a corresponding body part. To gales of laughter from the Q'ero, we learned we were saying, "breast." Agustín managed to sneak in "vagina" and "big breasts" before our lesson was over. We soon got even, when later that evening we gave an English lesson.

However, when it came time to sit for his private interview, to tell his initiation story, the prankster Agustín became "don Agustín," a paqo whom Juan Núñez del Prado describes as "the most brilliant young pampa mesayoq in Q'ero." Juan's opinion obviously is shared by many Peruvians, for don Agustín is in high demand with the people of the Sacred Valley. At the conclusion of our interview session at Urubamba, we were to drop don Agustín in Cuzco, where, with the new sacred year about to begin, he had many regular clients waiting for him to conduct despacho ceremonies, to offer prayers and blessings on their behalf, and even, perhaps, to perform healings.

Our interview was a paradox. Of all the Q'ero paqos, don Agustín was the most inconsistent in the chronology of his narrative. It took many attempts to determine which *karpay* came in what order and who was in attendance at these initiations. These details were never verified to my satisfaction, and I'm sure that if I asked don Agustín to once again tell his story I would detect still other inconsistencies. However, in other aspects of our interview, don Agustín more than lived up to Juan's high praise. The sensitivity of his observations and the beauty of his phraseology survived the double translation. The depth of his commitment to the sacred path is everywhere evident.

I had the opportunity to meet and work with don Agustín three or four more times over the next several years. One special occasion was when he and don Juan Pauqar Espinosa came to the United States for two weeks in the fall of 1996 to meet with friends and supporters of The Wiraqocha Foundation and to meet with Hopi elders in order to join the energies of the North American and South American mountains, which form the "spine of the Mother." But I had very little unstructured time with him during this particular visit and could clear up only the most important confusions in the details of his story. Therefore, I cannot claim that the sequence of the story that follows is *exactly* how events unfolded. What I can assure the reader is that the meaning and spirit of these events were carefully reproduced, and I have no doubt the reader will reap many benefits from having shared this journey with so eloquent and sincere a guide.

• • •

"Our Holy Mother Mary was the first person to ever blow[1] into the coca leaves. She was given the finest coca by God; it was not like the coca that I and other paqos chew, but was of the finest quality. She blew into the coca and chewed it because her Son was lost. She was the first to work with the coca, and from that time to this day we, too, use the coca in order to invoke the Apus.

"Mother Mary's chewing the coca is very much like the story we told you about the paqo Garibilu Q'espi [see chapter 1], who cured many people by commanding the yellow fever, from which he suffered, to eat all the other diseases. He could do this because the Apus and Pachamama were inside his body, and because he has his estrella. The Apus chose him to be a paqo and gave him his estrella. In this same way, the father of my father was chosen by the Apus to be a paqo. But he did not want it, and he died. My father was also chosen by the Apus to be an alto mesayoq, but he, too, did not want to be a paqo. Because of his refusal, many of his children died. When he saw his children dying, he offered a despacho to a sacred lagoon, but this estrella did not have the power to solve his problem.[2] After a time, my father also died.

"When I was young, I was very sick. When I was sick, I had

a dream in which a *misti* appeared, a man dressed in white clothes riding a white horse.[3] He was totally and absolutely clean. He said, 'If you serve me from the tops of the hills, you will be well.'[4] This dream happened when I was nine years old. By then, my mother had a second husband, who was a paqo. My mother said to him, 'See what you can tell from the coca leaves about the dream of my child.' My mother's husband read the coca leaves and said I was being called to the sacred path. He said, 'This man in your dream is the Apu. It is the Apu who is calling you.' After this dream, I meditated about whether I would take the responsibility for the sacred path or not. I was very young. I did not fully believe or accept this dream. I did not yet know how to chew the coca leaves. Still, as I got older I went to consult with many different paqos, and each one told me that I had been given an estrella.

"I did not do anything, but about one or two years later I had a second dream about this same misti, and this time he gave me a fruit. He said, 'You will be the owner of this fruit.' But this fruit was not really a fruit, it was a flower. It was a fruit *and* a flower.

"I grew up and my thinking became more mature. About this time, I heard of a paqo named Bernabe Marchaqa. I went to meet with him. He was a pampa mesayoq, one of the best paqos of Q'ero. He told me these dreams were happening in my life because I was chosen to be a paqo but I had not accepted the call. He found that I had three estrellas, not just one. He knew that I was in the hands of three Apus. I asked him where I should perform my karpay, at the Apu Waman Lipa or the Apu Ausangate. But he took me to Q'ollorit'i to receive the first karpay, the initiation. In this karpay we offered a despacho for all the mistakes of my ancestors [for his grandfather's and father's refusals to heed the call of their estrellas]. We offered twelve k'intus. That's the way I began to find my path. Not because of my will but because of Bernabe Marchaqa.

"When I performed my karpay, nobody [no spirits] came to visit my mesa, only the bull. We saw a bull, who approached us. But the bull is very dangerous. Bernabe Marchaqa said to me that the bull is too dangerous, and I must not accept it into my mesa. If I accepted this bull I would have become a very powerful alto mesayoq, but only for two or three years. If I rejected the bull, then I could only be a pampa mesayoq but I would have my power until the day I die.

"I meditated for some time after this karpay, and decided to reject the bull and to become only a pampa mesayoq. I did not want to have only temporary power. So Bernabe Marchaqa and I performed another karpay. This one was also performed at Q'ollorit'i, and another powerful paqo was with us, the alto mesayoq Andreas Espinosa. During this karpay a bull again came to the place where we were making our offering. The bull is an animal who announces death. He calls death. Because of this we did not want to accept the challenge. To accept the messenger of the dead is a very dangerous challenge.

"The bull just showed up, and we could talk to him. But you cannot talk to a bull like you can talk to an estrella. With an estrella you can establish a dialogue. But you cannot with a bull. He talks to you only. That is why it is dangerous to accept the bull. The bull is sacred, but it represents the darker forces. Then Bernabe Marchaqa and Andreas Espinosa said that if I accept the bull I will have power for only two or three years. They suggested that I take the pampa mesayoq path and I would have power for my whole life. So I committed to being only a pampa mesayoq.

"After this my parents died.[5] But I performed a third karpay with Bernabe Marchaqa. Andreas Espinosa told me to go with

Marchaqa. He said, 'Go to perform the karpay and I will call your estrella to come talk with you.' It was during this karpay that I was told again I had three estrellas: the Apus Waman Lipa, Anqaschaki, and Qolqe Krus. Bernabe Marchaqa told me I had these estrellas, but he told me this from far away, not from close to me. This time the power did not come close because I was not totally clean, in clean clothes and having washed well. To meet an Apu, you must be totally clean. I did not know this rule, and I went dirty to the karpay. This was a mistake. Because of this mistake, I did not meet my estrellas up close.[6] The Apus also told me that because of this mistake I could not be an alto mesayoq. 'You are going to be only a pampa mesayoq,' they said.

"Later another bad thing happened to me because of this mistake. I met a woman, but this woman died almost immediately. We were together only three months. After my woman died, I did my final karpay to become a pampa mesayoq. Because of that karpay, I am a pampa mesayoq who reads the coca leaves.

"I will stop now to choose the coca leaves, to remember more details."

After a few minutes of rest, during which he made several k'intus, blew his prayers into them, and then chewed them, don Agustín resumed his narrative. He began by offering some perspective on how one becomes a paqo.

"It was almost five years from the beginning to the end of my training. But I worked with Andreas Espinosa only for the initiation rituals. The first two karpays my [step-]father asked him to do for me. Bernabe Marchaqa was also there. Then my parents died. The last karpay was only with Marchaqa."

Here don Agustín paused, then he intoned, as if offering us a cryptic mantra that seemed to explain every nuance of the decisions he faced in accepting his path as pampa mesayoq: "All the work I worked was not worked. All the wants I wanted were not wanted. Because of that I assume the responsibility that all the work I work must be worked, and all the wants I want must be wanted."

Then, without missing a beat, don Agustín swept away the mystery of the moment by resuming his narrative in a most pragmatic manner. "You are not a paqo because you want to be a paqo. No! It is because the estrella chooses you to become a paqo. The estrella chooses you," he emphasized. "Then you follow the will of the estrella. When you do that, you are rewarded with large herds, good crops, good health, and healthy children. You have a good relationship with your wife. You are able to perform successful healings.

"To receive your estrella you must be strong. You must be able to receive the impact of the estrella. The estrella comes like a truck! Because I was strong I was able to open my heart to receive the power in my heart. That's how I received my estrella."

Don Agustín paused again, his initiation story complete. After a short break, I asked him just what the duties of pampa mesayoq entail. The other Q'ero I had already interviewed had tended to answer such broad questions very concretely, often giving only a mundane detail or two. It was very difficult to get them to put their mystical practices into any generalized context or to discuss the impact or significance of their practices. Agustín was no different.

"I do despachos for health, love, and for business," he said, summing up his practice in one sentence. Then, remembering something more, he added, "And for the Apus."

"To honor the Apus?" I asked, wondering what exactly Agustín meant. But Juan Núñez del Prado did not even translate my question. To him it must have seemed a naive and perhaps even ridiculous question, for he proceeded to answer it himself. He often did this when he thought it was just easier to quickly educate me on a fine point rather than go through the rigors of the translation process, from English to Spanish and from Spanish to Quechua, and then back again. So Juan explained, "No, not exactly to honor the Apus. When a paqo does a despacho for the Apus it is to establish his personal relationship with the Apus."

I asked Agustín for what reasons people come to him to perform a despacho, hoping my question would encourage him to tell a story or two about his work and the people who seek out his services.

"I do work for people who want to learn harmony—a couple or a family or people who want to work together," he said. "Several times [when I was first a paqo] I thought I must only do the work of making offerings to my Apus and Pachamama. But this is wrong. And my wife became sick, because I was performing my duties in the wrong way. After that, I learned that I must work for everyone. Because of [what happened with] my wife, I learned I had to integrate my work, working with Pachamama and the Apus for health, love, business, as well as making offerings to the Apus. I must do all this work.

"So after that I worked together with my wife. When I learned to work with her, I learned I could work with the left side. When we worked together, my wife worked with the left side and I worked with the right side. But when she could not work with me, I found that I could still offer a despacho with my left hand to Pachamama and with my right hand to the Apus. So I learned to integrate the work.

"I must tell the truth," he said. "These are all the things I did."

Don Agustín's pronouncement, so heartfelt, brought us all up short. Don Agustín's sincerity and intensity were almost overwhelming. We felt truly grateful that he, and the other Q'ero paqos, were allowing us to probe into their private worlds. We also recognized that such a pronouncement signalled that the teller of the tale desired a break. As don Agustín rested for a few minutes, I turned to Juan for an explanation of the left and right sides in Andean mystical work.

I knew that paqos could be trained on what is called the "left side of the mesa" or the "right side of the mesa." But Andean understanding of the left and right sides does not directly equate with the Western concept of being left-brained (analytical, linear, and so on) versus right-brained (intuitive, creative, non-linear).[7] Instead it refers to being trained in the "magical" (left) or the "mystical" (right) sides of the work. The distinction is often hard to pin down in concrete terms, and is described differently depending to whom you talk. But Juan explained that in the most simple terms a paqo who works predominantly on the left side of the mesa is one who is "capable of handling the power and the vision in order to use it for practical purposes, such as healing." A person working predominantly on the right side has been granted the teachings that give him or her the "capacity to actually meet and communicate with supernatural beings and energies." Ideally, a paqo will integrate the two teachings and "pull the kawsay," the living energy, from both sides of the mesa.

Another important distinction to the Andean metaphor of left and right is that men are considered to have a natural capacity for the right-side work, whereas women paqos have an innate capacity to work from the left. In the sacred world of the Andes, traditionally the left side is associated with "femaleness." For example, the moon and the sea are considered to be on the left side whereas the sun and the mountains are considered on the masculine, right side.[8] Juan Pauqar Flores had explained previously that women work almost exclusively on the left "because the rituals they perform are heard more by Pachamama and the Apus." Juan Núñez del Prado explained this concept in Jungian terms: the right side can be equated with logos, which is the rational mind and the propensity toward interpretation; whereas the left-side work can be equated with eros, which is the "impulse to life, the capacity to easily establish relationships, and the tendency toward wholeness and nurturing." Thus, women paqos are considered to be naturally more adept at the left-mesa work—namely, healing work. Men, on the other hand, are better at the right-side work of communicating with the Spirit world to access information. What a paqo must do to become a fully realized mystic is develop both capacities, that of eros and logos, thereby easily working both the left and right sides of the mesa. Don Agustín, therefore, had honored his wife by relating how she had taught him to harmonize and integrate both of these mystical capacities, so that he could offer assistance to people as easily with his "left hand" as with his "right hand."

As we regrouped to continue the interview, I decided to remain focused on how a pampa mesayoq works with despachos. This complex ritual offering is the pampa mesayoq's speciality, and it is probably the most frequently performed ceremony in the Andes. There is an almost dizzying array of despachos, more than two hundred different kinds. Each type of despacho is used for a specific purpose and is comprised of different quantities and types of *recados*, which are the individual ritual items and natural objects that fill the offering bundle. General despachos are sold pre-packaged by specialists in Andean marketplaces, and despachos for specific purposes, such as love despachos, are made upon request. It takes years to master just the basic types of despachos. My questions to don Agustín attempted to determine how a pampa mesayoq decides what type of despacho to use for a particular situation and what might result from the despacho ceremony. For instance, do they always work? But somehow my meaning was lost in translation, and don Agustín launched into a description of how a general despacho is made. I reproduce that description here so that the reader will have some idea of just how complex the preparation of a despacho can be. (I did not reproduce the Quechua names for the Andean plants and seeds; instead I simply used the defining description don Agustín or the translators provided.) What does not come through, unfortunately, is just how beautiful the arrangement of these offerings are. The pampa mesayoq selects and arranges each item with exquisite care. A completed despacho can be a work of art, or what a friend of mine describes as a "nature mandala."

"For a despacho," don Agustín said, "you need all the recados. Coca leaves, incense, sugar, everything in the packet [a prepackaged despacho that paqos and others can buy in the marketplace]. You use white paper, and on it you must put twelve k'intus and make the form of a cross with sugar. You must put in white and red carnations and red wine and pisco. You can put the twelve k'intus on white cotton. Over the incense and sugar you put an aromatic plant, a grass, that comes from the coast; a llama fetus; candies, raisins or grapes; another type of Andean seed; rice or noodles [uncooked]; tiny silver and gold sheets of paper that are like little books; gold and silver thread; a tiny flute of gold or silver; certain dried fruits; a magnetic stone; and a small crucifix. You can put in a type of clay and a crumbled up coca leaf. Other types of seeds and plants. Vicuña fat. Yucca. Coca seeds.

"Over all this, to finish, you put another white and red

carnation. Then you have a little shell that serves as a mesa and another little cross to close the door [complete the making of the despacho]. In one corner you put two tiny candles, one red and one yellow. There are also many little figurines of metallic paper or metal: stars, houses, people, keys and locks, stairways, animals. You choose from among these according to the purpose of the despacho."

Don Agustín sat silent for a moment, trying to remember if he had left anything out. Juan took advantage of the pause to tell me that there were something on the order of 218 different items that may be placed into a single despacho.

Don Agustín, I believed, was going to tell us all 218! But we didn't have the heart to interrupt him, so he continued his list. "There are two kinds of people symbolized in those figures, single and married. There is also a figure with its two fists together, symbolizing the touch of power. There is also a figure of a little man made out of candy.

"When you have selected these, then you drip a little trago [a sugar-cane alcohol] over them. You sprinkle a little more red wine around the despacho. Then you fold up the despacho and tie it with white thread.

"There are two colors that are important to a despacho: red and white. For a despacho to Pachamama, you choose red flowers. For the Apus, white.

"Then you burn the despacho and the fire carries [its power and prayers] to the Apus. The fire is the vehicle that takes the despacho to the Apus."

I thanked don Agustín for his description of the contents of a despacho, then rephrased one of my original questions, which had remained unanswered: "How do you choose what kind of despacho to use in a particular circumstance? For instance, what are some of the ways they are used, say, in healing? Is there a story of one despacho ceremony that you could tell us?"

"The first way to use a despacho," don Agustín explained, "is as an offering. This is a positive use. But if there is sin or something dirty [hucha] in your house, then the despacho is used in another way. The despacho cleans the hucha from your house. That's another kind of despacho." Then unsure of just what information we were seeking, don Agustín asked us, "Do you want to know exactly how that kind of despacho is made?"

"No," I said, and thanked him for offering to share that information with us. "We don't need to know that, but it would be good to know more about some of the ways a despacho works. For instance, do they always work, or can the offering fail? What are some of the outcomes of a despacho ceremony?" I was interested in how don Agustín interacted as a paqo, as a pampa mesayoq, within his community. Therefore I pressed these questions, and Anamaria and Ricardo patiently translated.

"If a person needs the service of one pampa mesayoq," don Agustín explained, "then [he or she] goes to a different one."

I turned toward Juan, asking if I had heard the translation correctly. He assured me I had. We asked don Agustín to explain the logic of this process.

"The other paqo reads the coca leaves for you to see if the problem or healing you want [from a particular pampa mesayoq] is for the 'hand' of that pampa mesayoq. If the coca leaves say this work is for his hand, then the person goes to that pampa mesayoq."

I wanted to ask about conflict of interest between pampa mesayoqs here, but decided not to because I suspected I was imposing my suspicious, competitive North American attitudes onto the Andean culture—and the question became moot anyway, because my persistent queries had obviously tired Agustín.

"This is complete," he said. "There is no more now. I will speak more tomorrow if you want.

Doña Agustina Apasa

When I first arranged, through Juan Núñez del Prado, to dispatch a messenger on horseback to Q'ero to ask if several Q'ero paqos would agree to come down from their mountain villages to tell their stories for a book, I was hoping only that the Q'ero would agree to participate. Juan and I together formed a "wish list" of participants: we hoped to interview at least two alto mesayoqs (don Manuel Q'espi, don Mariano Apasa Marchaqa, or don Juan Pauqar Espinosa), one pampa mesayoq (don Agustín Pauqar Qapa), and the two Pauqar Flores brothers, who could talk about the history of Q'ero and the Inkarí myth with the most fluency. It was only later, after the messenger had been dispatched, that I realized our omission: there were no women paqos on our list. As I awaited the messenger's reply, I prayed that our omission would somehow be rectified. The only female paqo I knew was doña Agustina Apasa, the wife of don Mariano Apasa Marchaqa. I did not know if there were any others in Q'ero. When the messenger returned, having manifested our wish list, I was ecstatic, and dismissed any unhappiness about having no access to women paqos. Perhaps there would be another opportunity later to interview a female paqo, I told myself.

Needless to say, it was with great delight that I discovered, upon my arrival in Cuzco, that doña Agustina had accompanied her husband. My prayers seemed to have been answered. However, by the time we arrived in Urubamba, two days after my arrival in Peru and perhaps a week after the Q'ero had left their villages, it was clear that doña Agustina was very ill. She was coughing in deep, chest-rattling fits, and she often clutched her chest as if in pain. For our first two days in Urubamba, she either sat quietly in a corner of the interview room listening or slept in her room. Sandy offered her a potent herbal remedy, whose awful taste was inversely proportional to its reputed healing efficacy, but doña Agustina took one sip, spit out the wicked substance, and refused to ingest any more. Finally, on the third day, while in Urubamba having lunch, we convinced don Mariano that his wife needed to consult a conventional medical doctor. After lunch, Juan, Ricardo, and don Mariano escorted doña Agustina to a doctor's office, where it was discovered she had pneumonia. Injections of antibiotics and various other medications were prescribed. Despite doña Agustina's terror at receiving the injections, they seemed to help. By the next day she felt well enough to spend an hour or so being interviewed.

Doña Agustina is a quiet woman who smiles readily but who often shrinks from eye contact. Nevertheless, when she was with us during the group interviews, she was not afraid to speak up for herself or to set the men straight in a dispute. Once, the men were debating whether they had any more information to tell us about a particular matter. Doña Agustina interrupted, and with a dismissive sweep of her hand, she put an end to their discussion: "They do not know any more!" she exclaimed, laughing. "They have told you all they know."

Doña Agustina was not called to the path of the pampa mesayoq in the conventional way, through a vision or a dream or the call of an estrella (manifestation of an Apu). Instead, her first husband decided she had the potential, and so he initiated her into the sacred path. Today, now married to don Mariano, doña Agustina still does not work alone. She assists don Mariano, who was present during her interview, by choosing the coca leaves and making despachos. Although doña Agustina's story is unconventional, it is, nevertheless, extremely valuable, for it reveals her deep connection to the realm of spirit, where Pachamama advises her how to perform a healing. Her narrative, too, provides a unique insight into the powerful female spirits, the Ñust'as. These are the ancient Princesses of the Mountains, the supernatural female energies who form couples with the Lords of the Apus, the male spirits who inhabit the mountains. Although her story is short, doña Agustina tells it with her characteristic simplicity and directness, and occasionally she unleashes her sharp sense of humor.

• • •

"My [first] husband was a paqo, an alto mesayoq, and he performed three initiation rituals for me, asking for me to be given the power to choose the coca leaves. My husband said I must be a pampa mesayoq. He gave me the karpays. I did not receive an invitation to be a paqo in my dreams or any other way. It was my husband who taught me. He taught me to choose the coca leaves for Pachamama and for the Ñust'as. My first husband died and left me. My present husband [don Mariano] gave me three initiations also.

"I only choose the coca leaves for Holy Mother Earth and for the Ñust'as, the Princesses," doña Agustina explained. "Holy Mother Earth is distinct from the Mama Ñust'as, the Princesses of the Apus. When I perform healings I dream about the Lady of the Valley, who is the Pachamama. Pachamama tells me to perform the despacho this way or that way. I dream about the Ñust'as also, who are ladies of the high snow peaks. They teach me how to perform the rituals for healing or what kind of healing is involved in the particular case.

"In my dreams, Pachamama is floating, dressed in the style of the women of the valleys. And the Ñust'as are dressed in brilliant gold or silver clothing. Sometimes they are tenderly caring for a child. Sometimes they also come to me when I am choosing the coca leaves or making the despacho, and they do it with me. They teach me.

"Frequently these beings appear together in my dreams. Because I am chosen to be a pampa mesayoq, I think that I will be together with these beings from now until the moment of my death.

"This is all."

Doña Agustina adjusted her *lliklla* (shawl), drawing it around her shoulders, wrapping herself up tight just as she had so succinctly wrapped up her initiation story.

I thanked her for her story, then asked her how old she had been when her first husband had initiated her. She replied that she had been twenty years old.

Now that her initiation story was told, doña Agustina seemed hesitant to talk. I wasn't sure if she was feeling shy or if she was naturally taciturn. In an effort to get her to open up, I asked a deliberately broad question about how becoming a pampa mesayoq may have changed her life.

"Being a pampa mesayoq is good," doña Agustina told us, "because before, I was often very ill. I think that this illness was cured because of my work with the Ñust'as and Pachamama. Since I became a pampa mesayoq I have had good health."

Ricardo then spoke up, asking doña Agustina about the

circumstances of her first husband's death. This seemingly straightforward query prompted doña Agustina to reveal some significant insights into the perils of following the sacred path.

"My husband died very quickly. He was bleeding from the nose, the mouth. He was only sick one day, and he died. Because of that we could not heal him. If he had had a long illness, we could have used our power to heal him. But it was very fast. He died in one day.

"There were just the two of us. We did not have children. When this happened, even our thoughts were hanged.[9] He was an alto mesayoq. His death could have been a result of a mistake he made. The malignant, dark forces can eat you, can eat your energies.

"The next year I met Mariano," doña Agustina said, moving quickly from the subject of her first husband's death. "He gave me his karpays, and now we are working together."

Juan, perhaps in an effort to lighten the atmosphere, made a comment, half in jest, about doña Agustina's marrying well, since both her husbands were paqos.

Doña Agustina squared her shoulders and shot back, "I am sure that the Lady Ñust'as and Pachamama want all my husbands to be alto mesayoqs!"

We all had a good laugh, then we resumed with more pragmatic questions. "How many female pampa mesayoqs are there in Q'ero?" I asked her.

"There are no other women pampa mesayoqs who have been given the karpays except for me," she replied.

In a future interview with the male paqos I would learn that there also are no female alto mesayoqs in Q'ero, although don Juan Pauqar Espinosa's daughter has been called to the path and he has pledged to support her training. Generally, however, the present generation of women, according to these Q'ero paqos, do not want to face the challenges of the path. It isn't that they are incapable of becoming paqos, but that they choose not to exert the effort. And so, we were told, there are currently no female paqos except doña Agustina in Q'ero. If I had known this at the time I interviewed doña Agustina, or if she had volunteered the information, our interview may have taken a different tack. I would have loved to hear her defend her gender about their willingness to become paqos. But for some reason I, and no one else that day, thought to ask doña Agustina more about this curious lack of women paqos, and so we lost an opportunity to explore an important topic. Instead, I asked doña Agustina if she felt there are any differences between a female and a male pampa mesayoq.

"There are some distinctions," she acknowledged. "The woman pampa mesayoq works with the Pachamama and the Ñust'as. The man works with the Apus."

Following up on this line of questioning, Sandy asked doña Agustina if there were any differences in the way female and male paqos performed the rituals. But doña Agustina answered the question only in the most personal way: "I always work together with my husband. I never work alone. We do despachos and healings together." Implicit in that answer, however, was the assumption that because doña Agustina and don Mariano work together compatibly, there are few differences between how male and female paqos carry out the ceremonies.

Sandy put another question to doña Agustina, one that provoked a somewhat heated reply. She asked if doña Agustina has any difficulty managing her responsibilities both as mother and paqo. Doña Agustina replied in a rush of Quechua.

"One can see that there is no conflict," she retorted. "Both are part of my total life."

Juan provided commentary about her complete response,

which never was fully translated. "She was surprised by the question," he explained. "She said first that everything in her life is better because she is a pampa mesayoq. She is surprised. She said there is no conflict with being a mother and a pampa mesayoq."

"Well," asked Anamaria, "how does becoming a pampa mesayoq set a paqo, either a man or a woman, apart in the community? Are they seen differently, treated differently?"

"No," doña Agustina replied. "It's the same for both men and women, and we are treated no differently."

At this point Juan donned his professorial hat and gave us a mini lecture. "In the Andes, or anywhere, all of life is a path. In your life you can choose any path. For example, another person may choose the political path. And even with the sacred path, you are just following a path. She's just assuming a role as a paqo, but it is not separate from her daily life or identity as a mother. This is somewhat different from your culture, where there may be difficult role conflicts and hierarchies. This is even true here in some areas, for instance with my colleagues at the university. Some of them are preoccupied with how I can be an alto mesayoq and an anthropologist at the same time. They say to be both is to lose my objectivity. But for myself, there is not any conflict. Neither is there for doña Agustina. She is no different from someone who chooses to be a good sheep herder."

I understood what Juan was saying, but I also knew that doña Agustina, or any paqo, was very different from the "average" man or woman. The very fact that one is a paqo no doubt sets one apart; why should the mystics of Peru be different from the mystics of any other culture? There is no question that an alto mesayoq wields a lot of power in the community and is usually a rich man compared with his neighbors. Reason led me to believe that such distinctions were relevant to any paqo, even a pampa mesayoq. But I had not come to Peru to debate the sociology of the mystical priesthood. Time was precious, and I wanted to hear more of what doña Agustina's life as a paqo was like. So I asked her to relate a story about a healing she had done. "How do the Ñust'as and Pachamama help you to be a successful healer?" I asked.

Doña Agustina's answer revealed her to be a very clever, and diplomatic, woman. "I always work with Mariano," she began, giving her husband his due before she sang the praises of the supernatural beings. "The Ñust'as and Pachamama in dreams tell me how to perform the ritual: to choose a special kind of coca leaf, or how to pass the coca leaves over the body of the person, or how to touch the person to determine what the sickness is, or if we must bathe them with a specific herb. They also tell me how to offer a specific kind of despacho."

Here Juan expressed verbally what I had just surmised, that it was really doña Agustina, not don Mariano, who was in control of the ceremony through her Spirit guides. "I think doña Agustina really tells Mariano what to do!" he said. I was thinking, and I'm sure the others were, of an earlier comment one of the Q'ero had made about how women have the capacity to be the paqos with the greatest power. "We must ask Mariano if his wife tells him her dreams of Pachamama before they start the healing process," Juan insisted. "We must ask him if this is so."

Although doña Agustina could not have understood our English discussion, perhaps the repetition of don Mariano's name set her wifely antennae buzzing, because suddenly she spoke directly to Ricardo, asking him to tell us something.

Ricardo translated: "She says she does not want to talk too much. Although if we have precise questions for her, she will answer."

Juan, however, would not be deterred. "We must ask

Mariano our question." Since don Mariano was sitting nearby, quietly observing his wife's interview, Juan took the immediate opportunity and had Ricardo put the question to him.

Don Mariano's response was as skilled as it was sincere. "There are no secrets between our hearts," he said, rather gently putting us in our places. "If she has a dream she tells me, and if I have a dream, I tell her. We talk about our work. First we talk about it, then we perform the rituals together."

Doña Agustina nodded her head in agreement. From their words and their body language it was clear to me that their work truly is a collaborative effort, and their respect for each other was obvious and unquestioned.

"Is it possible to have them relate one specific case?" I asked. I had not yet gotten very far trying to get the Q'ero to tell us specific stories about their work. But I tried again, thinking specificity might provoke a response. "Perhaps of the *last* healing they did together?"

Ricardo put the question to them and translated their brief, even terse replies. "Mariano says that the last one was about a month ago, and doña Agustina does not want to be specific about it. She says only, 'When someone wants to be healed, we heal them.'"

That was good enough for me.

Chapter 7

Alto Mesayoq:
Master of the Hanaq Pacha

The alto mesayoqs of Q'ero, says Juan Núñez del Prado, are the most highly regarded in the Andes. Many of the alto mesayoqs from the Cuzco region journey to Q'ero to receive their final initiation. Even if they have received all the karpays from their own mentors, he explains, they go to Q'ero to be recognized and blessed by the Q'ero alto mesayoqs.

To be an alto mesayoq, according to Américo Yábar, is to "walk the edge of a sword," for the alto mesayoq must always maintain his balance between the world of *paña*, the ordinary, and *lloq'e*, the non-ordinary. With his characteristic verbal flourish, Américo says, "In the unfolding of the non-ordinary world, lloq'e is what connects the alto mesayoq with the mystery and enigma, and what connects him with the unfolding of the unknown energies. . . ."

Literally, *paña* is the Quechua word for "right" and *lloq'e* for "left." As the left side of the Andean path, lloq'e is the conduit through which one accesses the magical world and pushes the kawsay for practical purposes, such as healing. Paña, as the right side of the of the path, is the conduit to the mystical union, or communication, with the world of Spirit. The concept of left and right sides in Andean mysticism is fairly complicated, and one must be vigilant in defining the terms according to the context in which they are used. Here, Américo is putting them into the context of what we in the West would call left-brain and right-brain capacities. Remember, Andeans refer to the sides of the body rather than to the brain hemispheres. So lloq'e as the left side equates with the right brain, or the intuitive and the magical, whereas paña as the right side equates with the left brain, which is more practical, rational, and analytical. Hence, Américo's reference of these terms as "ordinary" and "non-ordinary" states. Immersed in the world of lloq'e, the alto mesayoq learns to "see" in a non-ordinary way. To be *qawaq* is to be a literal seer of energy, an expert healer, and a visionary.

An alto mesayoq's training typically begins only after he or she has received the call to the sacred path, such as surviving a lightning strike. Anthropologist Washington Rozas Alvarez writes, "The *Apus* choose *paqos* through lightning, and it can choose any person. The person is chosen by being struck by lightning, whose first ray kills him, second dismembers him, and third resurrects him. Also, when a person is in any mundane place, like at his farm, lightening can call him by striking very close to him. He will feel chosen, *qoñiruna*, which means 'person chosen by the ray.' After this, he will look for a Master from whom to receive the *karpay*, which is the initiation."[1]

An alto mesayoq's training is long and arduous, often spanning a decade. "Not everyone can go through the trials and tests just because they want to," Rozas writes. "[I]n order to become a *paqo*, the *Apus* choose from all of the apprentices who are on the path toward becoming a member of this sacred society, who are like priests. Many of them fall behind halfway through, and some at the door. Only the chosen ones are the ones who can go on to receive the *karpay*."[2] Such training for the chosen ones has many prerequisites that involve not only spiritual and physical challenges but monetary ones as well. An apprentice must provide payment to a Master teacher in money, alpacas, llamas, and personal labor; and provide such staples as coca, liquor, wine, candles, despachos, food, and chicha during the training period. These requisites can prove a hardship for most Andeans, who barely eke out a living for themselves and their families from the stony soils of the high mountains.

Once consecrated, however, an alto mesayoq enjoys a privileged and respected role within the community. Because of the vision and wisdom he receives from his allies in the spirit world, particularly the Apus, he is called upon to oversee the political and social welfare of the community, and is often called upon to mediate disputes and to settle conflicts. The alto mesayoq's main role, however, is mystical. Through his dialogue with the Apus and interchanges with the refined energies of the hanaq pacha, the alto mesayoq accesses the very fabric of space-time, where he is able to "push the kawsay," the animating energy of the physical world, on behalf of those who seek his counsel. According to Rozas, alto mesayoqs of the second level (llaqta alto mesayoqs) are sometimes referred to as *Atum-Cheqaqs*, or Men of Great Truth; and those of the third level (suyu alto mesayoqs) as *Atum-Aqulleqs*, or Great Knowers. Fourth-level alto mesayoqs—kuraq akulleqs—can access even more far-reaching energies, those of the cosmos, and can work these energies on a planetary scale. Kuraqs may have awesome powers, from making the clouds part at will, to being in more than one place at a time, to prophesying the future.

There are three more "levels" to the alto mesayoq path beyond that of kuraq akulleq but there are currently no priests working at these levels. These levels involve prodigious healing capacities, heightened levels of awareness, and refined modes of consciousness that have not yet manifested in space-time on Earth. Yet these three levels of being are part of an Andean prophecy, already discussed in detail in chapter 3, that is unfolding at this very moment and in which we may all play a part to further the spiritual evolution of humankind.

Don Juan Pauqar Espinosa

The alto mesayoq Juan Pauqar Espinosa, age 42, was the first Q'ero I interviewed privately in order to get the personal story of a paqo. I was nervous and unsure of myself, despite all the good advice I had received from Juan and Ricardo and the experience I had gained during our group interviews. In many ways I was fortunate that don Juan went first, because of all the Q'ero he was the most at ease and personable. Don Juan, despite being a powerful suyu alto mesayoq, is as mischievous as a puppy. He is quick to smile, and his smile is irresistible, reaching from ear to ear as he utterly abandons himself to whatever amusement is at hand. He and don Agustín were often in cahoots on some prank or joke. I remember an incident that occurred one evening at dinner that perfectly illustrates don Juan's penchant for hamming it up.

The Q'ero have prodigious appetites, and because food is scarce in their villages, they do not waste a single morsel. They certainly didn't during our stay in Urubamba, where, if it was offered to them, they would finish any food left uneaten on a plate—whether they liked it or not. Each evening, dinner became almost an adventure, because the Q'ero were being exposed to such unfamiliar "culture" as cutlery and to a wide variety of unfamiliar foods. One night for dessert we were served strawberry Jell-O. The crimson Jell-O was itself odd to the Q'ero, but it came served in tall, stemmed, glass dessert cups. The cups of Jell-O sat untouched on the table, the Q'ero surreptitiously eyeing me, Sandy, and Anamaria to see how we actually went about eating this strange, jiggling food. I think it was Sandy who took the first taste. Still, none of the Q'ero followed suit. It was obvious they were very unsure of themselves.

Finally, don Juan decided he would take on the challenge of the Jell-O. With five pairs of Q'ero eyes intently focused on him, he carefully palmed the delicate stemware with one hand and picked up the dessert spoon with the other. Then he gently shook the cup. The Jell-O wiggled and jiggled, and don Juan burst into laughter. The other Q'ero, Sandy, Anamaria, and I laughed not only at the ludicrousness of the situation but because don Juan's laugh is so contagious. His cheeks screw up into brown apples as his smile streaks across his face, from eye to sparkling eye, like a comet streaking across the night sky. His expression simply radiates pure delight.

I couldn't decide if don Juan was deliberately hamming it up or really was having trouble, but his next move had us all in stitches. He probed the Jell-O with his spoon, gouging out a small gelatinous cube. It skidded this way on the spoon and that way on the spoon, his hand reacting as quickly as possible but always just a fraction of a second too slow. His tongue was plastered to his lower lip in the intensity of the moment, like a six-year-old's when he is learning to print his name. Finally, after another round of juggling, he managed to scoop—although slam dunk may be a more accurate description—the Jell-O into his mouth. The reaction of his facial muscles was instantaneous, so fast that I suspect they occurred independent of the motor centers of his brain. His face instantly screwed itself up—eyes scrunched closed, lips fused together, and cheeks pushing toward his forehead—into the most expressive "Yuck" response I've ever seen. Everyone again erupted into gales of laughter—and don Juan proceeded to eat three servings of strawberry Jell-O.

During our interview, don Juan's penchant to play the clown was far less evident; still, he immediately put me at ease by calling me "sister" and expressing his belief that our project was very important to the Q'ero. He even toasted with a shot glass of pisco to our success. He then gave me a gift of a beautiful khuya from his mesa in order to connect our *poq'pos*, or energy bodies. I have reproduced these private moments because they so beautifully express don Juan's spirit, and they demonstrate how natural it is for the Q'ero to reach out and share their love and wisdom.

• • •

Don Juan raised the shot glass of pisco and offered a toast: "I hope we will do this project with all success, these things we want to do." Then he tossed the pisco back in one gulp and placed the glass on the coffee table. He reached over and retrieved his mesa bundle from where it sat next to him on the couch. He held the cloth bundle to his lips, closed his eyes, and began to pray. Ricardo whispered that don Juan was having a "personal interchange" with his mesa, the ritual bundle that contains the khuyas, or power stones, that connect him with his teachers, human and non-human, and hence his power.

Don Juan finally lowered his mesa to his lap and withdrew a small cloth from the confines of the outer wrapping of the bundle. He held the finely woven, gray and maroon cloth, which was carefully folded into a rectangle, flat on the palm of his hand, and began to speak.

"Dear sister, I will talk as an alto mesayoq, and for your work I want to offer you this." He moved the small cloth bundle toward me. I was sitting on a chair next to the couch, but I quickly moved to the couch, facing don Juan, knee to knee.

"I give you this as a gift, so that you can carry something of me with you. This is to guard your khuyas. We are here because God has willed it. This gift is so you never have pain, so you are lifted up high. Take this so that you will always be well. As you grow on the path, I will be happy. With the blessing of the Holy One, we will grow together, because our God, Jesus Christ, has told us we must share the things we know. He said that we should not divide or keep our work separate. He said that everyone must love one another with the same heart."

I was deeply moved by don Juan's words, and as I accepted his gift I asked Juan and Ricardo to translate for me. "Tell him that as he is about to share his knowledge with us, I will carry his words with the same love with which I will carry his gift."

"I will be very happy if you do this," don Juan replied.

As the interview proper began, Ricardo translated our instructions—that we wished don Juan to tell us his initiation story in whatever way felt most comfortable. When he was finished we would ask questions.

Don Juan needed no further prompting, and he began his narrative with a prayer.

"Oh Lord of the Heavens, I am an alto mesayoq because it is Your will that I be on this path. Help me to talk about the things You have taught me.

"Let the words I talk be talking. Let the work I work be working, Lord, because it is Your will.

"We are human beings. The only difference is our clothing. But we are all human beings, with love for each other.

"It is the will of God that I am an alto mesayoq. The will of

God first showed itself to me through lightning. This happened when I was herding llamas in the pasture. I was just a boy when I was touched by lightning. I was only eight years old. My memory of that day is not clear, but when this event with the lightning occurred, I was watching the llamas. I was following them when I saw hail coming toward me. I saw the wind, which was coming to meet me. The moment the wind met me, the lightning struck. This wind entered me like a ghost. That is when the lightning struck. My hat was thrown from my head. It flew very far, and I thought I would die within one hour.

"When I awoke, I was completely disoriented. I got up and I started to walk. I walked straight and did not look to either side, and there in front of me I saw my mesa.[3] I only saw it. I did not touch it or carry it. If I had taken the mesa with me, I later learned, at that moment I would have become an alto mesayoq, for the mesa comes with much power.

"My father was a little ugly [bad tempered], so I did not tell him what happened. I did not tell my father because he would not believe me. Because I did not discuss this with my father, I did not know the meaning of this event or what to do. Afterwards, I learned that if something like this happens to you, you must eat all your food without salt and you must only go into houses without smoke, into clean houses. All these things must be done, but because my father did not understand these things and I did not tell him, I did not know I was supposed to do any of these things.

"With this turn of events, I told my mother. But my mother could not give me force [help me], because being a mother, she could not be above her husband. So we did not do anything. When I explained what happened to me to my mother, she understood it. But we didn't do the right things. And so I very quickly became ill, with congestion in my lungs. I was ill for a long time.

"Then a paqo named Andreas Espinosa met my path [we crossed paths]. He saw my path in the coca leaves. At that time, I was fourteen years old. Because I was fourteen years old, I had consciousness about what was happening. This alto mesayoq, Espinosa, said, 'Because you are young and, therefore, strong, you must be ill for no [physical] reason.'

"Andreas Espinosa read the coca leaves and said that we must do a karpay. The coca said that after this karpay I would have a dream, and I would find in my dream what I would become in this life."

Here don Juan jumped ahead in time, explaining the consequences of his choice to follow the sacred path. "With this karpay, I became healthy. I recovered my intelligence. This was good. From that time to now I have been well. Even though I do not have a lot of livestock, my life is good."

Don Juan quickly resumed the chronological telling of his story. "Andreas Espinosa recommended that we go to perform the karpay and that then I would meet my mesa. He said I must go without fear, because if I go with any fear I will not meet my mesa. If I have no fear, it will be waiting for me. So I went, and I found my mesa.

"The karpay was performed in the name of Q'ollorit'i at a little snow peak called Waman Lipa, which is the spiritual equivalent of Q'ollorit'i. Later, we performed another karpay, and for it Andreas Espinosa said that it was necessary that we go to Q'ollorit'i to become cleansed and purified. It was necessary for us to be *ch'uya kanaykipay*, to become totally clean [physically and spiritually].

"When he said this to me, he said that he cannot perform this karpay for me without payment. I must pay him one cow."

Don Juan paused, perhaps to let the import of that price sink in. Juan Núñez del Prado whispered to me that one cow in those days was a fortune.

"I thought to myself," don Juan said, resuming his story, "I thought instead that I would pay him one llama or one alpaca.

"We made an agreement that he would come one afternoon, but he never came. That was very sad. I was alone, without much family. My brother was a man of weak character, and nothing could be done. Very quickly I became ill. For one month and three weeks I was ill.

"And then some people arrived [in our village] and they took a picture of me. They gave me the photograph, and I gave it to my brother, for his own initiative, so he would go and find a consultant, another paqo, and ask him why Andreas Espinosa never came to perform the initiation. He went to a paqo, but this paqo was a pampa mesayoq, not an alto mesayoq. He should have gone to an alto mesayoq, but he went only to a pampa mesayoq.

"This pampa mesayoq explained why Andreas Espinosa did not perform the karpay. He explained the reason for my illness. He said that Andreas Espinosa did not perform the ritual because I did not pay him the cow. Then this pampa mesayoq offered a *pago* [despacho used as a ritual atonement or payment] for me. The pampa mesayoq said we must do two different kinds of despachos and we must use different *recados* [ritual items] in each."

Here don Juan paused again. After a moment of silent consideration, he became philosophical. "About these words which I am saying—God knows what I am talking about. I cannot say more than the truth or less than the truth. I am saying the things I must say. To become an alto mesayoq is very expensive. There are many people who have the capacity to become alto mesayoqs, but because of the expenses, they cannot. I have a daughter who has the capacity to become a great alto mesayoq. I will bear all the costs for her. The cost is a cow, or an alpaca and a llama. And something in money. During the time you study, you must pay for food and drink, too."

Having told the hard truth about the mercantile realities of the spiritual path, don Juan resumed his personal narrative. "This pampa mesayoq said that Andreas Espinosa did not have the force to complete the karpay. So this pampa mesayoq said, 'Come with me to Q'ollorit'i. We will go together. There we will perform a despacho.'

"So I prepared for this. I cleaned myself, purified myself. When I arrived at Q'ollorit'i, I said inside myself the things I must say [offered prayers]. When I was carried by this pampa mesayoq to Q'ollorit'i, we first arrived at the Holy Place of the Virgin. We rested there.

"When you first arrive at Q'ollorit'i, you must go to the sacred lagoons to bathe and clean yourself. At the sacred lagoon, the pampa mesayoq bathed me, totally naked, just like I left the womb of my mother. After he bathed me, we went to the Holy Place of the Virgin. There we did a full despacho.

"Later, after we offered the despacho, we read the coca leaves. They said, 'You are finding your path.' And the coca also told me what was my mistake with Andreas Espinosa. They told me in what way I offended him. They said it was because of that mistake [not paying him the cow] that don Andreas did not complete my training.

"This pampa mesayoq also told me that alto mesayoqs can be proud and arrogant. And Andreas Espinosa was getting old. So Andreas Espinosa did not teach me, even though he later became my stepfather when he became involved with my mother for a year!

"This pampa mesayoq was named Martín Herrillo, and he

had only one leg.[4] God must bless this pampa mesayoq for what he did for me.

"After we performed all the despachos at the Holy Place of the Virgin, we went into the sanctuary of the Lord of Q'ollorit'i. Then the pampa mesayoq said, 'You must have no fear. Everything is done, and now you must wait. The Lord of Q'ollorit'i will meet you in your dreams.'

"At that time, the chapel of Q'ollorit'i was only a small chapel, not like it is now. He told me I must wait alone inside the door of the chapel and perform my despacho without any fear. This was in the middle of the night. I listened for noises, but I did not hear any. I took a sip or two of pisco to animate myself so I would not have any fear.

"It was the middle of the night when a big noise arrived on the roof of the chapel. Then I heard the ghost of the wind. There was noise on the roof like the hooves of livestock, but there were no livestock! It was clear it was the ghost of the wind, which suddenly arrived as a noise on the roof of the chapel.

"Then the ghost was wailing like the siren of an ambulance. I knew that this thing that had arrived must be the Lord of Q'ollorit'i himself! He talked to me, telling me, 'Any Christian person who comes to you, you must give him your attention. Even if he is not a Christian, you must help him, too. And the times you come to me, you must come clean, free of any impurities. If you come like this, I will help you.'

"Then my brother came with the pampa mesayoq to see what had happened. My brother and this pampa mesayoq, don Martín Herrillo, they had become totally worried when they heard this noise. They thought that maybe a meteor had crashed, and maybe I was dead, because the noise was so loud. They came, and my brother said he was very worried about me. They arrived at the moment I was full of doubt.

"Then we went down [the mountain] to don Martín's house, and even don Martín said he had been worried for my life. Don Martín read the coca leaves, and he saw that everything was all right. He said, 'You are on your path, and you will be well.'

"Don Martín saw in the coca that everything was complete, everything was good. He told me I must also read the coca.[5]

"Don Martín said, 'From now on, you are *ch'uya*, totally clean.'

"Then I chose the coca leaves in a sacred way. I drank some pisco. Then don Martín said, 'By now, you must be happy.' Martín Herrillo saw that, which was the truth."

Remembering this poignant moment with his teacher, don Juan suddenly and spontaneously began to sing. The song's simple but haunting melody transfixed us, and we understood that we were witnessing an expression of profound love between paqo and maestro. Several of us, including Juan, were reduced nearly to tears as don Juan finished the song and told us simply but reverently, "This is my teacher's sacred song, which he sang for me at that moment."

After we composed ourselves and thanked him for sharing his teacher's song, don Juan drank a shot of pisco and resumed speaking.

"Don Martín recommended, 'Now that you are *ch'uya*, don't forget me. You know that I am lame. See me. Help me in my fields. I do not ask payment, like the others. Give me what you will.' Then he sang his sacred song for me."

Don Juan paused yet again, this time to light a cigarette, which he absentmindedly puffed during the remainder of the interview.

"Don Martín also told me, 'When you talk about these things, you must talk alone. Because you can share your words in the wrong places. They can become confused.'

"Then we returned to my house, to drink and eat. After that, don Martín, the master, saw an alpaca in my flock that he admired. It was the best one. Because the master was very kind to me, I offered it to him, even though this was my most prized alpaca."

It was clear from the waning intensity of don Juan's voice and from his body posture that the interview was drawing to a close. It was late, time for bed, and there would be no time for follow-up questions. But we were very pleased with don Juan's sincerity and how forthcoming he had been in relating his initiation story. He had started his session by giving thanks to God, and now he closed it by acknowledging his teachers.

"I have a lot of gratitude to Andreas Espinosa, because he started this thing, even if he did not complete it. And I have a lot of gratitude to Martín Herrillo, because he completed my initiation as an alto mesayoq."

Don Mariano Apasa Marchaqa

Mariano Apasa Marchaqa was the unstated leader of the group of Q'ero who had assembled to tell their stories. Although he was not the oldest, he was the recognized elder because of his reputation as a gifted *kuraq akulleq*, a fourth-level, master paqo. Of all the paqos in Q'ero, only don Manuel Q'espi is held in higher regard than don Mariano, and there is even some dispute here, because don Manuel is *kamasqa*, that is, he was "taught" the work of the sacred path by Christ, in a vision, not by apprenticing to master teachers.

Don Mariano also is one of the most public of Q'ero paqos, because he works with two or three mestizo students of the Q'ero who bring groups to Peru, from the United States and Europe, to study Andean mysticism and he has traveled to the United States himself. Working with these groups has become a significant source of income for don Mariano, and this relationship has raised some eyebrows about his integrity.

As much as I love working with the other paqos, I hold a special fondness for don Mariano, because he was the first paqo I met, and at that first meeting he seemed to see into my heart. It was because of him, in some unexplainable way, that I was here now, trying to help the Q'ero preserve at least a small part of their knowledge before it became distorted and sensationalized by misguided tour guides and overzealous Western teachers.

Don Mariano, however, is a hard person to get to know. He is open and sensitive, and yet there is a reserve about him that makes him less approachable than others. He can sit unmoving, his face utterly expressionless and inscrutable, for hours. Then the next minute he can be smiling, talking and laughing, reaching over to embrace you, thanking you for some small kindness. After a few shots of pisco, don Mariano can be everyone's best friend.

Don Mariano also is almost painfully honest, and his ego does not seem to unduly influence his sacred work. Whenever we asked a question that may have pointed out a contradiction in the Q'eros' explanations, he would refuse to reconcile that contradiction just to save face. For instance, in a long and complicated discussion about prophecy, it became clear that the Q'ero were denying any ability whatsoever to predict the future, even though other Q'ero paqos, such as the great alto mesayoq Andreas Espinosa, now deceased, and don Manuel Q'espi, have held or now hold portions of Andean prophecy that predicts, very specifically, the potential spiritual evolution of humankind. Don Mariano insisted it was not possible to know about such things. We questioned him further, trying to pin things down by being concrete. When reminded of predictions he had made to me and others at Mollomarqa in 1994 and to Sandy when he read her coca leaves—very specific predictions, by the way, that had come true—he acknowledged that he had indeed read the coca leaves or made such predictions. But still, he insisted, it is not possible to foresee the future.

We finally understood that the contradiction was colored by the fine points of semantics. There was a significant difference in the Q'ero concept of "future time" as it relates to an individual and as it relates to the collective. And there is an important distinction to be made between seeing someone's future potential—the possibilities that are likely for that person—and predicting events that will unfold in a person's future. This discussion is presented in detail in appendix II. I reiterate it here only to demonstrate how scrupulous don Mariano can be when representing the scope of his abilities.

I interviewed don Mariano last, after all the other Q'ero had told their initiation stories, as a sign of respect for him. We gave him free rein to tell his story as he saw fit, and we did not often interrupt him, preferring instead to hold our questions until he had completed his personal account. Like many of the other paqos, don Mariano began his interview with a prayer.

• • •

"God, I will talk about the wisdom You have given me. I will talk only about that. I will not talk about any other things. I will tell only the truth.

"Primarily things like this happened to me. When I was a young man, nineteen years old, I saw a condor flying around above me. Soon there were many of them following me wherever I went. Later, not only the condor, but the hummingbird began to follow me. They followed me all the time, the condors and the hummingbirds. I wondered why they were following me. And later, after the hummingbird came to me, there came the bull. I said to myself, Why is this?

"I first contacted, and then consulted with, Bernabe Marchaqa, who is a good pampa mesayoq. I asked him why these animals were following me. I am the nephew of Bernabe Marchaqa; he is my blood relation, the brother of my father. So I asked him why these animals were following me. He read the coca, and he saw there that this [the path of the alto mesayoq] was the path for me. He said that he was not very good at reading the coca for people who are close blood relations. But he said that even though he was only a pampa mesayoq, he would give me a karpay. Then he gave me the karpay.

"At the time he gave me the karpay, the condor, the hummingbird, and the bull did not come to meet me in the right way, and they did not talk with me.

"I asked Bernabe why they did not come to me in the right way and why they were not talking to me," don Mariano explained, "because after the karpay, even though they did not talk with me, they did not leave me in peace. Everywhere I went, they followed me. When I asked this, he told me, 'This is happening because I am only a pampa mesayoq. Therefore, the condor, the bull, and the hummingbird did not come in the right way and did not talk to you. You must go to Andreas Espinosa, because he is an alto mesayoq and he is my contemporary.'

"Because of the recommendations of my old men [Bernabe Marchaqa and don Mariano's grandfather], I went to don

Andreas Espinosa. He performed another karpay for me, and this time the condor, bull, and hummingbird talked, but they did not talk through my mesa. They only talked through Andreas's mesa.

"Andreas Espinosa gave me the karpay at Q'ollorit'i for three consecutive years. Even after performing these three karpays, these beings did not talk through my mesa; they talked only through don Andreas's mesa. But don Andreas told me, 'You must wait. You must persevere. Finally they will talk through your mesa too, and then you will meet each other.'

"Because I was done with the work with Andreas Espinosa, I went to consult with don Fabian Apasa, another alto mesayoq, who is from Qocha Moqo. With him I performed the karpay three times more. I worked with Fabian Apasa for three years, trying to learn the *wachu*.[6] But still the bull, hummingbird, and condor did not speak to me.

"Because neither Andreas Espinosa nor Fabian Apasa was able to help me speak directly with these beings, I went to don Manuel Q'espi, who said to me, 'Let's go together to Q'ollorit'i to see the Lord of Q'ollorit'i. When we do this, the condor, the hummingbird, and the bull should stop lying to you.'[7]

"And so when don Manuel took me to meet the Lord of Q'ollorit'i, the mesa of don Manuel spoke. The voices of these beings were speaking through his mesa, but little by little their voices began to pass over to my mesa. When this happened, Manuel Q'espi said to me, 'Good, now you must place your mesa on the right side of mine.' And when we put the two mesas together, side by side like that, the beings spoke first through the mesa of don Manuel and then through mine. They said, 'Let us go talk.'

"But when my mesa started to talk, a *kukuchi penitente* arrived and started to talk through my mesa. He arrived at my mesa, but not at don Manuel's mesa, because don Manuel is a very experienced and mature paqo."

Juan interrupted the interview at this point to explain to me that a kukuchi penitente is a person who has passed on but who cannot enter the hanaq pacha, the upper world, or heaven in the Christian tradition, because of the hucha he or she carries. When Juan finished his explanation, don Mariano resumed his story.

"After that, finally the right beings arrived at our mesas. The Apus spoke through don Manuel's mesa, and they expelled the kukuchi penitente from my mesa and started to speak through my mesa as well." This time I stopped the interview, inquiring of Juan whether the animals who were speaking were really the Apus. Juan shook his head in confirmation, then explained that the condor, hummingbird, and bull were physical manifestations of the spirits of the Apus. When communication was finally established through don Manuel's assistance, don Mariano was able to speak directly to the Apus. Don Mariano resumed his initiation story.

"They talked to us from the two mesas. Often during a new paqo's work on the path, the kukuchi penitente will come to his mesa first, before the Apus do. When the Apus arrived at my mesa, they pulled the kukuchi penitente from my mesa; after that only the Apus spoke. When the Apus pulled out the kukuchi penitente from my mesa, the Apus said to me, 'Now we are finally meeting.' And so when the Apus were in my mesa, little by little they began to speak more and more strongly.

"I worked with Manuel Q'espi for six years, and he gave me three karpays, and then he said, 'Now you are ready to do the karpays by yourself.'

"When I started doing karpays [working by myself as an alto mesayoq], I had an assistant, and every time I went to do the karpays, I would do them with him.[8] We also worked together with don Manuel Q'espi, because each year don Manuel goes to Q'ollorit'i to renew himself. To renew yourself is to perform a new karpay each year at Q'ollorit'i. Don Manuel does this every year. Part of doing the personal renewal karpay is bathing in the sacred lagoon at the glacier of Q'ollorit'i. It is called the Bañu Qolqe Punku [Bath of the Silver Door]. This is the place where the paqo takes his bath of renewal."

Here don Mariano paused and refreshed himself with a shot of pisco. Then he resumed his narrative, making an aside about his own growth as a paqo before picking up the thread of his story about his continued work with don Manuel Q'espi. "After this time, I began to walk the path under my own power. To walk in the *wachu* [sacred path] was very difficult for me.

"When we went to Q'ollorit'i with don Manuel, we offered a karpay despacho at the side of the sanctuary, the temple of Q'ollorit'i. We offered twelve k'intus, which are placed around a shell. This is a karpay despacho. It is simpler than many other despachos.

"For five years, I have been working with my wife, going to Q'ollorit'i for cleansing and purification. At that time, however, when I went to the Q'ollorit'i temple with my assistant and don Manuel, we went inside the temple first and offered candles to ask the Lord of Q'ollorit'i for power. We asked the Lord of Q'ollorit'i, 'Lord, give us Your *munay*, *llank'ay*, and *yachay*. Give us Your will and love, Your force.'" I recognized these Quechua words, and didn't need Ricardo and Anamaria to translate. They are the three stances of an Andean paqo, meaning, respectively, the capacity to love, to perform physical labor, and to wisely use the knowledge gained through personal experience.

With the retelling of that prayer, don Mariano rather abruptly concluded his initiation story. There were many areas we wanted him to expand upon, and we spent the rest of the evening in a question-and-answer session. To begin, Ricardo asked which Apus spoke through don Manuel's and don Mariano's mesas.

Don Mariano explained he was able to communicate with the Apus Waman Lipa, Santo Domingo, Q'anaqway, and Qolqe Punku. These Apus, he explained, are the *Mamarit'is*, the snow-covered Apus, the beings who are the mothers of the glacier Sinak'ara itself.

Juan was interested in don Mariano's training with don Manuel Q'espi. "It is said," Juan related, "that don Manuel has twice met with Jesus Christ in person, at Wanka and at Q'ollorit'i. Have you ever had this experience?"

"Yes. This is the truth," don Mariano said, shaking his head in affirmation. "The times I have gone with don Manuel Q'espi to Q'ollorit'i we saw the Lord of Q'ollorit'i and we talked with him. When I went to the temple, we met and talked with the Lord of Q'ollorit'i. But I cannot tell a lie—I have never been to Wanka."

I was interested in knowing what the Lord of Q'ollorit'i, whom don Mariano equated with Jesus Christ, had said to him once their dialogue had been established. When Juan heard the question I wished to ask, he looked rather shocked, as if even thinking of probing into such a personal area was impertinent and potentially insulting. But feigning naiveté, I insisted that it was worth a try. "Sure, he might refuse to answer," I reasoned, "but I've asked off-the-wall questions before and we've received incredibly informative replies. Let's just try this question and see what happens." Juan finally assented and translated my question to Ricardo, who put it to don Mariano in Quechua. Once again, we were well rewarded for taking the risk.

Don Mariano leaned forward on the couch, his feet planted

wide and his elbows resting on his knees. His clasped hands hung out over the space between his knees, his body language rather like that of someone who was enjoying shooting the breeze with a buddy. However, his posture became curiously contradictory: he was relaxed and informal, yet as he began speaking he leaned toward us in a manner insistent and emphatic, as if his body could lend weight to his words.

"The Lord of Q'ollorit'i said to me, 'Now I am giving you your estrella. And now you are going to heal people who have disease. You will help to make the livestock fertile and productive. And you will be able to push the kawsay. You will be one who can push the kawsay, the life force.' "

I knew I needed help from Juan in fully understanding the import of the last part of don Mariano's explanation, and Juan did not disappoint me. "The most important aspect of the mystical path is the kawsay, the life force," he explained. "It is the living energy, which infuses everything. An alto mesayoq is one who works with this life force. He can push the process of life, move it, so it can make things fertile, give health, bring abundance."

Because don Mariano had paused, we had assumed that he had reproduced the Lord of Q'ollorit'i's message in full. But he had not. There was more.

" 'You must never do a bad thing to another human being,' " the Lord of Q'ollorit'i had said to don Mariano. " 'You must never look with bad eyes at another human being. If you can do that, all your livestock will flourish, all the diseases you treat will be healed, and you will have a good life. Now you are consecrated.'

"And now I am handling and working this consecration," don Mariano concluded.

Ricardo asked don Mariano if the Lord of Q'ollorit'i ever appeared to him in dreams.

"Yes," don Mariano replied. "He always appears like a silver cross with a hand at each side pointing downward. When he appears, he only says a few words: 'I give you the knowledge. Anything you do, you must do well.'"

I was anxious to shift the subject to how don Mariano shared this knowledge with North Americans and other tourists and seekers who have contact with him through his mestizo students. I asked how he viewed working with "Westerners," an inaccurate term, but one we used because it was an easy way to get our point across and was a term that to don Mariano generally meant any foreigner. I specifically asked if he understood why so many Westerners were coming to Peru seeking the mystical knowledge. Did he have a problem with that?

"I am always happy to meet Westerners, and I am happy with our work," he replied.

His answer was heartfelt, but I wanted to probe deeper. Juan cautioned me. "You are looking for something different. You want to know the *meaning* of this, but for him it is just the work. It must be shared. Let us ask him, instead, if sharing this work with Westerners is different from or the same as working with any others, with the peasants for instance."

Don Mariano's reply was almost immediate. "The Lord of Q'ollorit'i gave me the estrella. He gave it to me to do the work with Indians, mestizos, or anyone who comes to me. I work with any person who asks me."

I was still not satisfied that don Mariano understood my original question. Don Mariano works with foreigners more than any other Q'ero. Each year the Q'ero are having more and more contact with the West. They would soon be traveling to the United States to teach and perform ceremony. While I celebrate the dissemination of a cosmology and a teaching I find powerful, beautiful, and compellingly relevant to the modern world, there are teachers of Andean mysticism in the United States who are, I believe, describing the Q'ero in hyperbolic terms and misrepresenting who they are and the scope of their mystical system. It was important for me to understand how don Mariano viewed his increasing contact with the "West" and what he thought about the spiritual seekers of all kinds who were coming to Peru in increasing numbers.

"Let's try it this way," I suggested to Juan and Ricardo. "I don't know if this wording is going to work or not. But there are a lot of people now from North America coming to Peru looking for something they're missing in their lives or are curious about—the heart connection, to touch the kawsay, things like that. And this is don Mariano's opportunity to speak to them and to what they're looking for. Ask him if he has any message for those people who come here seeking these spiritual teachings."

Again don Mariano answered almost immediately. It was clear his answer was coming unedited from his heart. "If people come seeking the knowledge, I must share what I know with them. Because all people are children of God, and if someone is looking for this knowledge, I do not have the right to withhold it from him. It is not a good thing to withhold this knowledge."

Having worked with don Mariano on a number of occasions, I know he practices what he preaches: he is open, loving, and generous with his knowledge. However, there was some speculation in the United States that don Mariano was being influenced by, even corrupted by, American money, that he was in effect a party to commercializing the sacred knowledge. Even I had such cynical concerns—that don Mariano and others were bartering their ceremony to the highest bidder in order to relieve their crushing material poverty. I had had many discussions about this with Juan, and about how people like myself were part of the problem. Juan had spoken openly, admitting that corruption was always a possibility, but that anyone having contact with the Q'ero, and with other paqos, had to evaluate their personal experience with their heart and through their *qosqo*—their energy center—and then reach their own conclusion without imposing their cultural judgments on the paqos. He had also admonished me, with his characteristic gentleness, that neither I, nor any other spiritual seeker, could afford to be sentimental about the Indians.

After hearing don Mariano's response to my question, I was more than satisfied that Western money was not a terribly corrupting influence, and while don Mariano took a short break, I said as much to Sandy and Anamaria, who had shared many of the same concerns. Juan, listening to my comments, helped us understand the origins of such conflicts and how our view of what a "mystic" or "shaman" should be is colored by our cultural heritage.

"We [non-Indians] have a paradigm about the religious experience," he said. "We are looking for specific experiences; maybe the energetic transmission of the paqo's power or the experience of a particular ceremony, like the *Karpay Ayni*. This is our paradigm. But here, in the Andes, for the Indian paqos, the sacred work is just sharing and establishing interrelations and interchanges with persons. The things that happen to the person are very personal. For example, with Sandy, when she received the Pachakuti transmission from don Mariano, she felt the crown of her head opening and a light entering her. Obviously in the moment of that particular ceremony, the paqo opened her poq'po and she became available to receive the sacred light. That is her experience. It is the same with everyone—whatever your particular experience, you must trust it and try to learn from it, just as the paqo learns from his own experiences.

"That is one thing. The other thing," Juan continued, "is that in our [Western] paradigm, a prophet must give a message to the world. But that is only one way. I respect that way. But there is also the propensity for a teacher to become a guru, to gather followers to whom he imparts his 'secret' knowledge. But here in the Andes it is different. If someone comes to a paqo looking for the teachings, that paqo will freely teach him the knowledge he has. And that is all. There are no secrets. Nothing is closed.

"Still, following the sacred path is a challenge. You must undergo different and difficult challenges. Like don Mariano, he spent one year with one teacher, three more years with another teacher, three more with a third teacher, and six more with Manuel Q'espi. He was *working* to become a paqo. This is an incredible thing—to find the right teaching. The right teacher for me could be one person. The right teacher for you could be another. But it's an effort. Don Mariano doesn't talk about it, but with each teacher I am sure he must have paid or performed a service for them. But the important matter is that he was looking for the gift, and finally he found it. It was available to him, and now he makes it available to others."

As always, Juan's commentary gave us a broader perspective from which to understand the Andean mystical path. We were ready to return to don Mariano's story.

Ricardo had a complicated, and potentially sensitive, question he wished to put to don Mariano, and he wanted my permission to pursue it. A testy but diplomatic discussion followed.

Juan explained. "Ricardo is wondering if he should pursue a very complicated, ethical line of questioning. He wants to ask don Mariano about the Lord of Q'ollorit'i's admonishment not to do bad things to another person, not to look through bad eyes

Don Modesto, a Q'ero pampa mesayoq, prepares to offer sacred coca leaves to the wind spirits at Ollantaytambo, the Temple of the Wind. (Photograph by Eileen London)

The author and Juan Núñez del Prado with the Q'ero interviewed for *Keepers of the Ancient Knowledge*. Pictured from left to right are don Juan Pauqar Espinosa, don Agustín Pauqar Qapa, Joan Parisi Wilcox, don Julian Pauqar Flores, Juan Núñez del Prado, don Juan Pauqar Flores, and don Mariano Apasa Marchaqa. (Photograph by Sandra Corcoran)

Left: Machu Picchu.

Above: The valley beneath the glacier of Sinak'ara where the annual sacred festival of Q'ollorit'i takes place.

(Photographs by John S. Wilcox)

(Above photographs by John S. Wilcox)

Top left: The author and her companions ride through the Andes toward the Q'ero villages.

Bottom left: The Q'ero village of Chua Chua.

Above: Don Julian Pauqar Flores, a Q'ero pampa mesayoq and past "president" of Q'ero.

(Photograph by Sandra Corcoran)

Above: Kuraq akulleq don Manuel Q'espi, the elder of the Q'ero, at Q'ollorit'i. (Photograph by John S. Wilcox)

Top right: Don Juan Pauqar Espinosa gives the author a khuya from his mesa. (Photograph by Sandra Corcoran)

Bottom right: Don Manuel Q'espi gives the author the Karpay Ayni initiation at his house in Chua Chua. (Photograph by Elizabeth B. Jenkins)

Top left: The author's chunpi khuyas, which are used to open the five energy centers of the body.

Bottom left: The author's right-side mesa, used to connect her to her teachers and the sacred sites at which she has worked.

Top right: Don Manuel Q'espi performing a despacho ceremony of offering and thanksgiving to Pachamama (Mother Earth).
(Photographs by Joan Parisi Wilcox)

Bottom right: A despacho to Pachamama containing a variety of natural items. (Photograph by Sandra Corcoran)

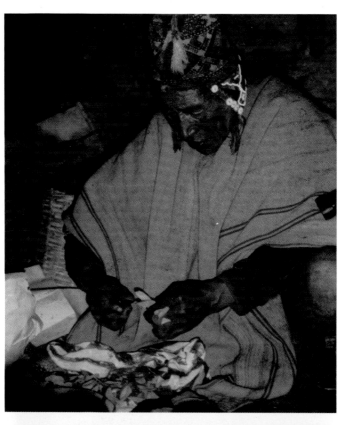

Left: Don Juan Pauqar Flores prepares a coca leaf k'intu for use in a despacho at the Wiraqocha Temple.

Right: Don Manuel Q'espi (on right) with his advisor, pampa mesayoq Juan Pauqar Flores, at the Wiraqocha Temple.

(Photographs by Joan Parisi Wilcox)

Above: Isidro, a Q'ero Shaman in training, releases sacred coca leaves with pampa mesayoq don Modesto at Ollantaytambo, the Temple of the Wind. (Photograph by John S. Wilcox)

Above right: Juan Núñez del Prado, an anthropologist and initiated kuraq akulleq, is the author's primary teacher and assisted her with the interviews for this book. (Photograph by John S. Wilcox)

Bottom right: The author and Juan Núñez del Prado observe a despacho ceremony by don Martín Marchaqa Q'espi and don Lorenzo Q'espi Apasa at Tipon. (Photograph by Eileen London)

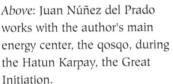

Above: Juan Núñez del Prado works with the author's main energy center, the qosqo, during the Hatun Karpay, the Great Initiation.

(Photograph by Sandra Corcoran)

Above right: Juan Núñez del Prado energetically bestows the sacred lineage to the author during the Hatun Karpay.

(Photograph by Eileen London)

Bottom right: Two Q'ero paqos speak with Juan Núñez del Prado at Pisaq.

(Photograph by Eileen London)

Above: Q'ero masters don Bernadino, don Sebástian, don Juan and don Manuel Q'espi with Américo Yábar at the Wiraqocha Temple.

Left: Américo Yábar, a mestizo who was trained and initiated as a kuraq by the Q'ero and teaches Andean shamanism around the world, pictured at the Island of the Sun, Lake Titicaca. (Photographs by Joan Parisi Wilcox)

The Apu Yanantin, symbolizing the union of two dissimilar energies.
(Photograph by Joan Parisi Wilcox)

at another person. Ricardo now wants to ask don Mariano about this, about how Mariano tells others what to do. Are you interested in that?"

I and my two women friends were unsure just what the point of Ricardo's question was. "He's asking about don Mariano's personal ethics?" Anamaria asked.

Juan nodded yes. "For me it's not a . . . I'm not comfortable here," Juan said. Then he turned to me, since these were my interviews. "It's up to you. Ricardo wants to know if you want him to ask this."

"Well," I said, feeling a little torn between what I saw as Ricardo's characteristic bluntness and Juan's perhaps overly developed sense of propriety, "I wouldn't censor anyone's question."

Juan wouldn't let me waffle. "Ricardo is asking if you are interested in this."

I made sure I understood Ricardo's question, that he wanted to know if don Mariano had ever violated the Lord of Q'ollorit'i's admonishment against doing evil to another person. "Juan," I replied, now speaking ex-academic to academic, "I don't know why I should be the censor. It's his question."

"But he wants to know if he should ask it on *your* behalf," Anamaria said, making clear to me a distinction I had missed in the translations from Spanish to English.

"Oh! No, not on my behalf," I said. "But if he wants to ask the question because he is interested, fine. I have no objection."

Juan translated the gist of our discussion to Ricardo, and Ricardo asked his question.

Don Mariano explained, not seeming in any way offended by the query. "The Lord gave me a recommendation to never do a bad thing to another person. If I do not follow the Lord's recommendations, I will make hucha for myself. If I don't follow these recommendations of the Lord, my work will not go well, my crops will go bad, what I want I will not get. I will become lost."

Ricardo followed up by asking if there are paqos who misuse their power to hurt people. If so, he asked, who are their allies? Do they have supernatural allies who grant them such power?

"Yes, there are such people," don Mariano replied. "But they do these things because these are the things in their heart. It is the expression of their heart. These men who do bad things, obviously they do not talk with the Apus or with God. Perhaps they pull power from the unclean places of the earth."

Don Mariano thought for a moment, and then resumed speaking. "Only a man with a spoiled heart will go in the wrong direction. The places from which this man gets his power are the spoiled places."

Then don Mariano turned to Ricardo and whispered to him. Both men broke out laughing. Ricardo explained, through Juan, that, confidentially, don Mariano had told him that even today there are some men like that in Q'ero. Then don Mariano asked Ricardo how he knew about such men. He chided Ricardo, suggesting that it takes one to know one! We all laughed, and sensing the mood change and the late hour, I uncapped the pisco bottle, declaring that we had had enough serious talk for one evening.

Chapter 8

Keepers of the
Ancient Knowledge:
Kawsay and K'ara

I can barely describe the anticipation I felt as I sat down with the Q'ero for our open discussion on the mystical system. I had been traveling in Peru and studying Andean mysticism for more than three years at that time, and yet this was the first time I had a Quechua translator at my personal disposal so that I could talk to my Q'ero brothers and sister one on one. The past three days of interviews had been fairly structured, focusing on recording personal initiation stories and gathering historical material about the Q'ero. Now was my chance to really interact with the Q'ero, to have a conversation in the best sense of that word. I had begun the interviews days before timid and uncertain, and I cannot claim that this day was any different. If anything, I felt a deeper sense of responsibility to "get it right," and I also felt tremendous time pressure, for there was an enormous amount of ground to cover but only a handful of hours left in which to do it. Still, the Q'ero and I had become friends over these three days; even though we couldn't speak each others' languages, we had become comfortable enough during our conversations to drop formalities and genuinely be ourselves. We were no longer separated by the personas of master/student, native/foreigner, or any of the other labels and perceptions that make for distance in a relationship. Instead, we had become individuals, with distinct personalities.

I could tell at a glance when doña Agustina was becoming miffed because she wasn't getting enough attention. I could tell when don Juan Pauqar Espinosa was bored, or when don Mariano was impatient, or when don Julian was becoming stiff from sitting too long. So as we launched into the most difficult but spirited part of the interviews—this day-long, free-ranging, and more philosophical discussion of the mystical system—it was in an atmosphere of respect, trust, and kinship that we talked.

During this discussion, I, and my companions, asked broad questions of the Q'ero and let them determine the course of our conversation. The logistics were daunting, with several Q'ero talking at once or in rapid succession. The interpreters had to be quick, and I, in an effort to capture speakers' words clearly, was shifting the large, rather heavy tape recorder from one side of the table to another until my arm was weary. Many times I had to halt a discussion so the interpreters could catch up. Obviously, these interruptions fractured the flow of conversation and sometimes derailed certain trains of thought. And the cross-conversation made writing these chapters especially difficult. Although I have striven to attribute information to its proper speaker, it would be too cumbersome to attribute every Q'ero response, as interesting as that would be for readers who would like to know just who said what. In the interest of a cohesive narrative, I sometimes have instead grouped responses and synthesized material into a coherent whole. You will be reading the actual Q'ero responses, but you may not be able to know, in a few instances, just who said what. I trust the reader will agree that this occasional lack of attribution is a small inconvenience in what is otherwise a fascinating glimpse into the Q'ero mystical worldview.

As we began, I asked Ricardo, through Juan and Anamaria,

to explain to the Q'ero that I wanted to know about the "basics" of their mystical system—such as sami and hucha, dreams and visions, the Apus and Pachamama—and about the fundamental beliefs and concepts underlying their energetic connection with the natural world. The Q'ero were as eager to discuss such topics as I was to listen. They began by declaring, "Let us talk! We will talk about all the things we know."

KAWSAY

Juan Núñez del Prado looked to me to determine our starting point, and after a moment's consideration, I looked to the Q'ero and said, "Let's start with *kawsay.*"

Kawsay, if you ask a Western teacher of Andean mysticism or one of the Q'eros' mestizo apprentices, would most likely be defined as "vital energy" or "living energy." It is the energy that animates the cosmos. But for the Q'ero, as you are about to read, kawsay is first and foremost a perceptual stance that one may take in order to deal with the banal realities of the everyday world. Only after discussing kawsay in the most pragmatic terms do the Q'ero even attempt to move on to more philosophic definitions. This kind of prosaic and concrete response is characteristic of the Q'ero, and I mention it here to remind the reader of the striking disparity of expectation one may experience when one is talking directly to the shamans themselves versus talking with or reading the work of their Western students, who translate and interpret the indigenous percepts in ways that satisfy the more analytic and conceptual modes of Western thinking.

Within seconds of my question, definitions and examples of kawsay were flowing, almost faster than the interpreters could keep up. "Kawsay is, for example, if we have a dream about a mestizo gentleman riding a horse—this announces that we will have success in the things we are trying to do," don Juan Pauqar Flores began, defining kawsay as something akin to good luck.

Don Agustín followed don Juan, nodding in agreement, and extending don Juan's definition. "Kawsay is living well, walking well." Don Juan resumed his example, picking up the thread of don Agustín's definition. "Kawsay is living in harmony in the family, with the children, with your spouse, with your work, caring well for your herds. It is to do well in everything, and everyone can see that you are doing things well."

Don Juan's brother, don Julian, concurred. "Kawsay is living well in the family, doing things in accordance and in union [with the larger order], working with the livestock and in the field, bringing order to all. It is having a conversation with your daughter-in-law or son-in-law and giving each other good words. It is making agreements, having a good dialogue, and sharing good words."

Here don Mariano interjected his thoughts, first flipping the folds of his poncho back and leaning forward, elbows on knees. His words shifted the definition of kawsay from the prosaic toward the more mystical. "Kawsay is all the things we have said, but when I dream of a fox, this is a good announcement to me. When I have a fox in my dreams that is going up into the hills, this is a very good omen to me. For example, last night I dreamed of a fox and the meaning for me is that my wife is going to recover [from her pneumonia]. This means to me that like the fox I will be above this difficulty."

Don Juan Pauqar Espinosa, until now content just to listen, also leaned forward from his place at the far edge of the couch to contribute his understanding of how kawsay announces itself in dreams. "If you dream of a baby, it announces good kawsay. When you dream of flowers, this means your herds will reproduce and flourish. So all dreams communicate something to you, and we should communicate these things with other people. I would have a conversation about such a dream with my wife or my children, because if I had a good announcement in my dream, after this dream we can all walk with happiness."

"I agree that kawsay is living in harmony," said don Agustín. "It is sharing food with another man, it is sharing drink with another man, it is even sharing with the pilgrims who have nothing at the moment they arrive to your community. Sharing with strangers is the power of kawsay. So it is living in harmony with all other people and caring for them as well. When you practice this, you will be loved by others."

Don Agustín's compelling definition stirred Ricardo to offer a story from his anthropological field work in the Andes. "When I studied in a valley in southern Peru," he said, "I was talking with my friends about Indian beliefs, comparing them with the Christian commandments. I asked them if the Indian tradition had what could be considered commandments. They said yes, and that the first one is to share with the person who does not have the capacity to ask you for help. This is a type of kawsay. If a stranger, a wanderer, comes to your house asking for food or drink, you must share with him or her. You must give that person a bed. Because it could be God Himself who is coming to test you.

"They told me that once there had been an earthquake in the region where we were working," he went on, "and only one village, Maqa, was damaged. In that town there had been a dog, scarred and diseased, in terrible condition. The villagers had expelled it. They hit it and kicked it. The dog finally left, and he wandered to another town. There he was given water and food and was helped. Because of that, the earthquake struck only in Maqa. Implicit in that legend is the lesson that God can come even in the form of an ugly and diseased animal to test your capacity for compassion."

Ricardo wanted to ask the Q'ero about the negative signs that come to one through dreams, but we decided this would take us too far afield at this early stage in our discussion of kawsay. Instead, Juan asked the Q'ero about the meaning of *kawsay pacha*. He explained that when he had first met don Andreas Espinosa and asked to apprentice with him, don Andreas had said, "First, I must see your kawsay pacha."

Three Q'ero responded, don Juan Flores, don Mariano, and don Julian. "To see a person's kawsay pacha is a test using the coca leaves," they said, "to see if your will and your feelings are [aligned] in the right direction, to determine if you believe that you are trespassing or if you have a lot of doubt. Reading the coca leaves, don Andreas wanted to see if you had the capacity to follow the path or not, to see if you had the capacity to grow on the path. This is the way we see the kawsay pacha." The verb the Q'ero were using was *qaway*, which means to see energetically, using one's mystical awareness not one's physical sight. It also implies a sense of diagnosing or examining.

I wanted to capitalize on this opportunity to examine kawsay from a more mystical perspective, so I asked the Q'ero if kawsay can be seen in things non-human—such as a tree, a river, a star, or an Apu—and if so, how.

Don Juan Flores replied that "kawsay exists in Pachamama and the Apus because they are alive. Even when we are chewing coca leaves," he said, "we are sharing kawsay with Pachamama and the Apus. Obviously, Pachamama gives us kawsay because when we work the land, she returns back to us food. This is kawsay. All the hills are alive; they all have kawsay. As well as the rivers. The water, the lakes and lagoons, the rivers, they are alive."

Don Agustín and don Julian spoke up, aiding don Juan in his explanation. "With water there is life. We drink the water and we live. But not only do we drink the water, we share it with the animals and the spirits who fly [birds]. The plants grow with water; even the wild plants like herbs and grass take kawsay from water. The rain carries the kawsay to the plants, to animals; but in the rivers, there is not only kawsay, there is also hucha, heavy energy."

Juan Núñez del Prado took advantage of a brief pause in the explanation to elaborate on the Q'eros' statement about hucha. "The rivers are ambiguous because they carry the hucha you have cleansed away from someone with your khuyas. Typically, you release this heavy energy into the river, so in that way you can find hucha in the rivers, but not in the lagoons or lakes, or in the rain."

SAMI AND HUCHA

The segue to hucha seemed as good a time as any to direct the conversation to the two types of energy: sami, refined energy, and hucha, heavy energy. I suggested as much, and Juan and Ricardo concurred. They framed the question by asking the Q'ero about the practice of *saminchasqa,* a practice by which one interchanges refined energy with an Apu or nature spirit by blowing into a k'intu (three coca leaves) or with an ritual offering of pisco.

The Q'ero talked among themselves for a moment, and Ricardo interpreted their varied examples of saminchasqa. "Blowing the coca k'intus to the Apus is giving sami to the Apus, it is the interchange of sami," they explained. "During Carnaval [a fiesta], we perform saminchasqa on behalf of the animals. Drinking ritually is also interchanging sami. If you are chewing coca in a sacred context, then you are giving sami. But if you are only chewing coca as you work, then you are doing *hallpay*, which is just to chew the coca leaves, like everyone else does."

Ricardo was preoccupied with the meaning of the word *sami*. Traditionally among the Q'ero, sami is refined energy. But Ricardo explained that he had heard several different definitions over the course of twenty years' anthropological field work. In one context he had heard the word sami used to mean "blessings" or "wisdom." For instance, in a story very much like don Julian's story of how God had offered Inkarí more *munay* (love), Ricardo had heard from a Native man he was interviewing that God offered to give the Inka sami. The Inka said to God, "But I have my own sami," and he went off to the jungle without having accepted God's offer of sami. The man who had told this story to Ricardo had said that if the Inka had received God's sami, he would have acquired more power than he had with his own sami. So, Ricardo explained, sami, in this context, meant some special kind of wisdom and knowledge, a new kind of power, a finer power than the Inka already had. The Q'ero, on the other hand, were giving us a practical explanation. Ricardo, ever the anthropologist, was wondering if he would ever be able to pin down a "precise" definition of sami.

I found Ricardo's commentary interesting for two reasons. First and most obviously, the more I knew about sami, the better I could formulate questions to put to the Q'ero. Second, and more importantly, sami is a fundamental concept in Andean mysticism, and any new knowledge acquired about it is important not only to those of us seeking to record and preserve the mystical system, but also to those of us seeking a deeper understanding of our personal work along the sacred path.

In an effort to explore the topic of sami more fully, Juan devised a question in the form of an example that he hoped would move the Q'ero from the concrete to the more philosophical. "On the Day of the Living and the Dead, November 1," he explained, "we commemorate our dead by offering them food, the things they liked when they were alive. When we offer these things to our ancestors, they come to eat. But they must eat only the sami, because you can see that they have left the food there. Nothing is moved. What is your opinion of this thing they are eating?"

Juan's question proved fruitful. The entire group of Q'ero spoke at once, offering their interpretation of this scenario. When we sorted out their comments, it became clear that their consensus, as expressed by don Juan Pauqar Flores, was that "sami is the essence of a thing. The souls come and eat only the essence."

Ricardo shook his head slowly in assent, as if a new understanding were dawning. He thoughtfully stoked the several days' stubble of beard on his chin. "My earlier story takes on more meaning with this explanation, because what was the offering of the Christian God to the Inka? He was offering his teachings, his wisdom, his words—which are his essence."

Juan Núñez del Prado agreed these definitions of sami as an "essence" and an "essential gift" were very important. Then he added, "The type of concrete question we asked is a good way to open up these very complex categories."

I was happy the anthropologists were happy, but I was interested in the Q'ero, not in the anthropological musings. "I don't have those concrete examples, like the Day of the Dead, at hand like you do," I said to Juan. "I'll rely on you to formulate questions using examples like that, but let's flip this discussion on its head for a moment and ask the same type of question about hucha." Ricardo asked the Q'ero to define hucha.

"Hucha," explained don Julian, "is speaking incorrectly,

fighting, instigating conflicts." When no other Q'ero offered a definition, I asked another question, hoping to elicit information about the "essence" of hucha. "How do they as healers cleanse hucha from people or things?"

Don Agustín began the discussion. "A person has hucha when dirtiness lands on him. If the hucha lands on a person, you must take it and pull it off him and put it in the river. The river takes it away."

"If you don't serve and honor Pachamama and the Apus, then hucha lands on you," explained don Mariano. "If hucha lands on you, bad things will happen in your life. You will have problems."

"Is hucha heavy, as in heavy energy?" Juan asked.

"Yes, hucha is heavy," don Agustín replied. "You have seen these people who carry packs on their backs for a living? They are carrying a lot of weight. You could say a person with hucha is carrying such a weight."

Ricardo was interested in who attracts hucha and how. "Who is a person who carries hucha?" he asked simply.

Don Agustín and don Juan Flores huddled in discussion, with the other Q'ero occasionally offering a comment. Finally they said, "If you are caring for livestock, but a fox or a condor eats your livestock, then you must be carrying hucha," they concurred. "Or when your llama falls over a cliff, or if it drowns in a lagoon, surely you are carrying hucha. If a person has those kinds of problems, then we tell him he is a *huchasapa*, a person who carries heavy energy, and he must go and cleanse himself in the sanctuary of Q'ollorit'i, or he must go to a paqo to be cleansed of his hucha."

"Perhaps this a good time to ask about mikhuy, because mikhuy can be a way to cleanse yourself or others of hucha," I suggested. Juan agreed, and for a few minutes we discussed how best to ask this question. It had become obvious during previous days' discussions that the Q'ero did not practice the hucha mikhuy technique [digesting heavy energy], but we wanted to ask them directly about this practice to try to determine exactly what they did or did not know. However, if we phrased the question to suggest that we knew how to perform mikhuy ourselves, which we did, then the Q'eros' tendency, judging from past behavior, would likely be to try to save face or please us by struggling to offer some knowledge themselves, even if they did not have any. We did not want to put the Q'ero in an awkward situation, nor did we want them to speculate. We only wanted to know of techniques that they themselves knew and practiced. Juan finally asked the question, using a phraseology we had previously found useful—formulating the question as second-hand knowledge. "Someone told us that there are paqos who have the capacity to digest and eat hucha. Talk about this if you will."

Again, a group discussion ensued. Finally, don Juan Pauqar Espinosa and don Mariano spoke on behalf of the group. "We agree that it is possible to eat hucha. But we only cleanse it. We offer the heavy energy up to the Apus. We do not eat or digest it. We just capture it, clean it from the person, and offer it to the Apus. First, we take the hucha and then we offer it up to the Apus. Then the Apus offer it to the *Taytacha*,[1] and the Taytacha decides how to get rid of it."

Juan Núñez del Prado considered their comments, then said, "I would like to tell them that don Andreas and don Benito taught me hucha mikhuy. I will ask them what they think about this. But we must be clear about one thing—*they* don't eat hucha. They agree on this. They only cleanse it."

Ricardo translated Juan's comments to the Q'ero, and then translated their reply in Spanish directly to Juan. Juan exclaimed, "It's a very practical answer!" He then let the rest of us in on the Q'eros' response. " 'We think this is a good tool. We think if you do this [hucha mikhuy] with another person, that person will become totally clean. We have shared with you the things we learned with our teachers. Because you have learned that practice, you must teach us how to do it. If you are able to share that technique with us, we will be very happy!' " Juan agreed to teach the Q'ero hucha mikhuy, and I decided that this was a good place for a break.

While the Q'ero and the others took some refreshment, I talked with Juan about how I should best continue the interview. "There are two other areas I want to talk about now, but I'm not quite sure how to do it since their answers are so practical. One is the related concepts of the *poq'po* and the *qosqo*, the energy body and the center through which energy is mediated. I'd like to try to get them to talk more philosophically, to explain these concepts in terms of the mystical cosmology before we talk about actual practices involving them."

Juan raised his eyebrows and lit a cigarette, two signs that I was indeed facing a challenge. "If the Q'ero don't know how to digest heavy energy, then they will not know how to use the qosqo to mediate energy. "Therefore," he advised, "we will ask only about the general concept of the qosqo."

"Well, maybe we should resume by asking about the *poq'po*, the energy body, since that must be where the hucha adheres when it lands on you," I suggested. Anamaria, who had been patiently translating from Spanish to English all day and now joined our conversation, asked if there was a way we could ask about the energy body in terms of the physical body, yoking the metaphysical to the physical in a way the Q'ero might better understand. Juan considered her idea and suggested that perhaps we could use the concept of the *vultu*, the ghost. Don Juan Pauqar Espinosa had talked about the ghost in his initiation story, about the wind entering him like a ghost and about the ghost making noises on the roof of the sanctuary building at Q'ollorit'i. "He used the term *vultu* for a field of energy yesterday, like a ghost," Juan said. "Let's start by using that word and let it lead us to the concept of the poq'po."

When we regrouped, Juan went ahead and asked the Q'ero about their understanding of the energy body, the poq'po, by equating it to a ghost. Juan Espinosa's answer, however, instantly dashed any hope we had for this approach. "The vultu was really the Apu," he said, correcting what he thought was our misinterpretation of his earlier story. The Apu, not being able to be apprehended directly, he explained, takes various forms, and the ghost on the roof was really the Apu.

"Just ask them outright if they know the term *poq'po?*" I said to Juan. I was a little exasperated with Juan's and Ricardo's academic approach, and I decided it was complicating matters unnecessarily.

Juan didn't think my question was such a good one, and because I couldn't speak Quechua I couldn't control the situation. I wanted to ask the question simply and directly, but Juan suggested that he ask the Q'ero about the poq'po using an example from his experience. He then proceeded to ask a question to the Q'ero directly, with a little assistance from Ricardo. Neither I, nor Sandy or Anamaria, knew what the question was. The Q'ero huddled in discussion, but it soon became obvious that Juan's question had not been answered.

I was quickly growing even more unhappy with the situation, so I wrested control. "Listen," I said, "try it this way. Simply ask them how kawsay is visualized. What is it they're seeing when they see a condor or puma in a vision or dream? If it's not the physical animals they're seeing in a vision, then what is it they're seeing? The animal's poq'po, or energy body?"

Ricardo put the questions to the Q'ero and listened to their long reply. I could see Ricardo become more and more animated, his excitement growing. It seems we had finally hit pay dirt.

Sandy, Anamaria, and I were frustrated because Juan and Ricardo suddenly seemed oblivious to us, their impassioned conversation in Quechua, which effectively cut us out. Unable to stand the suspense, I finally interrupted them, pleading for a translation. Juan turned to me, almost triumphantly, and explained that in answer to my question, the Q'ero had used a Quechua word and explained a concept that neither he nor Ricardo had ever heard before: *k'ara*. We had just broken new anthropological ground.

K'ARA

"It appears," Juan explained, the excitement of discovery still evident in his voice, "that the *k'ara* is something like the sami of a person, his or her essence. And *that* is what the Q'ero see [when they look at a person's energy body]. Ricardo is going to probe for more information."

Juan's explanation seemed anticlimactic to me, especially considering his and Ricardo's charged Quechua discussion. But I decided to be patient and let the anthropologists call the shots.

After an extended dialogue, mostly between Juan Núñez del Prado and don Julian, Ricardo reported that the Q'ero were saying that the k'ara is like a person's aura. "K'ara is connected to sami," Ricardo explained. "Sami is the essence of a person or thing, and the k'ara is the visible manifestation of sami. Hucha, however, has no visible manifestation."

Ricardo was still visibly excited, and we paused for a few moments so he and I could take some notes. He explained as he wrote that he had been searching for a clear definition of sami for twenty years, and now, because of sami's contrast to the k'ara, he felt he finally had a good grasp of what sami really meant. Despite my limited knowledge of the mystical system, I shared the thrill of discovery with Ricardo and Juan, but I honestly can't say I fully shared their sense of enlightenment. Mostly, I was simply happy the anthropologists were happy.

When things finally settled down, we decided we had to probe further about just who has k'ara and what forms it can take. Juan asked if paqos—such as Garibilu Q'espi, the great Q'ero paqo who had saved Q'ero from devastation by using the yellow fever disease to "eat" all the other diseases[2]—have k'ara. The Q'eros' answer, reproduced below, indicated that k'ara could be understood in at least two different ways: as an aura or energy body, in some cases almost like an etheric double of a person or thing; and as an inherent quality or power of a person or thing that could be invoked and utilized on behalf of others.

"Yes, Garibilu Q'espi had k'ara," don Juan Flores answered. "The moon has k'ara. The Apus have k'ara, and by invoking the k'ara of an Apu you can heal a person. Don Andreas Espinosa healed disease by invoking the k'ara of the Apu. The Apu has more k'ara than a paqo. My master, Andreas Espinosa, healed by invoking the k'ara of the condor and the Apu. But I don't believe that ordinary men have a k'ara."

Before we had a chance to inquire about don Juan's enigmatic final sentence, don Julian added to his brother's explanation: "Andreas Espinosa said to me, 'You must always carry the k'ara of the condor and the hummingbird.'"

Ricardo jumped in at this point to clarify an academic concern of his, whether k'ara is the same as or different from *kayk'ara*, a term that means crested or pointed. The Q'ero talked among themselves for a moment, their talk leading first to snickering and then to outright laughing. Don Agustín in particular seemed to think something was very funny. He partially covered his face with his hand and eyed us women shyly in the space between his fingers. Sandy, Anamaria, and I turned toward Ricardo for an explanation.

Ricardo looked uncomfortable. "They said that what they speak of is not kayk'ara, it is k'ara." he said, Anamaria translating his Spanish for us. We looked at Juan inquiringly. Something was going on again, and only we women were being left out. Finally, Juan revealed that the Q'ero had made an erotic joke as an example to Ricardo: a woman's clitoris is kayk'ara, they said, not k'ara! We all laughed, and most of us, male and female, blushed. If I remember correctly, we paused the interview at this point for a round of pisco. Once refreshed, we picked up where we had left off, exploring the concept of the k'ara.

"So they carry the k'ara of whatever animal they are working with, the condor for instance, or of the Apus they are in service to?" I asked.

Juan Núñez del Prado answered for the Q'ero. "Yes, to carry the k'ara of something means to be with it."

"Right," I said. "Don Julian was told to carry the k'ara of the condor and the hummingbird. But someone else might work with the puma. Would they carry the k'ara of the puma, of whatever their ally or totem animal is?"

"It seems like that," Juan replied

"Well, let's ask and make sure." I rephrased the question, and don Mariano answered for the group. We were surprised by his answer, but it was a pleasant surprise, because don Mariano provided an unexpected and fascinating tidbit of information. "No," he said, "in the puma the important thing is not the k'ara, because the puma does not have k'ara—the puma has a tail."

Although the others look confused, I understood exactly what don Mariano meant. I smiled with delight, thinking of a story Américo Yábar had told me about the puma's power, a story I considered to be little more than an example of Américo's penchant for hyperbole. I looked at Juan, and he was grinning as well. "To see the tail of a puma is very important," Juan began. "It's power is in its tail, not in its k'ara. Américo Yábar has a story—"

"I was just thinking of that story!" I interrupted. "The story of when he was a little boy and an old man in a village in the mountains where he was staying took him to a decrepit hut and made him sit by a window. The teacher took his poncho and twirled it round and round through the air, telling Américo to watch the window closely, for he was calling a puma. The puma did come, and its tail flashed with light and color, twirling around outside the window as the crazy old teacher twirled the poncho inside the hut. Américo said that was how he first learned that the puma's power is in its tail."

I mentally apologized to Américo for doubting his story. Then we pushed on, with Sandy inquiring whether the Q'ero worked with animal allies. Juan at first did not understand the notion of animal allies, so Anamaria explained that many Native North Americans worked energetically with animals who act as spirit guides, teachers, and protectors. It was clear there were some cultural and language barriers inherent in this line of questioning; and because I already knew that generally the Q'ero do not work with animal spirits like North American Indians do, instead seeing see them as manifestations of their Apus, I suggested that we hold off on the question for a while and stick with the issue immediately at hand—who and what does and does not have sami and k'ara. I was anxious to follow up on don Juan's statement that he did not think the average person has k'ara. I was confused as to how we can all have a poq'po, or energy body, and yet not all have k'ara, the sami that is visible in our energy body. Ricardo put the question to don Juan Pauqar Flores, but his answer was vague.

"If a man has the capacity to share good information and establish good connections with other people, he has sami. If he does not have this capacity, he has less sami."

I tried my question again, asking specifically about who has k'ara. The Q'ero consensus was that "only great men [or women] have k'ara."

"Wow! Does this leaves us common people with no visible energy body?" I asked.

Juan shook his head. "Yes, that's what they seem to be saying. Only great men or men on the path, paqos, have k'ara. But here is my opinion of what they are implying. Everyone has an energy field, and k'ara is a visible manifestation of that field, but only powerful paqos have enough k'ara for it to be *clearly visible*. It's kind of like the paintings of the saints, where they are shown with a distinct aura or halo around their heads. For the rest of us, it is too weak to be seen. But this is only my opinion."

"I wonder if k'ara is different from *kanchay*?" I mused aloud. "If I'm not mistaken, Oscar Miro-Quesada[3] uses the term *kanchay* to mean light energy."

"Let's ask them if the k'ara shines," Juan suggested.

Don Mariano responded, picking up the train of thought from which this whole discussion had ensued and then just as quickly losing it. "The condor has a red k'ara. But the puma, in the night, you can see it shine, but that is not a k'ara, it's the puma's tail."

"What is it that a *qawaq* sees?" I started to asked, knowing that a qawaq is someone who can see energy and auras, but before I could put my question to the Q'ero, Ricardo interrupted to tell us that the Q'ero were in disagreement. "Juan Pauqar Espinosa and Agustín feel bad to have to point out a disagreement with don

Mariano," Ricardo reported, "but they feel he has made a mistake. They say the condor's k'ara is shiny white, not red."

"There are two kinds of condors," don Agustín explained, the index finger of his right hand tapping the weathered open palm of his left hand for emphasis. "The leader of the condors is the *apuchin*, and only the condor apuchin has a k'ara, not the others. It is white. Condors live in a group, and the condor apuchin is the leader of the group. Only the condor apuchin has k'ara."

"What about the hummingbird? Does it have a color?" Sandy wondered aloud. "And what about the Apus?" I asked. "They have the greatest power and the most k'ara, but do they shine in different colors according to the level of Apu?[4]

Juan interrupted our stream of questions with a commentary: "Don Mariano's answer brought out a distinction between red and white light, and don Juan Espinosa and don Agustín established that the condor's k'ara is white. Ricardo is pointing out this contradiction, so now we should ask if all the k'aras are white light. Do you want to ask about this, or do you want to ask your question about the colors of the Apus?"

"Let's just ask them if the k'ara comes in different colors, and if so, what colors," I decided.

"There are different colors," began don Juan Pauqar Flores. "The Apus come in different colors. Some are white, others red, and still others black. People have different colors of clothing and the animals have different kinds of fur, so the Apus' k'aras have different colors."

"He mentioned green, too," Juan said, correcting Ricardo. "The order is white, red, black, and green."

Don Juan continued with his explanation. "We can see the color of the different Apus. There are some that are gold and yellow—there are actually two shades of yellow. We also see the color silver. All of these are the most powerful Apus—they are not equal, there are differences among them."

"Can we get some additional examples of different colors of k'ara?" I asked, fascinated with this line of inquiry. "What has a green k'ara, what has a red one? What's the significance of the colors?"

The Q'ero talked among themselves for several minutes, don Julian and don Juan Pauqar Flores often counting on their fingers, as if listing something. "If the Apu has the color white, that is a good sign; it has much kawsay," they agreed. "It has an abundance of quality because white is the highest color. Red is next, then comes yellow and then black, which is much, much lower.[5]

"White is above all the rest. White commands [has more power than] the colors gold and silver. Also green. An Apu that is yellow is one that contains the minerals gold and silver within it. A pampa [highland plain] that contains these minerals also has a yellow k'ara."

It actually took a lot of time and effort to sort the above information, and the Q'ero complicated matters by metaphorically equating the Apus of various powers and intensities of k'ara to the Peruvian political hierarchy. Juan explained that white equates with the *alcalde*, red with the *regidor*, yellow with the *alguacil*, and black with the *contordor* or *capitán*. I had no idea what he was talking about, and I did not take the time to pursue translations of these offices. However, I suspected a color correspondence of the k'ara with the *chunpis*, the four energy belts that encircle the human body. I wondered aloud to Juan if these belts might not somehow be associated with intensities of the k'ara or shifts in one's capacity to utilize the k'ara, and he agreed this was a subject ripe for exploration. Then Juan explained a further complication: that the Q'ero had also grouped the colors of the k'ara with the "sides" of the mystical path. According to the Q'ero, the colors white and red are grouped together, and yellow and silver are grouped together, and both these groups are considered on the right side of the path, connecting one to *paña*, the mystical realms and the side of the mesa from which one communicates directly with the spirits. Green and black are considered *lloq'e*, or on the left side of the path, which involves the more practical aspects of the sacred work and is the healing side of the mesa.

I was immensely interested in all of these equations, but I also recognized that I was in way over my head, especially since time was so short. I reluctantly decided to get back to basics, so I suggested we return to our discussion of sami and hucha. "Ask them if hucha is visible or has a color. I know they already said it doesn't, but if not, then how do they know when someone has hucha?" The question actually put to the Q'ero was, "If a paqo has the capacity to see [*qaway*], then what does he see when he sees hucha?"

"When we look at the coca," the Q'ero said, "if there are leaves folded over or broken, then we see that you have a mistake, you have hucha."

"Using the coca is an indirect way to see the hucha," Juan said. "Let's challenge them and ask about seeing it directly." He slightly reworded the question. "If one can see sami through the k'ara, then does hucha become visible there also?"

The Q'eros' response was unanimous and emphatic. "We do not see hucha directly. We find it using the coca leaves."

They talked briefly among themselves, and Juan filled us in of the gist of their conversation. "They are discussing their feeling that implicit in our question was the sense that there are people who have the capacity to see hucha. They feel a little embarrassed, because they do not have the capacity to see hucha."

Juan talked to the Q'ero for a moment, and then turned to us, explaining, "I said to them, 'This is not a problem because people have different capacities. People are not the same. There is nothing to be ashamed of.' But this just shows you the pressures that are being felt here."

"I'm curious about pulling hucha from another person's body, and I'm wondering about how we cleanse ourselves of hucha," Anamaria said. "Are they saying we always have to go to another person?"

"Well, they have the capacity to pull the hucha using an object, like their mesa or a khuya," Juan explained.

"And if they can't mikhuy, then they must have to go to another paqo," I surmised.

It was time for lunch, and as the Q'ero wandered off to the dining table, Juan took a moment to answer Anamaria's question more directly. "There is a complex but very important point to be made here," he began. "Sometimes a person receives, in the moment, the capacity to do something. Other times that person does not have the same capacity. When trying to cleanse someone, for example, the act depends upon whose 'hand' is the right one at the time. For example, if someone comes to Ricardo for a healing but he cannot handle it and then that person comes to me and I can handle it, they say that this problem is for my hand and not for the hand of Ricardo. This depends not only on your personal power but it depends—" Juan suddenly broke his train of thought and took a different route in his explanation. "This is speculation on my part. But Andreas Espinosa was recognized as the highest paqo in Q'ero, recognized by everybody here as such. But in one case, in the case of don Mariano, one of his karpays was not for the hand of Andreas Espinosa; it was for the hand of don Manuel Q'espi. This fact does not deny the power of don Andreas. It just tells us that don Manuel had some capability with don Mariano that don Andreas did not have. And because of that, the karpay worked with don Manuel. This point is very important, because if you remember in don Mariano's initiation story, the Apus spoke through the mesa of don Andreas, but even so Mariano's mesa did not speak. But when the mesa of don Manuel spoke, then Mariano's mesa spoke as well. So even if you are a powerful paqo, if the thing is not for your hand, you cannot handle it. The problem is for the hand of another person. It is the same with cleansing hucha I think."

As is usually the case with Juan, his explanation was more than a clarification, it was a teaching in and of itself. But we had had enough talking and teaching for one morning. We, too, were hungry and so we turned off the tape recorder and joined the Q'ero for lunch.

Chapter 9

Keepers of the Ancient Knowledge: The Three Worlds

When we resumed the interview after lunch and a brief siesta, I decided to inquire about the three worlds of Andean mysticism: the upper world, called the *hanaq pacha*; the middle world, the *kay pacha*; and the lower world, the *ukhu pacha*. I had barely begun the interview when I was caught by surprise. As the Q'ero described the hanaq pacha, they revealed that there is a Land of the Dead, and its "doorway" is a volcano! As with the discussion of k'ara, I tossed aside my long list of carefully planned questions and looked to Juan and Ricardo for assistance. We essentially gave the Q'ero free rein. As usual, we were well rewarded, for despite our meandering through this new, and unfamiliar, territory, we were not only able to add to our understanding of Andean mysticism, but we were provided yet another unique glimpse into the hearts and minds of the Q'ero.

THE HANAQ PACHA, KAY PACHA, AND UKHU PACHA

Don Juan Pauqar Flores answered my query about the three worlds first, with the other Q'ero quickly following suit. Their answer revealed how deeply the thread of Christianity had woven itself into the warp and woof of indigenous cosmology.

"The hanaq pacha is the house of the Lord, of God. It is also the place where the children who have died go; they go to heaven. The hanaq pacha is another type of *llaqta* [town or city], different from where we live. It is the place where the souls of men live; the world of the hanaq pacha is the world of the heavens, it is the blue world above us."

"Who lives there?" asked Juan. "The souls of dead babies, paqos, and the saints?"

Don Julian answered. "No. God is the only one who lives there. But when children die, the moment they die they transform into something like birds that fly up to heaven. Older people, men and women, when they die they go to a volcano that is near Arequipa."

We were all surprised by this answer, even Juan and Ricardo. As our resident anthropologists, they dug for more information, trying to retrieve the name of this volcano of the dead. But the Q'ero would only tell us that it was near Arequipa, in southern Peru. However, they were eager to offer more details of this world.

"There are the souls of the dead in this volcano," said don Agustín. "When you kill a sheep, the spirit of the sheep goes to the volcano. When you kill a llama, a cow, or a bull, the spirit of the animal goes to the volcano. The [human] souls in the volcano cry out, 'They're coming! They're coming!' The spirit of the sheep says, 'Baaaaa;' and that of the cow says, 'Mooooo!'[1] and the spirits in the volcano hear them and cry out in happiness, 'Good! Good! They are coming!' This is because all the people there are thinking, maybe they are coming for me!"[2]

"These [human] souls, when they first arrive at the volcano, they don't have anything. Those souls who have been there for a long time, however, they have a house, lands, and herds. When the relatives of the dead person care for the tomb of the dead person, putting flowers on it and tending it, then that soul will have a good life in the volcano, a good house and lands, and other good things.

"When someone is a messenger from this world to the other, then the relatives of the dead person can send messages and supplies through this man or woman. Drinks, food like quinoa,[3] and other things."

"Where is this volcano?" we asked, "In the hanaq pacha or the kay pacha?"

"The kay pacha," replied don Agustín. "But to this volcano town, only the soul of a dead person can go. A living person cannot go there. But still, to live in this volcano, your soul must climb the mountain, the sides of the volcano. It is very difficult. But only the soul arrives there; this is our shadow self."

"Why must the soul climb the mountain?" Juan inquired.

"This mountain has a red peak, and living human beings try to climb this mountain but they can never succeed in this. No one can climb it. If you try to, you will fall down. You may even die," don Agustín said.

"But why does the soul climb it?" we asked.

"At night, in your dreams, we can go to this mountain," don Agustín explained, still not directly answering our question. "It is possible in our dreams."

Juan again asked why the soul must climb the peak.

This time don Julian spoke up, explaining, "When we die, the soul has no difficulty climbing this mountain, which we cannot climb when we are alive."

"Are there other places where souls go after death, or only to the volcano?" I asked, wondering if the ukhu pacha was equivalent to the Christian hell or purgatory. Anamaria asked the question in a slightly different way. "Do both the good and the bad go there, to the volcano?"

Juan Pauqar Flores answered. "Everyone goes there. The good and the bad, but to be sure, the bad have more difficulty."

Ricardo and Juan asked about how one is determined to be either "good" or "bad."

Don Julian explained that "when we die, there is a door in this volcano. At the door is St. Gabriel. A soul knocks on the door, and St. Gabriel opens it. This is when the bad are recognized and sent back to the volcano."

Don Julian's answer seemed to indicate that the volcano was only a stopping point along the way to somewhere better, perhaps the hanaq pacha. The syncretism between the ancient, indigenous belief and Christian belief was obvious, so we surmised that the hanaq pacha was equivalent to heaven. Still, we couldn't be sure, so we asked for more details.

"The souls of the bad are sent back," don Julian explained, "and the souls of the good are allowed to pass through the door."

Obviously, we had not established that the door leads to the hanaq pacha. Juan Núñez del Prado explained the indigenous, although Catholicized belief that "if St. Gabriel does not permit the dead person to pass, he or she must return to their tomb. St. Gabriel is the messenger between this world and the next, and on All Saints Day, Peruvians pray to him to open the door for all their dead loved ones."

Don Julian explained further. "When these dead return because of their mistakes, they return to their tombs. They spend much time there. These souls, they are vagabond souls. They are beings who scurry around and scare you. They are wanderers."

Don Agustín added to don Julian's explanation, seemingly surprised that we did not know this information. "When these vagabond spirits are rejected by St. Gabriel, their relatives must

ask the help of a good paqo, who must make the person accept-
able to St. Gabriel. To do this, the paqo calls the soul and at the
same time calls St. Gabriel, and the paqo prays, 'Accept him!
Pardon him!' If the paqo is powerful, St. Gabriel will accept that
soul."

"What about a paqo?" Juan wondered aloud. "Can he pass
easily?"

"The paqo, like any other person, leaves relatives behind,"
don Julian explained. "When a paqo dies, his relatives must
arrange for another paqo to do the same work for this paqo as
he would do for any other person—make offerings to the Apus
and call to St. Gabriel to accept the soul of the paqo."

What about those souls who become wanderers? I wondered. What happens to them? I asked Juan, and he explained
that these vagabond souls wander around on Earth, and if you
accidently meet one you can catch a sickness, called *uraña*,
caused by fright and the shock to your nervous system. The disease takes the form of an ill wind, and you can be well one
minute and deathly ill the next.

Don Mariano provided further information. "Some kinds of
winds are the vagabond spirits' voices. If they infect you, you get
uraña and die. Some people have the capacity to identify a
vagabond spirit. If someone identifies a vagabond spirit, he
must call the owners of the soul [the deceased person's rela-
tives] and tell them that their soul is doing this. Then they must
do the work with St. Gabriel to change the situation."

As fascinating as our discussion was, time was growing short
and I wanted to move on to gather information about the kay pacha
and ukhu pacha. But Juan had several more "little" questions: "The
people in the volcano, are they happy? Sad? How is the way of life
inside the volcano? Is this the final destination for souls?"

The Q'ero agreed that "there in the volcano the souls do not suffer—because they have their houses. Each soul has its own house."

"Only the souls who are recent arrivals suffer," said don Agustín, " because they don't have a house."

Don Mariano agreed, adding, "The danger is if the volcano erupts. The souls work to prevent this, because such an eruption could be the beginning of the end of the world. Otherwise, in their world, they live very well. They live in harmony."

Don Agustín had other ideas. "The new arrivals have a time of *ñak'ariy pacha*, a suffering time, because they do not have houses. But they go to a Catholic priest, who performs a Mass, and afterwards, they will have a house."

Don Agustín seemed fixated on the houses of the afterlife, so we decided to switch topics completely. Wanting information on how the nature spirits occupy these various worlds, I asked if *Inti* (the sun) and *Mama Killa* (the moon) are in the hanaq pacha or the kay pacha.

Don Julian answered. "They belong to the kay pacha. But they must travel from one side of the sea to the other. They rise from the sea and go back to the sea."

"What happens to the sun during the night?" Ricardo wanted to know.

"During the day the sun gives his light to us," don Julian explained. "But then it must move on and give its light to other towns."

"What about the rainbow?" I asked. "Is it in the hanaq pacha or kay pacha?"

"*K'uychi* [the rainbow] is at the same time in the ground and above," don Mariano said. "The rainbow is in this world, the kay pacha, and also in the hanaq pacha. When the *Taytacha Inti* [Lord Sun] becomes sick, he has a rainbow around him. In this case, the rainbow is completely in the hanaq pacha. But usually the rainbow connects the hanaq pacha and the kay pacha."

"In water, like in fountains, you can see something like a rainbow," don Juan Pauqar Flores added. "This is a rainbow of the kay pacha. If you see this k'uychi, it is dangerous," he said, holding up his hand as if to ward something off. "You can get an inflammation of the mouth or you can get eye disease."

"What about the stars?" I asked, figuring that I might as well cover all the nature spirits of the hanaq pacha before I asked about those of the ukhu pacha.

Don Juan Pauqar Flores answered. "The stars are in the hanaq pacha, and they are young ladies who are dressed in their finest clothes. They are very elegant and dressed in many colors. In the heavens are not only the young ladies, but also the old ladies, like Venus. She is an old woman, old and large. Those like her are not young ladies—they are *qoyllurs*, not *ch'askas* [planets, not stars]. Where there are a lot of young ladies, there must be at least one old lady to care for them, to watch over them."

I was delighted with don Juan's answer, and although I had a million more questions about the hanaq pacha, the tick of the very kay pacha clock forced me to move on. I asked about the spirits of the ukhu pacha, the lower world, and once again don Juan answered.

"The ukhu pacha is lower than this world, lower than the kay pacha. There are some people who live there who are very small." Don Juan gestured with his hand, indicating how small these ukhu pacha people are by holding his thumb and index finger about two inches apart. "And also there are *qowis* [guinea pigs] there.[4] A guinea pig to these tiny people is like a cow or a bull is to us! Ten or fifteen of these people, with great difficulty, can kill a guinea pig to get food."

172 • KEEPERS OF THE ANCIENT KNOWLEDGE

"Are there supernatural beings there?" I asked.

Don Julian took over, explaining the structure of the ukhu pacha in relation to the three worlds of Andean cosmology. "The whole world is like a house with different floors. The lower world is like one floor. The kay pacha and the hanaq pacha are other floors. The *ukhupacharuna* [people of the lower world] live underground, inside Pachamama. And just as we have businesses, selling meat in the market, some of them have businesses too. But they sell the meat of the guinea pigs. They run after the guinea pigs; they are small enough to fit into the guinea pig holes, so they can hunt them. But we live in the middle world," he concluded.

"Can a paqo travel between these three worlds?" I asked.

"No," answered don Juan Pauqar Flores. "We don't."

"Then how do you know about the three worlds?" Anamaria wondered aloud.

"That's a good question," I said, "but it may be too abstract." I looked to Juan for help with formulating the question. Juan and Ricardo talked for a few minutes and then Ricardo put the question to the Q'ero. Because it was not translated, to this day I do not know exactly what the question was.

"We don't have the capacity to go to the hanaq pacha or the ukhu pacha," don Mariano answered, "but we can invoke the spirits of the hanaq pacha."

Don Mariano's reply was informative, but it raised other serious questions. "If the hanaq pacha is the place only of the souls of dead children and God, as they said earlier," Juan remarked, "then what spirits could they be invoking?" Juan put his question to don Mariano, but it was don Agustín who answered.

"In the hanaq pacha is God, Jesus Christ," he said. "We only invoke the power of God. Even a kuraq akulleq does not have the power to manipulate anything in the hanaq pacha."

"Well, where are the spirits of paqos and saints and such?" Juan asked. "In what world are they?"

Don Julian answered first, rather hesitantly. "It cannot be in the ukhu pacha," he said. "That is impossible. They must be in the hanaq pacha."

"So the paqos and the saints are in the hanaq pacha?" Juan and I followed up.

Again don Julian answered. "The saints are *unanchasqa*." Juan Núñez del Prado explained that to be *unanchasqa* is to be given an actual symbol of power, perhaps a scepter, or to have been warranted to act with power on behalf of a higher authority, such as by God. "In the beginning the saints were given the sign of power by God, by Jesus Christ, in the kay pacha," don Julian continued. "He said they must live in the kay pacha. Jesus said, 'St. Juan, you must live in this church,' and he was sent to that temple. So the saints now all have a place in a temple or chapel in the kay pacha."[5]

Juan suggested that this might be a good place to ask about the prophecy, about the spiritual evolution of the world. I agreed, and we had a long and challenging discussion with the Q'ero about prophecy, which I have partially reproduced in chapter 3 and more fully in Appendix II. By the end of that difficult discussion, we were all exhausted. It was clear that everyone was talked out and that the interview, having lasted more than five hours, was winding down. I had a million more questions, but knew I would not have time to ask more than one or two final questions. I remembered that we had not asked Sandy's earlier question, about whether the Q'ero work with animal allies in the same way that many North American indigenous peoples do. I put that question to the Q'ero as our final question, and don Mariano replied for the group.

"No. Everything helps, but we do not have the capacity to establish a personal relationship with a particular animal. Only with the Apus. We have the Apus."

KAWSAY PURIY: WALKING THE SACRED PATH

It seemed fitting that my interviews with the Q'ero would end with a restatement of their reliance upon and reverence for the Apus, those most powerful of nature spirits. After four days of intense discussion, I now understood unequivocally that the Apus were the primary energetic and spiritual links by which the Q'ero mediated the three worlds of Andean cosmology. The Lords and Ñust'as of the Mountains, because they cannot be apprehended directly, often dialogue with the paqos who are in service to them through the condors, hummingbirds, bulls, or pumas. But no matter their symbolic manifestation, they are the supreme nature energies of the Andes, their spiritual majesty mirroring their physical magnificence. As I packed up the tape recorder and collected the more than fifteen tapes that were scattered across the table, I considered don Mariano's final comment. It stirred the memory of a story that most of us who walk the Andean sacred path have heard in one form or another. This is more than a story, however. It is really a teaching, a forewarning, and a parable of preparation. One version of the story goes as follows:

One day a young paqo-in-training was walking down through the mountains. In the distance he could see someone approaching. Soon he could make out the figure of an old woman, slowly but methodically making her way up the steep path with the help of a wooden staff. When they met on the path—it being only wide enough to permit one person at a time to pass—they stopped to greet each other. "Where is it you are going, Mamacita?" the young paqo asked the elderly woman. She pointed toward the crest of the mountain. "Up there," she said. "I live over that mountain."

"You have come a long way," the paqo said, observing her weariness.

"Yes," she replied, "I have just come from a wedding." As she spoke, the old woman caught the paqo's gaze and stared deep into his eyes. The paqo was mesmerized by the intensity of the old woman's eyes, but he soon became very uncomfortable. He broke her gaze and nervously stepped aside to let her pass.

"Well, I'm sure you must want to be on your way, Mamacita," he said. "Will you be all right?"

"Yes, I will be fine," she replied over her shoulder as she once again set off. "I have made this journey many times."

During the remainder of his journey home, the paqo couldn't stop thinking about the old woman. He knew there was nothing strange about meeting a solitary individual in the mountains. Such things occurred all the time, for there was no other way over the mountain but on foot. One often met solitary individuals herding llamas or alpacas. Still, the paqo couldn't shake the feeling that something strange, almost momentous, had happened on the mountain but he had failed to see it. He decided to tell his maestro about the old woman.

His maestro listened, and then patted the paqo on the back, almost as if he were consoling him. "My son," he said, "you have missed a great opportunity because you could not see [*qaway*] what you were looking at. That was not a chance meeting you had on the mountain. That was not an old woman who crossed your path. That was the Apu! If you had truly been able to see her, you would have known it was the *Ñust'a*, who appears to those she favors as an old woman returning from a wedding to her mountaintop home. You missed a great opportunity, my son. For if one has the spiritual wisdom to recognize the Princess of the Mountain, she must grant one's wish."[6]

As I wrote this chapter, Don Mariano's final remark—of having a sacred relationship with the Apus, the Lords and Princesses of the Mountains—sparked my memory of this and many other mystical stories I had heard over the years from Q'ero paqos and my mestizo teachers. These are marvelous stories and myths of how the puma calls its prey using its dream body and how a shaman reads the changing face of the rainbow. According to William Sullivan—who, in his seminal book *The Secret of the Incas*, cracked the code of Andean cosmology and astronomy as encoded in Peruvian mythology—myth is a "vessel designed and fitted for essential cargo." Stories are "ark[s], whose builders had one and only one concern, the welfare of future generations."[7] The plethora of mystical information the Q'ero had related during the interviews—about the volcano of the dead and the glow of the puma's tail, about the k'ara of the Apus and the lives of the ukhupacharuna—all seemed "essential cargo" for the journey along the mystical path and into the heart of the kawsay pacha. What my discussion with the Q'ero was really about, I now realize, was not the transmission of cultural or mystical information, but the joining of energies—male and female, North and South, Western and indigenous, modern and ancient. I had begun the interviews seeking factual information about Andean mysticism, but I have concluded writing about this information knowing that facts alone cannot provide a road map into the mystical and shamanic worlds. At most they are signposts to guide us in our practice, safe havens where we can momentarily place our trust before we make the next plunge into the unknown. No matter his skill as an alto mesayoq, don Mariano at heart has only his trust in his relationship with the Apus to guide him during his journey through the shamanic world; yet through that relationship, because of that trust, he gains access to the cosmos, to spaces exterior and interior, to multidimensional realms beyond time and space. The Apus are his doorway, a distinctly Andean one. But we can all find a doorway. We have only to choose one, to trust it implicitly, and then to step through it into the fullness of being.

Part III

The Flight of the Condor: Putting Andean Shamanic Practices to Work in Your Life

Chapter 10

Hucha Mikhuy: Cleansing and Digesting Heavy Energy

I sat across from Américo at Mollomarqa, his ancestral home high in the mountains above Paucartambo. "What is this energy we are learning to work with?" I asked him. The spirit of my question was more informational than pedagogical. I was not in the mode of a paqo seeking the techniques and advice that would advance my training, but in the mode of a writer hungry for information for an article on Andean shamanism. "Tell me about energy," I urged.

Américo responded enthusiastically to my question, his words translated as quickly as he spoke them. "The universe is a filament within which we as individuals are surrounded by the infinite. We are all points that are surrounded by the great infinite. We are dealing with questions and answers that move like the wind. We are in transit through this existence . . . touching the infinite light . . . connected to the cosmos with bridges of filaments.

"In respect to the ancient traditions, there are filaments that have been accumulated wisely in esoteric places and maintained through magic and the occult—an alchemical reaction! Our process of spirit has maintained the vision of those lights. They are now willing to open, to illuminate the night, and especially the night of the planet. All the traditions have spoken, the powers have spoken, the myths have spoken, the Hindus, the Mayas,

the Hopis—all the great traditions have spoken of this. The Andean lamas—who almost never come down from the mountains—maintain an incredible receptivity to the cosmos. They have an incredible but simple understanding of and connection to Pachamama. They are connected to the mystery and the enigma; they are connected to all the great spiritual traditions of the planet. They may not know formal names, but they know absolutely and correctly the goals. A connection exists from the Andes to the Himalayas, because they truly and authentically work with the spirit of the wind, which is the messenger from the mountains and of Pachamama. Therefore, we are oriented by those filaments. Those filaments, through an unconscious way and a superconscious way, are being put out at this time to the great altars of the world, the great mystical places of the world— it is the time of the gathering.

"Right now everything is truly connected because it is all a great ball of energy, of spirituality within the planet. The spiritual energies are all connecting to each other. What is actually happening is that the world's spiritual energy is being moved, to the point that we can actually produce the will and intent of the world's great teachers. Bubbles of energy are being connected by the will and intent of the great teachers, who know the prophecies. . . . There's a development, a growth, of consciousness. It is not only a matter of individuals situating themselves, but of us collectively situating ourselves in a new place. It actually touches on that expanded consciousness."

When Américo gave me this information, I had approached him as a journalist, coming from a place of intellect rather than of heart. Eventually, he stopped responding to my questions in a serious and thoughtful way and just played with me, almost parodying my intellectual stance. This was during my first trip to Peru, when I was very new to the Andean sacred path. A year

later, Américo would finish this conversation at the Island of the
Moon, the place of the female shamans. At that time and place
I was in a completely different frame of mind—and energy body.
I had been intently studying the tradition and energy techniques.
I was a paqo now, not a journalist. During the first half of a
month-long training in Peru, I had traveled to the Q'ero villages
and Q'ollorit'i with Juan Núñez del Prado. Then for two weeks I
had traveled around Peru and Bolivia with Américo and four
North American women paqos, all friends. Américo had been
training us in the left side of the mesa, in the practical and magical arts. One day, on Island of the Moon, he had unknowingly
finished his conversation about energy, in a most emphatic way.
I had already learned more fully how to sense and control my
energy body, but I still lacked a sense of the power this control
afforded me. I knew how to be in conscious interchange with
the kawsay pacha, but, like a child in a candy store, I was indis-
criminate in appetite and self-control. Américo very succinctly
gave me, and the other women present, advice that I quickly
took to heart and that would, much later, sustain me during a
very difficult and emotional period in my personal life.

"Everything we're doing now," he said, "[is meant to help us]
arrive at our energetic body, accumulating energy from anywhere—and that's the only avarice I allow my sisters. Do not
waste it! Waste your money, spend your money, but do not
waste your energy, do not spend your energy unnecessarily."

Juan Núñez del Prado describes our energy body as the *poq'po*, the bubble, a term his teacher don Benito Qoriwaman used. This energy bubble extends outward around your physical body and has a surface to it, like a skin. Your poq'po protects you, by mediating the amount and kind of energy to which you are exposed. For instance, your *poq'po* accumulates heavy energy, called hucha. There is no way to avoid this. But if you occasionally cleanse your poq'po, hucha has less chance to build up and affect your physical body. Juan identifies three primary tools from various spiritual traditions that he considers particularly useful for cleansing your energy body and empowering you: prayer, meditation, and *hucha mikhuy*. Hucha mikhuy is the process of "digesting" or "eating" heavy energy, but in the Andean tradition, you can also cleanse your poq'po by simply releasing hucha. Both techniques are described below. In either case, when you cleanse your poq'po of hucha, you also infuse it with *sami*, refined energy, which empowers you.

As Américo Yábar said, we want to expend our energy wisely. One way we can do that is by being cognizant of "dissimilar" and "similar" energetic relationships, called, respectively, *yanantin* and *masintin*, as discussed in chapter 2. When we are attuned to the yanantin energy of a situation or person, then we can begin to identify what is different about us or incompatible between us. We can be alert for and respond to energetic states that may cause problems in our relationship, creating hucha. From this awareness grows opportunities for discovering points of similarity and mutual contact from which we can begin to harmonize the energies to empower both parties. We can use the hucha mikhuy technique, for example, not necessarily to change the relationship—because many relationships, such as male and female, will always remain yanantin—but to cleanse the energy exchange of hucha that may result from having to engage such dissimilar or potentially incompatible energies.

All cleansing is mediated through the *qosqo*, the region around your navel that is your "spiritual stomach." It is different sizes, and can be located in slightly different places, in different individuals. The exercises that follow will help you locate your qosqo and begin to sense and control it. At first, these exercises may appear deceptively simple. On the one hand, they *are* simple; for the primary activity is focusing your attention and intention. On the other hand, gaining *conscious* control of your qosqo takes effort. Remember don Mariano's advice to me? It was, in a nutshell, "Work hard." His is good advice. The key to self-mastery is *practice*. It takes diligence and commitment to learn to sense and control your energy body. Therefore, truly master an exercise before you move on to the next one. The results of such mastery—being able to consciously push the kawsay to create harmonious energetic interchanges in your life—are well worth the effort.

I'd like to point out, however, that creating energetic harmony in your life does not mean that you will have banished challenges and ambiguities from your life. Unpredictability and uncertainty are the twin faces of possibility and creativity. To use the words of Dr. Deepak Chopra,[1] we want the energy from the "field of infinite possibilities" to play through our lives, opening us to the magical potentials of ourselves that we may be incapable of even imagining within the domain of the rational. Energetic harmony, however, ensures that in the flux of the creative possibilities of our lives we maintain well-being and develop a conscious fluidity that allows us to embrace or flow through the unpredictability. In addition, we develop a spiritual alertness that allows us see opportunities and to take risks, increasing our courage to make the most of opportunities for individual and communal growth.

Therefore, I urge you to take your time and master each exercise—and this chapter is nearly overburdened with exercises! There is no shortcut to mastery, for sensitizing yourself to and learning to control your energy body is fundamental to all Andean mystical or shamanic practices. The beginning exercises are aimed at first helping you to feel and access your poq'po and to control your qosqo, your primary energy center. Then you will attempt to explore the kawsay pacha using only your energy body. Once you have achieved success with the initial techniques that attune you to your poq'po and to the kawsay pacha, you can go on to learn to cleanse your energy body of hucha and empower yourself with sami.

ACCESSING YOUR ENERGY BODY

EXERCISE 1: Locating Your Qosqo

Sit quietly where you won't be disturbed. Take a few minutes to settle yourself, perhaps with meditation or a breathing technique, then place your dominant hand over your belly, around your navel area, a few inches above the skin or clothing. Bring your awareness to the space between your hand and your stomach, feeling the warmth that is generated by your body. You should be able to distinguish an area of energy, an especially concentrated warmth or perhaps a tingling sensation or a sticky, pulling feeling. When you do, perceptually note its edges and boundaries. This area is your qosqo, the primary energy center or "eye" of your poq'po. Once you have sensed this area, move your hand farther away from your skin or clothing, a little at a time. Sense the warmth extending outward. This is your energy body extending outward and your qosqo opening, creating a larger energy center. You should practice sensing your qosqo and pulling it outward until your arm is fully extended. At this point, your qosqo is considered wide open. Practice moving your hand outward from your body and back inward, expanding and contracting your poq'po, and opening and closing your qosqo. Remember, the qosqo can be visualized as an eye, whose pupil dilates as it lets in more light and contracts as it lets in less light. It can actually be open or closed at any point in the extension of your poq'po. Your poq'po could be extended but your qosqo could be barely open. You may want this to be the case in a situation where you are probing, or "tasting," an unfamiliar or disharmonious energy. You would want to "taste" it cautiously, a little at a time. Usually, however, the two movements go hand in hand: as you extend your poq'po, you more fully open your qosqo. Fundamentally, opening and closing your qosqo is largely a matter of intention. But you can learn to sense the degree to which your qosqo is open or closed by using your hand to sense its edges and parameters, noting how these shift as you intend your qosqo to open wider or to close.

When you have consistently achieved control of extending and withdrawing your poq'po and opening and closing your qosqo with your hand, stop using your hand and begin using only your intent. Simply intend that your poq'po extend or contract. Command that your qosqo open or close. The next series of exercises, the Hours of Power, in which you practice sensing the energies of the natural world with your poq'po, will help you determine whether you have gained *intentional* control of your energy body.

THE HOURS OF POWER

The fundamental practices of Andean shamanism are not so different from the shamanic practices of other systems or other cultures, and in its reverence of nature it is not different at all. Work with any indigenous people and you will find that the fundamental shamanic techniques are ones that teach you to be aware of the essences of nature and your connections to them. It is crucial to learn to sense the energies of nature, and then to discern the nuances of energy between one place and another. It's easy to feel the difference between the energy of an airport and that of a city park, and between the city park and an isolated mountain peak. But it is another thing entirely to feel the difference between one park bench and another, between one niche in the mountain ledge and another only a few feet away.

The following exercises are ones that you may have come across countless times in many different traditions. They are exercises to sensitize you to the different energies of nature. However, you will learn to sense these energies using your poq'po and to mediate the energies through your qosqo.

I begin with an exercise I practiced many times with Américo Yábar, which he calls the Hour of Power. I have also practiced this technique, in a completely different way, with Paul Crane Tohlakai, a Navajo friend and teacher. I have not personally practiced all of the techniques exactly as they are described here, especially over the time periods described, but I have developed them for use in this book based on energy sensing techniques I have practiced in other ways and under different circumstances in Peru and elsewhere.

Américo and Paul both designate the periods of sunrise and sunset as the hours of power. These are the transitional times when the "veil between the worlds" is thinnest. We know that there is in fact no veil between the worlds, because in the kawsay pacha energy flows freely. However, because we are so adapted to, some might even say trapped by, the perception of a linear space-time, we tend to perceive seams in the fabric of the energy world. The transitional hours of sunrise and sunset are powerful times when these seams are most visible, and so we use this visibility to paradoxically lift the curtain of our perceptions to see the seamlessness behind the seams.

The sun, called *Inti* in Quechua, is a powerful generator of energies, and its energy is most obvious to us in the form of heat and light. Our sense of touch (hot/cold) and vision (light/dark) are drastically affected as the sun moves across the horizon. Américo, in his characteristic poetry, simply says, sunrise and sunset are times when the "power of the world floods the spaces of our being." And so a good place to start sensitizing yourself to the kawsay pacha is by working with your poq'po at sunrise and sunset. However, *Mama Killa*, the gentler energy of the moon, is the sun's counterpart. It is the Feminine complement to the sun's Masculinity, and is itself a powerful nature energy. An exercise to sensitize you to its energy follows those concerning the sun.

EXERCISE 2: Harmonizing with the Setting Sun

Practice this exercise for at least one month. It is also a good idea to practice it during different times of the year, perhaps for one month during each of the four seasons. Make sure you are settled comfortably out of doors at least ten minutes before sunset. Dress comfortably, according to the season. It is not important that your skin be exposed in any way. Choose a place that is as free of distractions as possible, and it is not a good idea to begin practicing this exercise on the shore of an ocean or lake, as the water energies, which are particularly powerful nature energies, may pull your awareness from the sunset. Let the sunset be the focus of your environment.

Settle yourself by meditating for a few minutes. If you do not have a meditation technique, then simply focus your awareness on your breath and try to empty your mind of everyday thoughts and concerns. Once you are settled and relaxed, attune yourself to your poq'po and open your qosqo, a little at a time, focusing your inner awareness on the sun. (If you don't yet have intentional control of your qosqo, use your hand to draw it outward and fully open.) Keeping your eyes closed, feel the sun and its movement with your energy body. Try to sense the sun's dimming, its sinking. Reach out with your energetic perception—Américo would say to reach out with your energy filaments, which extend outward like threads of light from your qosqo—to "see" the effect of the sun's changing light on the sky and landscape. Continue gently probing with your energy body until you "feel" that the sun has gone down. Your skin will probably give you the first clues to the sun's setting, as the air temperature may cool. And even with your eyes closed, you will be able to discern a lack of light. That's fine, attune yourself to what a sunset feels like physically. But also awaken all your other senses. What does the sunset look like through closed eyes? What does it taste like? Smell like? Notice these sensory impressions, then release them and attune yourself to the energetic feeling you sense through your qosqo. After a month of sensing sunsets, you should be aware of the myriad nuances of the movement of energy of a setting sun.

EXERCISE 3: Harmonizing with the Rising Sun

Repeat the exercise above, for one month, during sunrise. How does the energetic "feel" of the environment change as the sun rises and infuses your world with its light and heat? How does a rising sun feel energetically different from a setting sun? Is there a different "taste" to the energy?

EXERCISE 4: Harmonizing with the Moon

Choose a time of night when the moon is high in the sky, and over two consecutive months go outside at the same time of the evening and repeat the technique described above, only this time with the moon. Be sure to give yourself at least twenty minutes and keep your eyes closed as you sense the moon. Attune to your poq'po, open your qosqo, and see if you can sense the changing conditions of the moon. When does a cloud cross in front of it? Did you feel that shooting star to the left of it? (You may never know if there really was a shooting star, because your eyes are closed!) During the course of a month, how does the moon's energy change with its phases? (It's helpful to repeat this exercise for at least two months in a row.) How is the moon's energy different from the sun's? Can you "taste" the difference between a masculine nature energy (sun) and a feminine nature energy (moon)?

The moon, you will remember the Q'ero telling us, has a powerful k'ara. I will not be surprised if you find this exercise the easiest and most intense of any in this chapter. It was for me. As I recounted earlier in this book, I first merged with the lunar energy at Aguas Calientes, the ancient baths of the Inkas, in 1994. I was in the baths at night, doing ceremony with a group of Westerners. Our only light was from the milky glow of fat white candles stuck here and there in pools of wax on the concrete between the two pools. The night sky was brilliant with stars and the moon. At one point we each went to the edge of the large pool we were working in and began to meditate, our instructions being to touch the energy of the moon. "Throw your energy filaments to the moon. Connect with her magic. Become reborn in the light of the night," Américo urged us. "Go! Go be with the mother of the stars, the mistress of the night." After only minutes, I felt my poq'po enlarge and illuminate. My qosqo opened wide, and my awareness was huge, immense. Soon I was pure awareness, and as Mama Killa and I merged energies I felt an infinite tenderness coupled with an intensity of bliss that was nearly overwhelming. I was utterly immersed in this bliss, and although I felt these emotions in a distinctly physical way, I was totally without body—until I was suddenly and explosively snapped back into my body by my teachers. "Seeing" (*qaway*) my energy body, the two of them had waded over to me. One touched me on the chest, over my heart, snapping me back to physical reality. He whispered a personal comment in my ear about what they had just "seen" in my energy body and the quality of the work I had done over the last week, and then he gave me a simple instruction about my further training. I'm sure my teachers had good reason for pulling me back from my reverie and grounding me, and I was not resentful. Still, for hours I remained filled with the most exquisite refined energy I have ever experienced. The spell of the moon was broken, but the essence of that experience is one that is always with me.

EXERCISE 5: Harmonizing with the Stars

Repeat this same sensing exercise for one month but instead of focusing on the moon, focus on the stars. You may choose one star on which to focus your energy "attention" or simply give yourself over to the entire field of stars. In urban and suburban areas, which receive so much artificial light as to drown out starlight, this may be a perceptually challenging exercise, at least to your rational mind. We want to see what we're connecting with. Although energetically it doesn't matter if you can physically see the stars or not, it is preferable that they be visible, if for no other reason than their beauty, which inspires us to practice, practice, practice!

This is a glorious exercise in Peru, where the darkness of the countryside makes the night sky blaze with fist-sized stars. The Milky Way is a great glowing road across the hanaq pacha, the great Shaman's Road in the mystical tradition. Américo says that "the eyes of the shaman shine brighter and are more charged the more he is able to move the power of his filaments in the direction of the stars." I have heard it said by an alto mesayoq from Lima that we each have one star that belongs only to us, which is the star of our destiny. If you can identify this star and incorporate its energy, then you can read the story of your present and future life in it. As you practice this energy-sensing exercise, can you find your star?

What you have been doing in these exercises with the celestial energies is experiencing the refined energies of the hanaq pacha, a powerful part of the kawsay pacha, through your poq'po, or energy bubble or body, rather than through your physical senses. You also have been exercising and sensitizing your qosqo. As you touch these energies, you inevitably pull refined energy into your energy body, increasing your capacity for power. As you can see, it takes time and effort to develop the perceptual power of your energetic body. But as you have also no doubt found, the effort is worth it!

KAY PACHA NATURE ENERGIES

It's now time to focus on the kay pacha energies. Although the sun, moon, and stars, because they are physical entities, can be said to be "in" the kay pacha, their energies, being celestial, are also associated with the hanaq pacha. A tree is definitely more of the kay pacha than a star. So now repeat the same basic perception exercise—eyes closed and sensing through the awareness of your poq'po and qosqo—with any object in or aspect of nature. Try a tree, a lake, a river, the wind, the rain, the snow, sand, grass, a flower. It may be beneficial, depending upon your development so far, to choose one object and practice with it repeatedly until you really have a sense of its energy vibration. Then move on to a different type of nature energy. As other energies present themselves, such as rain or snow, a perching bird or sleeping cat, take advantage of the opportunity to sense them. However, I recommend that you *not* choose an element of nature that is associated, by some people, with the ukhu pacha, such as a cave, a snake or spider, or a burrowing insect.[2] There are particular nature spirits associated with various terrains, and some are "less friendly" than others, although that anthropomorphic judgment isn't really fair. Words truly are inadequate to describe these energies, but it may be more accurate to say these energies are less "wieldy" for some people, especially if you bring a culturally based perception of negativity or darkness to these entities. Remember, there are no "good" and "bad" or "positive" and "negative" energies in Andean cosmology, just light/refined and heavy/dense. It is advisable to stay with the lighter, more refined energies for now.

EXERCISE 6: Harmonizing with a Nature Energy

When you choose an object in nature that is an entity unto itself, such as a tree or a hill or a rock formation, do not touch it, if possible. For instance, if you have chosen a tree as the object of your exercise, do not sit with your back against it.

Instead sit about three feet away from the trunk, facing it. For a less substantive nature entity, such as sand or rain or wind, immerse yourself in it. Push your feet into the sand, face into the wind or rain.

Settle yourself for a few minutes using whatever relaxation technique is most comfortable and effective for you. Then attune to your poq'po and open your qosqo. As you make energetic contact with the natural object, be alert to subtle changes of temperature or density at your qosqo area, and to colors and textures that may "appear" in your inner vision. Don't try to analyze any of these sensations, just experience them and let them go. Of course, if at any time you feel uncomfortable, pull your poq'po in closer to your physical body, close your qoqso until it is just a small opening, and end the exercise by cleansing yourself, feeding the discomfort down into Mother Earth. If you still feel uncomfortable in any way, lay down on the ground, belly to belly with the Mother, and release all your hucha out through your qosqo. Remember, when you release hucha you are feeding the Mother, and she is always hungry! As you release hucha, also "pull" refined energy in through your head or crown chakra.

An additional note if you choose eventually to work with a stream, river, or waterfall: In the Andes these water spirits, especially those of the waterfalls, are called *phasi runa*, literally the "people of the water vapors." They "appear" to different people in different ways, but are generally sensed as mischievous, joyful energies. Work with them especially to overcome inhibitions and to enhance creativity. Remember, too, that hucha can be released into river water, so you may sense the hucha of others that has accumulated there.

Once you have "merged" with a particular nature energy, and it may take some time—one of my friends on the Andean path trained with a Native North American medicine woman, and she had to sit with one nature energy for a year before she could move on to another!—choose a new one and repeat this exercise. How many different nature energies can you "taste?" Do some feel more compatible with your personal energy than others? If so, examine the differences between compatible and incompatible energies, and be alert for those same "clues" in your energetic interchanges with the people in your life.

CREATING ENERGETIC HARMONY: HUCHA CLEANSING TECHNIQUES

You are now getting a good, intuitive sense of your poq'po and its primary energy center, the qosqo. You no doubt are learning to control both by extending and withdrawing your energy field and by opening and closing your energy "stomach." If you feel ready—and honor your feelings here as to whether you feel ready to proceed with more intensive energy work—you can begin to learn how to cleanse heavy energy from yourself and others in order to harmonize your energy relationships and interchanges. First, learn to release heavy energy.

You probably have accumulated enough hucha over the course of your lifetime—and we all accumulate more in countless ways every day—to keep yourself busy cleansing yourself for some time. Remember, only human beings generate hucha, and we all accumulate it as we interact in less than harmonious ways with others and so move out of equilibrium with our core self. Hucha is heavy energy, but "heaviness" is a relative term. What creates heavy energy for you may not create it for me. My teacher Juan Núñez del Prado tells the story of his work with kuraq akulleq don Manuel Q'espi at Macchu Picchu, where they were working in the sacred baths, Juan releasing his hucha into the water with don Manuel "anchoring" him in the practice. Don Manuel sat at a cistern situated higher up the terrace from where Juan was sitting, and Juan turned toward don Manuel, wondering aloud if he would be bathed in don Manuel's hucha as the water flowed down and over him. Don Manuel's face crinkled with laugh lines as he dismissed Juan's concern, declaring that his hucha was sami to Juan! With humility Juan silently turned back and began the hucha cleansing practice, having learned a gentle lesson from master to student about the relative apperception of hucha according to the state of one's energy body.

The most obvious ways to determine what heavy energy you carry in your poq'po is to acknowledge where you are experiencing physical pain or how you are carrying emotional discomfort or fear. Another way to identify hucha is to examine the yanantin and masintin relationships in your life. Anywhere these relationships are causing difficulties is an area ripe for energetic cleansing. When you have identified hucha, then you can consciously release this energy out through your qosqo, feeding it to Pachamama and drawing in sami.

EXERCISE 7: Releasing Hucha

The first cleansing process, which is a *release* of accumulated hucha, is deceptively simple. Just sit quietly, attune to your poq'po, open your qosqo, and feed Pachamama your hucha, "intending" it to move downward and out of your poq'po through the root center (*siki ñawi*) at the base of your spine. Extend the energy filaments from your qosqo into your own poq'po, probing for dense spots in your energy body where hucha may be encrusted, or sensing a dragging effect in the flow of your energy, or detecting "hot spots" where hucha may be concentrated. Then draw the hucha into the opening of your qosqo and down and out your root chakra.

While you feed the hucha downward, simultaneously open your crown chakra (at the top, or crown, of your head), align yourself with the hanaq pacha, the upper world, and draw refined energy, sami, in through this chakra. Feel the sami suffuse your energy body. It is important that you not "empty" yourself during this cleansing process; therefore, when you release hucha, you always want to simultaneously fill yourself with sami.

The hucha release process is flexible and can be individualized in whatever way is most comfortable and useful for you. Simply open your qosqo and intend that the hucha in your bubble flow through you and down to Pachamama, who is the great digester of hucha. Draw sami in through your crown to empower yourself. You will intuitively and energetically know when the process is complete. When it is, close your qosqo and honor Pachamama for her work on your behalf. You may want to make an offering of sugar or sweets, foods Pachamama loves.

You may find that it will take several sessions to cleanse the hucha you perceive in one part of your poq'po or associated with just one aspect of your life. Respect your intuitions and stay attuned to the feelings of your energy body. However, particularly heavy energy—old patterns and deep psychic wounds—may resist the release process and call for a more penetrating kind of cleansing, that of hucha mikhuy.

EXERCISE 8: Performing Hucha Mikhuy

Releasing hucha is one way to cleanse yourself. *Digesting* hucha is another, more advanced technique. Basically, the difference comes in the intensity of the cleansing and way that the energy is mediated through the qosqo. In the releasing technique described above, you are really cleansing the surface of your poq'po, the "skin" that acts as a protective barrier for your energy and physical bodies, where most of our hucha accumulates. In the hucha mikhuy technique, you cleanse hucha that has penetrated this surface—usually the most entrenched patterns and emotional pains, which you have been carrying for a long time. With this technique you also can reach out to others, cleansing their poq'pos as you digest their hucha. In some ways the hucha mikhuy technique shares similarities with the process Carlos Castaneda calls "recapitulation," in which one retracts or recovers one's energy filaments from the people and events of one's life and so reclaims one's power.[3] Castaneda's recapitulation process is time-consuming and highly ritualized; hucha mikhuy is not.

Digesting heavy energy begins the same way releasing heavy energy does: you attune yourself to your poq'po, open your qosqo, draw the hucha into your qosqo, and feed it out your root center and down to Pachamama. However, there are two main differences. First, the hucha you draw in through your qosqo may be your own or someone else's (or, even, from a place or an object). Second, instead of being connected to a source of sami, such as reaching up to the hanaq pacha to pull in sami through your crown chakra, in hucha mikhuy you extract sami from the hucha energy stream itself. In effect you "split" the single flow of energy into two streams, one of hucha and one of sami. You then release the hucha downward to Pachamama and direct the sami upward through your spine or energy centers to your head. You are pulling refined energy from the flow of your own or someone else's hucha, empowering yourself (and Pachamama) as you cleanse yourself or another person. *This double flow of energy is the key to knowing when you are actually digesting hucha as opposed to simply releasing hucha. If you do not feel the double flow, then you are not digesting energy.*

No doubt you are right now asking yourself two questions: Is hucha mikhuy difficult to learn? And, how can sami can be extracted from hucha? I, too, asked those questions, and was provided enlightened answers by my teachers. The answers are linked, so bear with me as I answer them in a linear fashion. First, let me address the question of difficulty. Simply put, hucha mikhuy is not difficult to learn—simply *command* your qosqo to do it, and it will! As for our other question, we have to remember that hucha is energy—it is just incompatible or disharmonious energy. Américo Yábar would call it disordered energy. It is not bad or useless or contaminated energy. The hucha that someone else carries may indeed be sami for you, just as don Manuel's hucha was sami for Juan Núñez del Prado. Juan likens hucha to food: our physical stomach knows how to digest food without our telling it to, and from that food it will absorb nutrients and expel anything that is indigestible. In response to both questions, Juan told me, "You do not have to teach your physical stomach to digest the food you eat. In the same way, you do not have to teach your spiritual stomach to digest hucha. Just command it to!"

Still, some of us are allergic to certain foods, and our bodies do not respond well when we ingest them. Can we be "allergic" to someone else's hucha? Yes and no. If you attempt to mikhuy someone's energy and you cannot detect the split stream or you feel sick, that may mean that the other person's energy is so incompatible as to be indigestible for you *at the present time.* Try again later, perhaps after you have cleansed more of your own hucha and so strengthened your own energy body with additional sami. Remember Juan's metaphor of the stone in the garden? If you feel the "stone" is too heavy for you to move, just leave it until you are stronger or until you can get help.

Enough talk. Now it's time to try hucha mikhuy—starting

with yourself. Sit where you will be undisturbed, settle yourself for a few minutes with meditation or breathing, attune to your poq'po, and open your qosqo. Now command your qosqo to eat your hucha. Sense the hucha energy flowing in from your poq'po through your qosqo, and the stream splitting—the heaviness flowing downward to Pachamama and the light energy, the sami, flowing upward to your head. Continue practicing this until you can clearly feel the double flow of energy. If you do, you are *digesting* your hucha.

Because mikhuy can cleanse at a deep energetic level, it may take several sessions to cleanse only one area of your poq'po. If you begin to feel light-headed, that may be a sign that it's time to stop this particular mikhuy session. You may be drinking in too much sami! If you really go overboard, you may even feel a little drunk. As always, listen to your energy body and your physical body and respect their feedback. If you feel lightheaded, then open your crown chakra and release the excess sami, intentionally sending it to someone you know who may need it.

Sometimes, if you are touching a particularly deep wound in your life, you may need to be "anchored" by another person well-trained in the hucha mikhuy technique. Again, remember that stone in the garden? If you can't lift it, you may need someone else's help. If you are cleansing a deeply held, painful energetic wound, you may need someone else's assistance to get the hucha moving or simply to provide emotional and energetic support. This person can assist you in digesting your heavy energy by mikhuying you as you mikhuy yourself. He or she can also monitor your emotional reactions and physical state as you digest your hucha, and can support you by sending you sami from their own energy body or from the hanaq pacha.

Now that you have practiced digesting your own hucha—

and you have *mastered* that technique haven't you?—you can begin to think about performing mikhuy on others.

EXERCISE 9: Performing Hucha Mikhuy on Others

Hucha mikhuy generally achieves three outcomes: it feeds Pachamama what she loves best, hucha; it energetically cleanses the other person, lightening him or her; and it empowers you. However, mikhuy has nearly unlimited uses, most practically for divesting a tense or troublesome situation of its heaviness. When you mikhuy with good intentions—*why else* would you digest anyone else's hucha?—you are in effect spreading peace and joy. Juan told me of one situation where he used mikhuy to make a bad situation bearable. He was in line in a bank in Cuzco, which was crowded with angry customers. It seems the government had experienced a fiscal crisis and had not paid government workers for several months. Now they had partial paychecks in hand and the bank was packed to overflowing. Juan described the lines of vocal and impatient customers, including the one he was standing in. He began to mikhuy the energy of the people in his line. Soon, he said, on either side of him were lines of grumbling customers, but the people in his line were smiling and passing the time in pleasant small talk.

So when would you perform mikhuy on others? Any time heavy energy is accumulating: whenever you feel a relationship is out of harmony, during an argument with a spouse or coworkers, at the scene of any kind of accident, when your child is uptight and tense from worrying about an exam—the situations that may benefit from mikhuy are endless. However, you should begin learning to apply this tool by *practicing on people emotionally close to you and with whom you have a positive and nurturing relationship*, perhaps a good friend or a family member. The better you know the person and the more securely and lovingly bonded you are with him or her, the easier it will be to cleanse that person of hucha.

The mikhuy technique is the same as described above, except you open and extend your qosqo to touch the other person's poq'po. Open your qosqo a little at a time, gaining a sense of the other person's bubble slowly and in increments that are comfortable for you. If you are truly touching another person's poq'po, then you will fully empathize with that person, feeling his or her hucha through the guise of the same pain or depression or fear as does that person. Once you have connected to the person's poq'po, command your qosqo to digest the other person's hucha and feel the double flow of energy (the hucha moving down to Pachamama and the sami flowing to your head).

As with most energy work, to perform hucha mikhuy on another person, that person neither has to be in close physical proximity to you, nor does he or she have to know you are performing this cleansing. Undoubtedly, however, he or she will feel the empowerment that results from the cleansing. Let me repeat that: he or she will feel the empowerment that results from the cleansing. Mikhuy is an act of *munay*, of love and empathy. I stress this point because someone once asked me how mikhuy differed from "spiritual vampirism." It should be clear to you by now that mikhuy is an act of selflessness, not selfishness. It never drains another person, only empowers him or her, Pachamama, and the person performing the technique. It is an act of service, of *ayni* (spiritual reciprocity).

After you have perfected your mikhuy technique on people to whom you are emotionally connected, move to people with whom you have fewer emotional attachments, to those who are emotionally neutral for you. This might be someone at your place of work whom you are not in close contact with or a neighbor whom you don't see very often.

Finally, when you feel ready, begin to mikhuy those people who push your buttons. Who do you think is the biggest jerk alive? Which person raises your blood pressure by just walking into the room? Who is your worst enemy? Anyone to whom you feel a strong aversion is someone with whom you have probably generated hucha. You no doubt need to cleanse your own bubble before you attempt to cleanse his or hers. But once you have cleansed yourself, go ahead and cleanse this person's poq'po. Then watch and see how your relationship changes.

Juan tells a story from his own life that illustrates how powerfully mikhuy can change the dynamics of an unhealthy personal relationship. He had a colleague at the university who was openly hostile to him. The man was jealous of Juan and was loathe to even be in the same room with him, never mind talk with him. Juan's feelings toward this man were mutual. Unfortunately, they worked in the same department and were forced to share an office, along with many others. They disliked each other but there was no way they could avoid each other.

After years of slights and cold shoulders, Juan, now that he was on the sacred path, learned the hucha mikhuy technique and decided this colleague was the perfect candidate on which to test this technique. He began by releasing his own hucha, and then he performed mikhuy on this man's poq'po. For eight months or more, Juan patiently practiced mikhuy on this man. Nothing changed—until one day, as the two passed in the hall, the man spontaneously said, "¡Buenas dias!" to Juan, something he had not done in all the years of their working together. The man caught himself, stunned at this greeting that had escaped his lips, and he stopped short in the hallway. Juan strolled past him, tipped his hand, and replied, "¡Buenas dias!" That spontaneous greeting broke the ice, and before long this man began to greet Juan when they arrived to the office in the mornings.

Within weeks he invited Juan to attend a department meeting he was running. When the opportunity arose, Juan reciprocated. Soon the two were on speaking terms, and now, many years later, they are great friends.

EXERCISE 10:

Tasting Other Energies Through Mikhuy

Mikhuy is generally used to digest hucha, which is a distinctly human energy. However, it can be used to "taste" other "flavors" of energy as well. Using your qosqo, you draw in and "digest" the energy of a place or an object using the same technique described above. I don't recommend that you try mikhuying unfamiliar energies, at least not until you have truly mastered hucha mikhuy and feel empowered in every way. I myself have never tried to mikhuy anything other than hucha. However, I relate one last story to illustrate just how powerful a technique mikhuy can be. This story was first told to me by a friend and an impressive paqo in her own right, Elizabeth Jenkins. I asked Juan about it, and he recounted it to me firsthand, and gave me permission to retell it. Juan gave such consent hesitantly, for Peru is a center of UFO activity and has an ardent UFO community, and he has no desire to participate in debate about the UFO phenomenon. However, his experience is unique and not only demonstrates the power of the mikhuy process but raises many provocative questions about the possible nature of at least some UFOs.

Juan had been driving his VW Beetle when he spotted the unusual flying object moving slowly just above the horizon, over the valley surrounding Cuzco. The object was huge, silver, and cigar-shaped—obviously not an airplane or blimp. Fascinated, Juan pulled over to watch it. He stared in excitement and disbelief, visually following the metallic craft as it floated slowly over the valley. The longer he observed the craft, the more Juan was sure that he, an "agnostic" when it comes to the UFO phenomena, was having a real UFO experience. As he tracked the object, he remembered the teaching of don Benito Qoriwaman, who had told him that everything is energy and that he should taste and experience every kind of energy he could. Well, Juan reasoned, a UFO was energy and he wasn't likely to get another chance to taste this energy—so he opened his qosqo and began to mikhuy the UFO. To his surprise, it began to grow smaller and smaller. As he "ate" the UFO, he felt energy accumulating within his body, building to an intense pressure in his skull, until finally he had digested the entire UFO! It had completely disappeared.

Juan described the result of his experiment with disbelief and humor. "I felt as if my mind was blown!" he exclaimed. "I've never taken LSD, but I walked around in a mental haze for four days, as if I had eaten many doses of LSD!" When asked what he thought the UFO actually was, Juan said the only conclusion he could reach is that it was "a blob of free energy," simply another, although unusual, manifestation of the infinitely creative kawsay pacha.

Chapter 11

Language of the Stones: Working with Khuyas

Don Mariano Apasa, and his wife, pampa mesayoq doña Agustina, had just completed an engaging despacho ceremony. The ceremony capped a pleasant day at Hatun Q'ero, the ceremonial village of the Q'ero. We had arrived on horseback, exhausted and dirty, after several hard days' ride through the mountains. This morning we had slept late, washed our bodies and hair in the village courtyard, and then resumed our energy work in a leisurely and pleasurable way. After lunch, my seven companions and Juan Nuñez del Prado had headed off for the stream on the other side of the village from where we were camped. I had stayed behind, for I had badly injured my right knee the day before and was recuperating, the swelling from the torn cartilage having been treated the previous night with a poultice made from a local herb known for its anti-inflammatory properties. Laying on a blanket in the sun, I had amused myself by coaxing Q'ero school children to sing into my tape recorder. They erupted into giggles every time I played their Quechua songs back for them.

While my companions were learning to sense and make energetic interchanges with the water spirits, don Mariano had appeared. He emerged from around a thicket of bushes near the stream, quite unexpectedly, for this was not his home village. Juan had arranged for him to come work with us after dinner, and we had just now finished the despacho ceremony, which don Mariano had dedicated as a blessing for us for the rest of our trip. We were to leave the next morning to continue our journey to Q'ollorit'i, a sacred festival held at the base of the glacial Apu Sinak'ara.

After the despacho, don Mariano, who sat cross-legged in the shadows in a corner of the tent, spoke quietly in Quechua to Juan, who translated don Mariano's request to us. "He asks that those of you who have mesas, pass them forward."

Five of the eight of us had mesas. We dutifully passed them forward, and Juan placed the cloth-wrapped bundles in a semi-circle before don Mariano.

Don Mariano reached out and retrieved one of the bundles. He held it with both hands, brought it to his lips, and lovingly peppered it with kisses. Then he held the bundle a few inches from his lips and began to gently blow into it, almost caressing the mesa with the breath of his blessings and prayers. He was oblivious to us as we sat watching him intently, fascinated with this act of munay, or heart. The only thing that existed for don Mariano was the colorfully wrapped bundle of khuyas. Slowly he brought the mesa to his right ear and cocked his head, his face a study in concentration and receptivity. He was listening to the mesa. As a kuraq, he had the ability to speak to and to listen to a mesa. What were the khuyas telling him? We couldn't know.

One by one, don Mariano repeated his actions with each of the other four mesas. He remained silent until he reached the last mesa. As with the others, he covered it with his kisses and blessed it with his breath. But then, after listening to its message for a moment or two, he declared simply, "This is a mesa of power."

Juan translated don Mariano's statement, and appended his own question. "Whose mesa is this?" It was Eileen's. An environmental scientist from the Boston area, Eileen had been on the sacred path for nearly two years. This, however, was her first trip to Peru. Juan asked her what the mesa contained. She explained that it held mostly khuyas from the American Southwest and from the Yucatan.

Without further word, don Mariano returned the mesa bundles. Then he turned his cinnamon-colored face toward us, and, being a man of few but direct words, counseled us with characteristic bluntness: "You are all paqos on the sacred path. Continue to work hard, and one day you may even become more powerful than me."

Through don Mariano's words and actions, I gained a new respect for mesas and the khuyas they contain. Until now, I had not really understood the mesa as a true repository for power. And I held the work of the khuyas to be one of the more improbable aspects of Andean shamanic work. Later in this trip to Peru, however, I would receive specific training in the khuyas from Américo Yábar, a master of the stones of power. But it was don Mariano, who had approached our mesas as he would have those of accomplished paqos, who had given me the first, and perhaps most important, teaching. Even though Eileen and most of the rest of us were novices, he had sensed that our mesas were accumulating power or had already done so. I knew that it was through our mesas that we, too, could more easily push the kawsay, the energy of the living cosmos. We were beginning to acquire the tools of a shaman.

Stones and rock formations are afforded a special status in Andean mysticism. It's not surprising that the feature that is most ubiquitous in the Peruvian environment—stone— would be an energy the mystics come to know intimately. Over the millennia, stones have counselled Peruvian shamans well, and so stones of power, called *khuyas*, have many uses in a shaman's mesa. Their primary use is as healing tools, as an aid to cleanse hucha from the body. As you have already read in this book, many Q'ero have not been taught the hucha mikhuy technique, and so instead, many of them use khuyas to cleanse hucha from a person. But stones are also repositories of information, and an Andean shaman is always alert to a stone that wants to speak to him or her. Most Andean paqos have mesas that are comprised primarily of these stones. The energy of a sacred site can be carried through a stone the paqo acquires at that site; khuyas are also passed on from teacher to student. If a paqo wants to counsel with that teacher, all he or she has to do is work with the stone that once belonged to that mentor. The exercises below teach you how to identify stones of power, learn from them, and work with them for healing.

RECOGNIZING A KHUYA

Américo Yábar is a recognized master of the khuyas. He can speak for hours, days even, about stones of power. I have been fortunate to work with him in places like the Island of Moon, which is known as the island of the female shamans and is located in Lake Titicaca, where the shore is covered with the most exquisite stones imaginable. The sheer numbers are amazing, but what really overwhelms you is their diversity. It's hard to believe that so many different kinds of stones can be jumbled together on one isolated island in a land-locked lake.

There are almost as many uses for a khuya as there are types of stones. Américo can list the kinds of khuyas and their uses until your head spins: *ch'aska rumis*, star stones with which you work with light energy; a special black stone used to heal heart problems; spiral stones used to charge energies or to extract hucha, and on and on. By listening to the stone and examining it closely, letting your imagination and intuition "read" the stone, you can discover how to use its energy.

"A stone is a field of energetic action," says Américo, "of magical action that you express, that you sustain in the language that the stone is connected to—to the moon, or to Pachamama, or to Mama Qocha [ocean or large lake]. The stone gives you a description of the field of consciousness and a field of magical action—you must follow it, pronouncing it as you experience it. Because it is like poetry. And poetry, we must all remember, is the antecedent of shamanism. They are both a door. And you play, and you play, and suddenly you go in. You go to the other side! And sometimes it's very hard to come back. Because when you do, nothing tastes as good! Because you have accumulated energy, you've become a specialist at lending it. So that's our work!"

All Andean shamans work with khuyas, and they are a tool that requires special attention. Although you can decorate your living space with stones, the ones you use as khuyas should be kept wrapped in cloth. You can then work with an individual stone from the bundle or the entire bundle itself. Very often a healing mesa is not even opened, and the entire bundle is passed over a patient's field. Khuyas also like to be "fed" every once in a while. To feed a khuya, you sprinkle it with pisco, wine, or some other kind of alcohol. Américo, Mr. Flamboyance himself, says khuyas especially like to drink fine cognac! I also usually smudge a new khuya, even one that a teacher has given me. Smudging a stone, with the smoke from sweetgrass, sage, or natural tobacco, cleanses it and makes the stone ready to unfold its new, and unique, relationship with you. But before you can work with khuyas, you have to first acquire them and then establish a relationship with them. You must approach them and consider them as living beings, fully conscious, and then you will be well on your way to becoming, like Américo, a master of the khuyas.

EXERCISE 1: Messages Inscribed in Stone

Not all stones are natural khuyas, but all have the potential to be. Stones with strong energy, with left-side energy that can be used for practical purposes such as healing, usually make themselves known—all you have to do is listen. If you're like most people, you have probably collected pretty or unusual stones as you walked the woods or the beach. Somehow we all feel the pull of stones, even if we have no explanation for our affinity for them. If you have any special stones that you've collected over the years, use them for this exercise. Otherwise, pay attention as you walk out-of-doors (or even indoors; one of my most important khuyas was jumbled in among scores of fist-sized stones decoratively lining a planter in a mall in Arizona!) and listen for a stone that is calling you or drawing your attention. Open your qosqo to receive these kinds of invitations. The call can be as overt as a visceral or energetic pull to your physical body or it can be as subtle as your eye simply being drawn to one particular stone in a pile of many stones. When you have received such an invitation from a stone, then collect it, leaving an ayni offering behind: a pinch of tobacco or sage, a strand of your hair, whatever—it is the intention of thanksgiving that counts.

Once you have received the invitation of a stone, you are ready to begin establishing a dialogue with it, to begin to receive its teachings. Initiate this work by sitting quietly with the stone and holding it cupped in both hands against your body at your qosqo or heart. Establish an energetic link with the stone for a few moments, gaining a sense of its energy. Don't project your energy into the stone; instead, simply open your qosqo, allowing yourself to receive the stone's energy and to perceive its qualities. Once you've established an energetic link with the stone—this might happen in a matter of seconds or of days—then begin to acquaint yourself with it by visually studying it in careful detail, letting your eye find its own way and your imagination play with its shape, size, texture, and coloration. Américo would tell you that once you "enter the subtleties of the stone's existence and its essence" the images you will receive and forms you may superimpose on the stone are not coincidences. It is from these usually visual images that "the messages begin," according to Américo. "Touch the stone," he would urge you, as he did me. "Focus your attention on the lines and take it to you, then you will begin to receive the message of an entirely different energetic body. It is very important to take into account the physical form and the projections of the stone. Understand that in the stone, in its form, are expressed subtle memories of other times that get lost in the night. That's why you see faces, images in the stone, markings, impressions, and so many other things and situations that come to be and are expressed in the dark folds of the stone." At this point in the practice, you should become visually and kinesthetically intimate with the stone. You can even run the stone over your body (does it feel different on the soles of your feet, the palms of your hand, the cheek of your face?) or even taste it (make sure it has been washed!).

Let these images and the form of the stone guide you to its use as a khuya. Some khuyas are used in healing specific maladies—heart problems, blood maladies, depression, anxiety,

214 • KEEPERS OF THE ANCIENT KNOWLEDGE

and so on. Other khuyas have more general applications, such as cleansing hucha or releasing energy blockages. Many reveal mantras or rituals that should be used with them. While only a particular khuya can tell you for what purpose it needs to be used and in what ceremonial way—you will discover these messages in the next exercise—Américo has taught that there are also fundamental, almost universal, physical forms that equate certain khuyas with particular healing practices. Allow the visual and energetic examinations of the stone to guide you to your particular khuya's use, but generally:

- A spiral or circular projection or protrusion indicates both a charging stone and an extracting stone. You can "charge" someone's energy body by using this stone at their temples or at their chakras points to infuse sami. You can extract heavy energy from their energy body and into the khuya at these same points.

- A smooth stone that has concentric layers, especially circular ones, building up over it is a good meditation stone. It can also help ground and center anyone with an excess of disharmonious energy. Simply let them hold it or run it through their field to achieve the desired effect.

- A stone with a natural hole all the way through it is a powerful guardian and teaching stone that may hold many powerful secrets and may reveal many of the mysteries of life. Use it as a dreaming stone as well, allowing a powerful dream or desire to slip through the hole into consciousness or into manifestation in the physical.

- A stone with square or rectangular lines on it is a doorway stone, and it can be used to help you shift awareness and perception to new possibilities or to release resistances and open blockages.

- A stone that has three almost identical markings—three protrusions, three "doorway" lines, three layers to it, is a three-worlds stone. It can be used to harmonize your abilities to work with the energies of the three worlds: the ukhu pacha, kay pacha, and hanaq pacha. It also represents the three "stances" of an Andean mystic—munay, love; llank'ay, physical work and strength of will; and yachay, wisdom grounded in experience—and so can help you harmonize your abilities to these three areas of life.

- A triangular stone can be a three-worlds stone or one that mystically connects you to the Apus. This latter association is especially relevant, of course, if you discovered the khuya in the mountains.

- A stone that has a face in it, whether human-looking or otherwise, can be a teaching stone or a guardian stone, providing very specific instruction or protection. If the khuya is in the shape of an animal, insect, or bird, connect with the energies and symbolic disposition of that creature to acquire those characteristics in your own life or to transmit those qualities to others as you use the khuya on them.

Once you have identified the khuya's purpose(s), let it also tell you how to work with it. Some stones transmit their power by simply being held during meditation; others want to be run through your energy field; still others may want to be held close to the body or kept under a pillow during sleep. A typical method of working with khuyas in healing is explained in exercise 3, below. But first, there's more to learn from your khuyas.

THE KHUYA AS TEACHER

Not all stones have intricate markings or features. Some are plain, polished, and smooth; they are generally nondescript. However, any stone that calls you has a meaning and message for you, and is willing to be put into service as a khuya. After you have visually and tactilely examined a stone, receiving any images from it, it is time to listen to it in a deeper, more profound way. Only the stone can tell you how it can best be used. And in the case of a guardian or teaching stone, only the stone can reveal its message to you. To listen to a khuya, to hear at least one of the stories it has witnessed in its long existence, to discern its use in your shamanic practice, and to discover its teaching in your life, you simply place the stone over your qosqo and meditate, opening your awareness to the stone's.

As a newcomer to the Andean path, you will no doubt find it easiest to approach the khuya meditation from the "left side" of your perceptual body, from the magical side of the mesa. Most khuyas, because they are used for practical purposes such as healing, naturally work with the left side. Américo says, "The important thing is that you approach the stone with your left side open, and that you link your memory with the memory of the stone, and allow the stone itself to tell you its qualities." Having your "left side open" means nothing physical—it does not mean that you hold the stone on your left side or with your left hand or even that you intend to be in your right brain (the left side in Andean terms). It simply means that perceptually and energetically you are intending to interchange energy with the stone for the left-side, magical purposes, which in the Andes, as I have said, is *practical* work, such as healing. These are the easiest messages to discern from a khuya. You could just as easily approach the khuya from the right side if it is a khuya that seems useful for right-side work. For instance, your teacher may give you a khuya, perhaps as part of an initiation, whose primary purpose is to link your mesa to the teacher's and to his or her lineage. That kind of energetic interchange is a mystical connection, one of communication rather than of application, and so is said to be of the right side. Left-side and right-side work can become confusing for beginners on the Andean path, but suffice it to say that a khuya can have one or more specific left-side (practical) uses and also have a right-side (communicative) use. But it is easiest to begin by approaching khuyas from the left side, and that is what you should be doing now.

EXERCISE 2: Stones Speak

Sit with the stone, meditate to quiet your rational mind, and begin to perceive the khuya's energy. Let images, colors, and symbols float through your awareness. Unlike the last exercise, where you sought to interpret a jumble of images, in this exercise don't become attached to any of them. Don't judge or try to interpret them. Just let them drift through your awareness. Soon you will slip into the space of receptivity, and you will touch the khuya's bubble. You will begin to "hear" the khuya's "voice." That voice may be auditory, or it may be visual, like a movie running inside your head (perhaps the disjointed symbols will suddenly become cohesive and coherent); it may even be a kinesthetic voice, with sensations and feelings suffusing your body. When you are in that space beyond your rational thoughts, the stone will tell you its story and/or how to best use it in healing or shamanic work; all you have to do is listen. My and Américo's advice would be to listen not with your head but with your heart. "Khuya," after all, means "affection" in Quechua, and your first bonding with a khuya, your first energetic interchange and revelation, can be as sweet as meeting a beloved.

An alternative, or adjunct, to the above exercise is to sleep with the stone under your pillow or pressed against your qosqo. Ask it to tell you its story, to reveal itself and its qualities, during the dreamtime. Sometimes it is best to "meet" a khuya using both techniques, as we tend to listen differently through our subconscious self, which is "awake" during sleep, than through our conscious self. I have found both techniques equally powerful. I slept with the khuya don Mariano gave me under my pillow for almost a year. Through it, don Mariano counseled me, most often in the form of dreams, and helped me make important decisions at crucial points in my early training along the Andean path. But I first heard a khuya's story by meditating with one held at my qosqo. I was at Sullistani, a sacred site in southern Peru where the great circular burial towers of the shamans reach up like stone dreams into the hanaq pacha. I picked up a stone that called to me, but at the last moment, before I went off to meditate with it, Américo pushed another small, very nondescript stone into my hand and insisted I meditate with it instead. I did, and an incredible scenario unfolded before me. Like a movie projected onto the screen of awareness, I saw a very old shaman perform a drinking ceremony with an elaborately fashioned *kero*, or ceremonial cup, as he prepared himself to die. He was old and tired, and he was asking the spirit world to take him. It was night, and he stripped off his clothes, exposing his sinewy body to the cold and wind. He made his prayers, drank something from the ceramic cup, then smashed it upon the stones and laid down to die between the very two boulders I was now stretched out between in my meditation. But during the freezing night, death rejected him. The next morning, finding himself still in the body, the old man accepted the will of Spirit and he made a long prayer to *Inti*, the sun. He carefully gathered up the pieces of the kero he had smashed the night before, wrapped then tenderly in a cloth, dressed himself, and returned to join the several people, perhaps family members, who had been keeping vigil throughout the night down below the stone towers. With them, he returned back to his village, where he lived in service for another three years. The stone told me of his eventual death, how his family wrapped his body and returned it to Sullistani, and where his body was buried, in a surprising place not far from the stone funerary towers.

I still have the other stone, the one I originally picked up, but I have not yet worked with it, even though I have had it in one of my mesas for more than three years now. I feel the time has not yet come for that stone to speak to me. One has to have patience with the stones. You will know when the right time comes to listen to them, or when they are ready to talk with you.

THE KHUYA AS HEALER

Khuyas, as described earlier, are one of the major healing tools of Andean paqos. They use healing and power stones to cleanse hucha from a patient's body. You too can try this. First, identify a stone that has healing capabilities (see the exercises above). Then prepare the healing stone by infusing it with sami, the refined mystical energy. You should perform this charging cere- mony before any new stone is used for healing, although you can periodically charge a well-used khuya using the same method. (Actually, you can charge any khuya for any purpose using this technique, but it is especially good for healing. If your intended use is not healing, simply substitute the other intention at the appropriate point in the ceremony.)

EXERCISE 3: Healing Stones

To charge the khuya, center yourself, entering a meditative state of awareness, then hold the stone up toward the hanaq pacha, skyward, in your right hand. Your hand is becoming a living "mesa," or altar, allowing you to directly touch the mystical energies and connecting you to the right-side work of communicating directly with the spirit realm. Then "intend" sami into the stone, feeling the flow of refined energy sweeping into the stone. Now move the stone down and into your left hand, which should be at about shoulder height. Your left hand is the left side of the living mesa, the side of the magical energies, where practical, healing work takes place. As you move the stone down into your left hand, "intend" a transfer of healing energy from the right side of the mesa to the left; that is, you are transforming the mystical energies into the magical. Now, with the stone in your left hand, touch it to your heart center and infuse the stone with munay, the power of love grounded in will, through which all healing takes place. The khuya is now ready to be used in an actual healing.

Have your "patient" lie down or stand in front of you. Ask him or her to enter a restful, receptive, and meditative state. Prepare yourself by centering yourself or meditating for a few minutes while holding the healing stone cupped in both hands. You can blow your prayers or intentions through the stone toward the hanaq pacha. Then open your qosqo and tune in to the patient's energy body. (If the problem is psychological or emotional, still scan the patient's energy body, as described below, to see where the stress or dysfunction is being held in the physical body.) Beginning at the patient's head, run the stone slowly over the person, perhaps touching him or her, perhaps not; only you can determine what the "right" technique is by staying in energetic interchange with the khuya through your qosqo. Run the stone down the person's field in slow, sweeping motions, touching the khuya to the floor or ground for a moment at the end of each sweep. By touching the stone to the ground, you feed the hucha it has collected to Pachamama. You can also rinse the stone in a bowl of river or lake water. Continue cleansing the patient's energy body, paying particular attention to any areas you feel are particularly dense or encrusted with hucha. Tell the person to visualize the heaviness leaving his or her body and entering the stone, and ask him or her to visualize refined energy streaming into his or her field through the crown chakra. When you are done, cleanse the healing stone by touching it several times to the ground (indoors, the floor), rinsing it in river or lake water, or by smudging it. Never use the same stone on more than one person without first cleansing it between sessions.

Chapter 12

Manifesting Intentions Through a Despacho

I was nervous. Unsure. Feeling inadequate. I was about to make and offer my first despacho for a group of new-comers to the Andean path. The group of six were my first real students. I had agreed to teach them the rudiments of the Andean path over a long weekend. Having always avoided the role of teacher, I had dreaded this day. But it was inevitable. Nearly five months before I had talked privately with my teacher Juan Núñez del Prado, asking him what the next level of my training should be. His answer surprised me. "I have taught you all I know. Your training is complete—except now, to fulfill your initiation to the fourth level, you must pass on the knowledge. You must now teach it."

I instantly rejected Juan's counsel. First of all, I knew he was being kind, if not outright modest. He had decades of experience on the sacred path, and he had loads more to teach me. Second, I was a writer. I would pass the teachings on through the written word, not the spoken word. But Juan rejected that explanation. "You must teach," he told me again.

The universe, or my Higher Self, soon saw to it that teaching opportunities came my way. Finally I relented, and agreed to teach a small group of six people in Reston, Virginia. The weekend had gone well, and I was closing the training by teaching about despachos. I was about to make and offer an Apu despacho. But I felt unworthy. No false humility here. I truly felt unsure of myself. I had seen despachos made dozens of times in the Andes, and I had assisted my teachers in making them. But I had never made one entirely by myself. I was confident I could explain the meaning of most of the recados, the ritual nature items, as I placed them in the despacho, but I was nervous about making it correctly and of having the energetic intent that would open the Apus to receiving it.

Then, as my husband assisted me in sorting the recados, I remembered a story Juan had once told. He had been working with don Benito Qoriwaman, receiving despacho training. Don Benito had demonstrated the proper selection and placement of the ritual items many times to Juan, and Juan, having traveled the Andes and worked with other paqos, had observed hundreds of despachos being made. When don Benito finally commanded that Juan make and offer his first despacho, Juan felt confident of his ability. He carefully constructed the nature mandala that is a despacho, sure that his technique was impeccable. But he had hardly finished when don Benito brushed the despacho aside, spilling its contents, and declaring it unfit as an offering to the Apus. Juan, stunned, had no idea why he had failed, and don Benito offered no explanation. Time and time again, Juan prepared a despacho, and each time don Benito rejected the offering.

Finally, in anger and spite, Juan began to throw together a despacho. "I'll show him!" he said to himself, impulsively and angrily selecting and placing items in the despacho. Finally, the offering was complete, and Juan folded the paper and tied the bundle closed. He waited for don Benito to once again reject the despacho. Instead, don Benito smiled with satisfaction. "Wonderful," he declared. "Finally! Finally! Instead of trying to make a despacho like I do, you have made one of your own, filled with your own intent, energy, and passion."

Juan instantly understood that, while there is a technique to making a despacho, what is most important in such an offering is the authenticity of the maker and of his or her energy. The only correct way to make a despacho is the way you make it, not the way your teacher does. Juan's lesson became mine, and I proceeded to make a beautiful despacho—and an authentic one.

Don Agustín Pauqar Qapa explained some of the many ways a pampa mesayoq makes and uses despachos; you will remember that there are more than two hundred different kinds. General despachos to Pachamama or the Apus are usually offerings and thanksgivings. They also may be pagos, or payments, used to atone for a mistake or misjudgment. Despachos also have very specific purposes: as healing tools, to attract wealth, to enhance one's love prospects, to foster business success, and so on. We in the West cannot simply go to the marketplace, as an Andean can, and order a love despacho or a prosperity despacho, but we can, nonetheless, use despachos to align ourselves with our intentions.

THE PRINCIPLES OF INTENTION AND EMBODIMENT

In the Andes, "embodiment" plays a significant role in manifesting one's desires. At the sacred annual festival of Q'ollorit'i, where more than fifty thousand pilgrims gather at the base of a glacier more than sixteen-thousand-feet high, there is an area set aside specifically for making dreams come true. In the Andes, the mystical and shamanic work are referred to as *pukllay,* or sacred play, so my traveling companions and I called this area at Q'ollorit'i the "play area." If one wanders into it, one is wandering into the land of dramas and dreams, a place where even though people are lighthearted and laughing, their intentions are decidedly serious. Legend has it that if you enact your heart's desire—be it a new truck, a business, a visa to the United States, a marriage partner, or a baby—you will be granted your wish if you see the Lord of Q'ollorit'i in a vision or a dream, or if your request is made with sufficient ardor to be heard by the spirits of the Apus. The enactments are so serious that vendors sell any accoutrement that might be needed to embody your dream: a land deed, play money, a plastic wedding ring or truck, a miniature house. As you wander the area, you might be pulled into a drama, to act as a "stand-in" for the desired lover, or the real estate agent who will sell that dream house, or the immigration official who will stamp that prized visa. You, too, can engage in sacred play, embodying your dreams and desires using a despacho of intention. In one of the exercises below, you will see how I combined the Andean despacho offering with intention and embodiment techniques to manifest my dreams.

While we in the West have neither the *recados* (ritual items) or the knowledge to make a despacho as an Andean paqo would, we can adapt their use to our own culture without changing the intention of the original ceremony. The instructions and stories below will help you use these beautiful offerings, what my friend Elizabeth Jenkins calls "nature mandalas," in your own life.

EXERCISE 1: Making a General Despacho

You can make a thanksgiving or offering despacho to send your prayers and thanks to the Pachamama or to the Apus (whichever mountains in your area you feel connected with) by adapting the ritual items from an Andean despacho with those that are native to your area. The generic elements of an Andean despacho are listed below, with suggestions for easily obtainable substitutions.

I always begin ceremony by preparing myself with meditation, smudging with sage or sweetgrass, and/or by praying to the six directions (the four cardinal directions, Mother Earth, and Creator). A despacho ceremony is no different. So after you gather all the items you need, stop for a moment to prepare yourself to enter sacred space.

In order to determine which items you will need, you first

have to determine how you will offer the despacho, by burning it or by burying it. The smoke of a burning despacho takes your offering to the Apus; burying a despacho honors Pachamama. However, depending upon your circumstances, it is perfectly legitimate to make a despacho to Pachamama and burn it. The difference is not in how you offer the despacho but in what items are used in its preparation and to which spirit you are directing your attention and intention. Most despachos contain a half shell, like that from a clam or scallop, and a cross at their center. The shell represents the feminine energies and the cross, placed in the "bowl" of the shell, represents the masculine. Generally there are two important distinctions between an offering to the Apus or to Pachamama, as outlined below. Note that although each of the two types focuses on the masculine or the feminine energies, you should place items of both energies in every despacho to harmonize the energies:

- Apus: An offering to the Apus contains white flowers and twelve k'intus. It usually does not contain very much food. Choose ritual items that represent masculine energy or the hanaq pacha (sky).
- Pachamama: An offering to Pachamama contains red flowers and eight k'intus. It contains lots of sweet foods, like sugar, cookies, and candies. Choose rituals items that represent the feminine energies and the kay pacha (earth).

The description that follows for making a despacho is one of many, many possible formulas, and it is a Westernized adaptation of an Andean despacho. Let your intuition guide you in this ceremony. Here I present the fundamentals of the procedure, but you can be as creative as your heart leads you to be.

A despacho always starts with a rectangular piece of white

paper. Next, place a shell at the paper's center with the "bowl" of the shell facing up and the widest part facing away from you (always use a half shell). The shell represents the feminine and the cosmic circle or wholeness. Always offer an item to the despacho with focused intention, with mindfulness. Next offer the cross, which represents the masculine energies and the four sacred directions. It is placed in the bowl of the shell. The k'intus are the next crucial component. Because you will not have access to sacred coca leaves, you can substitute any ceremonial plant leaf, especially fresh bay leaves, laurel leaves, or olive leaves. With your fingers, form a k'intu of three leaves, stacking one leaf atop another and making sure the leaves are as healthy and perfect as possible. The veins of the leaves, each leaf's underside, should be facing down. Hold the k'intu up and pray over it, blowing your prayer through the k'intu in a soft breath. Make as many k'intus as you need for your intention. As stated above, usually twelve k'intus are offered to the Apus, because there are twelve sacred Apus in the Andean area and because twelve is the sacred number of Peru, representing the twelve royal panacas, or lineages of the Inkas, among other things. Offer eight to Pachamama. As an adaptation, you could offer four k'intus if you want to honor the sacred cardinal directions, or six for the six directions. Place the k'intus around the shell, or around the center of the white paper in a clockwise direction, one at a time as you make them.

Next, you will offer the flowers, or, if you prefer, you can wait and lay them on top of the finished despacho just before it is closed. There is no specific number of flowers required; a few will do. Offer red flowers to Pachamama and white flowers to the Apus. If red or white flowers are not available, any color will do, especially pink or purple flowers for Pachamama and yellow flowers for the Apus. You can offer the entire flower, sans stem, or pull the petals from the flower and arrange them in beautiful circular patterns around the center of the despacho.

When the shell, cross, k'intus, and flowers have been offered, you can begin to lay in the other objects, being very mindful of which item you are selecting, why you are selecting it, and praying over it before you place it in the despacho. Some items that find their way into most despachos are

- White cotton to represent the clouds.
- Colored threads or yarn to represent the rainbow.
- Tiny squares of silver and gold foil or shiny paper. Silver = feminine energy and the left side of the sacred path; gold = masculine energy and the right side of the sacred path. Usually both colored squares are placed in a despacho.
- Tiny metal or paper figures representing people, animals, keys, houses, and so on. They are selected according to the reason for the offering or thanksgiving. Since these aren't readily available outside of Peru, you can omit them, or you could cut small figures or symbols out of magazines or draw what you need.
- Sacred plant items, such as seeds, grains, grasses, herbs, and so on. You can consult books of herb and plant lore to find the symbolic meanings of many plants and seeds. Sage, sweetgrass, and natural tobacco are also appropriate offerings.
- Food items to feed the spirits, especially rice or crackers for the Apus and brightly colored candies and sweets of any kind for Pachamama, although add a little bit of both sweet and more substantial foods to either kind of despacho.
- Alcohol of some kind. Sprinkle over the despacho periodically. Red wine is especially good but you could sprinkle water as well.

- Small stones or stone fragments, especially crystals or minerals, and a magnetic rock if you can (or a piece of rock that is iron-based). Meteorites are very powerful offerings.
- Fragments of natural items, such as starfish arms, animal fat, a bit of fur or animal hair, a claw. Consult an animal lore book to discover the symbolic meanings of various animals, and do not hurt or harm any living thing in an attempt to secure matter for an offering.

Place anything else you want into the despacho, always being tender with the item being offered and taking care to intuit how and where it should be placed. Despachos are always works of art. Take your time, and work through your energy body rather than your rational mind.

When you have completed making the despacho, it is time to close it—to "close the door" or "close the mouth" as some paqos would term it. There is more than one specific method to folding a despacho. Some paqos fold the sides in first, usually the left side first, followed by the right. (Note: You are actually working with the pointed tips of the paper's corners.) Then fold the bottom of the paper up over the center of the despacho, forming the "mouth," and finally fold the top of the despacho down to "close the mouth." Another common method is to fold the despacho closed as you would a mesa cloth. First fold the bottom up, then the sides in, then the top down. Then tie the despacho closed with string or yarn: white for an Apu despacho, red for a Pachamama despacho, although like everything else I have said, you can also use whatever color yarn you desire if it has specific meaning for you. A common string combination is yellow and white (or silver), the colors representing the masculine and the feminine.

If you are working in ceremony with other people, the person who made the despacho can now take the despacho bundle, cover it with cloth, making a mesa bundle, and run it over the bodies (connecting through their poq'pos) of all the participants, blessing them with the power of the despacho and asking them to release their hucha into it before it is offered. If the despacho-maker has a mesa, the offering should be kept wrapped in with the mesa until it is offered. When it is time to make the offering, the despacho-maker then takes the despacho to the fire or to the place where it will be buried, and offers it.

MAKING YOUR DREAMS COME TRUE

Embodying your desires is a powerful way to focus your intentions and to engage kawsay. I have taken the Peruvian penchant for embodiment and the power of the despacho ceremony and combined them. I've only done this once, but that experience was powerful enough for me to pass this method on to many other people. Let me recap a very complicated set of circumstances that led up to my embodiment despacho.

My husband and I moved back to my home state of Massachusetts in 1988 and bought a condo at the pinnacle of a tremendously inflated real estate market. Unfortunately, the market soon fell and we, and thousands of others, were left with property whose value had fallen below the balance of our mortgage. A few years later, when we decided we wanted to move, we were left with next to no options. Several attempts to sell the condo failed, and real estate agents weren't even interested in listing the property. About the same time, we decided we wanted to go to Peru to hike the Inca Trail. We were in training as paqos and we wanted to enter Machu Picchu our first time in the same way the shamans of old did, after walking in our Medicine Bodies and dying to our old selves along the Inca

Trail. The trip was expensive because we had to gear up almost from scratch. We needed everything from hiking boots to a four-season tent. I put that desire in the sacred pipe, a Native American practice, during a New Year's eve ceremony, but I still didn't see how it would be financially possible. There were several other desires high on our list at that time, but selling our property and going to Peru were the two most important ones. So we decided to prepare an embodiment despacho. This is a powerful tool, and we did not undertake it lightly, but this seemed the appropriate time to ask the cosmos to push a little extra kawsay our way. Basically, we wanted to manifest a "miracle" or two!

On a raw March afternoon, we opened sacred space, placed the white paper upon the carpet in our living room, and began to carefully and mindfully construct our offering. We decided we wanted to "gestate" our dreams in the womb of the Mother, so we prayerfully prepared a Pachamama despacho that we would bury. We didn't have a shell, so we started with the k'intus. We offered eight k'intus of fresh bay leaves. In went the red flowers, the sweets, and so on. Then we began adding our personal embodiment recados. First we put in a picture of Machu Picchu and asked to be able to afford to go during the coming year and to have the physical and spiritual stamina to walk the Royal Road to this sacred citadel as paqos. Next we concentrated on the desire to sell our condo. We began by putting an extra key to our front door into the despacho. For good measure I had cut our address out of the phone book, and I placed this scrap of paper in the despacho as well. We asked the universe to provide us the key to a new home at a new address, wherever it was "meant" for us to be. Then we put in a dollar bill, asking for the financial means to fulfill our desires. I put in an old wristwatch, and we asked to be taken off our time and to be put in sync with the universe's time. My husband offered prayers for a new job and then added his business card to the despacho. We put in several items more and then closed the despacho.

Even though it was a frigid March day, we bundled up and drove to a nearby state conservation land area, where we hiked in with our qosqos open, letting our energy bodies lead us to the proper place to bury our offering. I had a small garden trowel with me so we could bury the despacho. We walked for a long time, not paying attention to trails. We often found ourselves turning into the sun, weak though it was. At one point we walked through a burned-out area, noting the metaphorical significance of the previous year's new growth that was just becoming visible. Finally, my husband pointed to a rocky ledge—actually he pointed down over it—saying this is where we had to bury the despacho. I was hesitant about climbing down this steep and slippery grade, snow patches still dotting the rock. But my qosqo told me he was correct, this was the place, and so we carefully climbed down. When we reached the ground on the other side, we soon discovered that the trowel would do us no good. The ground was frozen solid. Still, we called in the six directions and meditated for a minute, preparing ourselves to somehow make the offering. Then we started prying at the rocks that were laying around, hoping that one or two would lift free and we could at least cover the despacho. But the rocks were frozen solid and wouldn't budge—except one. One rock lying next to a pile of rocks moved, and to our delight it revealed a little "cave" in the rock mound. My husband pushed the despacho bundle into it—it just fit. It was as if this space were made for our offering. So we made the offering and then, as we closed sacred space and hiked from the area, we detached from the form of the outcome. To detach means that while you hold the "space" for your intentions, you don't fixate or ruminate about the actual manifestation of your desires. You let the universe perform its magic, letting Pachamama gestate your intentions and birth your desires into manifestation. The *form* that manifestation takes may be quite different from any you envision; you must trust in the infinite wisdom of the universal energies (and your Higher Self) to know best what you need for your personal growth.

By early May, through a series of coincidences that are too long to explain here, the opportunity for us to go to Peru to walk the Inca Trail in a spiritual way had presented itself. We scraped together the money to outfit ourselves and we began to train for the high-altitude trek. I received an unexpected and lucrative free-lance writing assignment, so we were able to amass all but $2,000 of the money we needed to go to Peru.

But there still had been no movement on the sale of our property. We did not have the condo on the market, so we knew we were giving Spirit a huge task in finding a buyer for it. We shouldn't have doubted. One evening in early June, just after dinner, the telephone rang. My husband answered. It was a real estate agent "cold calling" people in our condo building with units of our description, inquiring if they were interested in selling. He had a client, a recent widow, who wanted a particular type of condo unit in our building, which was nearly brand new and was handy to public transit. She had cash, so no banks would be involved. The only catch was we had to be out in three weeks, so she could move in immediately after closing the sale of her house. No problem, we said, come on over. She came over, she loved it, she offered us a price no real estate agent said we could get considering the market. We signed the purchase and sale agreement on July 4, Independence Day, and before long the sale was complete. After we paid off our mortgage, we had exactly $2,300 left, just what we needed for our trip. We flew to Peru in August and took our first step on the Inca Trail at Chillca. At the end of the trek I met don Mariano, who predicted that one day I would write this book.

Every single desire we embodied in that despacho manifested within about a year.

EXERCISE 2: Making an Embodiment Despacho

The general techniques for making your own embodiment despacho are contained in Exercise 1 and in the story above. Because each person's desires and dreams are uniquely personal, I hesitate to outline a single method for constructing an embodiment despacho. You simply need to open your qosqo and make an *authentic* despacho. Begin by following the general format for any despacho (white paper, perhaps a shell and cross, flowers, and so on). Then embody your intentions and desires in any way that resonates for you. However, the two steps I insist you not skip are to first carefully sort out your desires before making the despacho and to detach from the form of the outcome after you offer it. The universe works in mysterious ways, so they say. But you have to be prepared for the outcome the universe determines. What I didn't tell you in the story above is how we found our new home, which turned out to be an apartment. It was spacious and situated on beautiful grounds, once an apple orchard. But we didn't especially like it because it was part of a huge complex. However, we had had only three days to find a place in this particular area because out of the blue my husband got a new job, his dream job. Professionally, socially, and spiritually our new location was a boon, but an apartment in a huge complex is not exactly what we had in mind when we asked for a new home. And on the way to getting there—to this new job and residence—we looked our dream land in the eye and had to walk away. Walking away from an opportunity to buy a beautiful spread of land with a community of spiritually minded people in Arizona was the hardest thing we ever did, but our poq'pos said, "No!" loud and clear, and we had to listen. Actually, it was only a few days after we paid attention to our poq'pos and withdrew from the land purchase that the real estate agent called and we sold our condo.

So as you prepare your own unique embodiment despacho, be prepared to be detached from the form of the outcome. Pushing the kawsay, living in mystical union with the cosmos, means living with conscious fluidity. You have to always acknowledge that the universe may have plans for you that currently aren't even a glimmer in your eye. . . .

And so you're now ready to prepare your despacho of intention. As you consider which desires and dreams you wish to manifest, I will leave you, and close this book, with the words of Américo Yábar. He gave me this message in Lima, in 1995. I had just spent an amazing month in Peru, two weeks working with Juan Núñez del Prado journeying to the Q'ero villages and Q'ollorit'i, and two weeks on an incredibly wild and profound adventure all over Peru and into Bolivia with Américo and four women friends. One day, near the end of our trip, Américo abruptly took my tape recorder out of my hands and left the room where we had all been sitting talking. He came back fifteen minutes later, returned my recorder, and said only that he had recorded a personal message for me. I would like to share this message with you now, for it not only offers good advice for anyone about to perform ceremony to embody a desire, but it expresses the attitude of Andean paqos in a way only Américo can. He speaks from the heart, as do the Q'ero and Juan and all the others who have reached out through these pages to you. Read and reread these words, and remember them, for they reveal the stance of the shaman and the heart of the Andean mystic:

"To the stars of the morning, only give love. Love opens your consciousness. It gives you jewels that touch the heart. Fear paralyzes you, makes you unable to act. The more paralyzed you are, the more fear you have. It's a vicious cycle.

"The fragrance of the flowers is abstract and is connected with love. Love gives you wings. It turns you into an eagle. It allows you to see from high above, and at the same time it makes your body humble. It helps you relax in life. It gives you courage to experiment in life in all its different dimensions.

"Love is a *k'uychi*. It's like a *k'uychi*—a rainbow in which are clearly visible all the different colors of feeling, which transport your heart to the hanaq pacha. A rainbow contains all the colors of life.

"Think of liberty. Think of the infinite. Don't think of small things, of trivialities. Trivialities are very small, they're very silent—so silent that they are like cockroaches scurrying around. Fear always makes you think small, but love never thinks small. Love is able to sacrifice everything. Just think of the impeccability of the eagle flying into the wind, into the unknown, into the mystery.

"And also have humor—that laughter under the stars, that laughter by the sea. Grasp the grandest emotions of life. This is the sense of humor that ought to be man's future religion. Don't allow miserable opinions to sway your vision of the world and of life.

"Be happy. Be happy. Be happy.

"Believe in love, in life, in God."

Appendix I

The Q'ero as Shamans and Mystics

In this book, I call the Q'ero and their cosmology both mystical and shamanic, which may be confusing to those readers who are familiar with the academic distinctions between the two concepts. Generally, a shaman is one who enters an altered state of consciousness to "travel" the multidimensional universe and to retrieve information for prediction, healing, insight, and so on. A shaman may use ritual, dance, drumming, psychotropic substances, and other techniques to induce the altered state. He/she may travel outside his/her physical body to other realms of existence, where he/she may meet totem animals or spirit guides in order to receive guidance and information. Usually, the shaman undertakes the spirit journey or performs a specific ritual for a well-defined purpose, striving for a particular outcome.

A mystic, on the other hand, generally is one who has a solitary and profoundly personal transcendent experience of merging with the natural world and the larger ground of Being, realizing the oneness of All. In that contemplative moment, the ego is overcome, the boundary between self and other dissolves, and one experiences unity consciousness. The mystic, therefore, usually is not associated with magical practices and ritual (other than, perhaps, inward-reaching disciplines such as meditation and yoga), nor is he/she necessarily seeking guidance, teaching, healing, and the like as a direct result of the transcendent experience, although such outcomes are often associated with an experience of mystical union.

The Q'ero, and other metaphysicians of the south-central Andes, technically could be called shamans, for they undergo rigorous training and initiations into the metaphysical work, often perform ritual for an intended purpose, and sometimes commune with nature spirits with the intent of receiving a teaching, guidance, or other information not otherwise available to them. However, the Q'ero practice *fundamentally* is much more mystical than it is shamanistic. The Q'ero do not purposely enter altered states of conscious with the express intent of journeying or retrieving information. They do not employ the shamanic techniques of drumming or ecstatic dancing; they do not use psychotropics to induce altered states, as, for example, do the shamans of Amazonian Peru. Instead, the mystics of the south-central Andes develop their *energy body.* They learn to interchange energy with the *kawsay pacha*, the cosmos of living energy. Their "goal," if we may use that term, is to always be in *ayni*, or reciprocity, with all the other energies of the kawsay pacha. Therefore, they seek mystical union more than they do shamanistic control of the multidimensional world of energy. From that mystical union, they, like the lamas and gurus of the East, often develop suprahuman abilities—but the development and use of these abilities is not the *intent* of their practice.

We can best understand the Q'ero, and the Andean tradition in general, within these anthropological definitions by acknowledging how these metaphysicians blend shamanic practices with a mystical worldview. This is most clearly expressed in their concept of harmonizing the left and right sides of the mesa, as discussed in various places in this book. Briefly, *paña*, the right side of the sacred path, is the mystical aspect of the work—

direct, personal communion with nature and the energies of the cosmos. It is, ultimately, a transcendent work. *Lloq'e*, the left side of the sacred path, is the work of the magical, the practical techniques and rituals that are undertaken for specific purposes and for seeking specific outcomes, such as divination, healing, rainmaking, and so on. As such, the Q'ero metaphysical cosmology, and the larger Andean sacred tradition, is at once mystical *and* shamanic, and I use both terms liberally, and nearly interchangeably, with reference to the Q'ero.

Appendix II

Lost Knowledge: The Q'ero and Andean Prophecy

In order to understand certain portions of the Q'ero interviews and the logic of certain of our questions concerning the prophecy, a little background information is necessary. As was explained in more detail in Part II, the Q'ero and most other indigenous peoples of Peru have over the past several hundred years incorporated beliefs and traditions from their Spanish occupiers and the Catholic Church. The Catholicism of the Q'ero, however, is not the doctrine one finds in the modern, mainstream Church. It is, instead, a unique blend of Peruvian indigenous cosmology with sixteenth-century Catholic dogma and certain heretical teachings. One such borrowing is the Joaquinist formulation of a tripartite history: that the historical epochs can be defined according to certain spiritual criteria as the Age of the Father, the Age of the Son, and the Age of the Holy Spirit. Theologian and cleric Joaquin de Fiore's three epochs are based on a complex, apocalyptic, and ecclesiastical scholarship of the twelfth century that I will not reproduce here and that has not, to my knowledge, survived in any meaningful way in the Andes today. However, Andeans use distinctly Joaquinist terminology to describe three ages of history—the *Dios Yaya Pacha*, the Age of the Father; the *Dios Churi Pacha*, the Age of the Son; and the *Dios Espíritu Santo Pacha*, the Age of the Holy Spirit—and, as Juan Núñez del Prado has discovered, they equate these ages with distinct stages of the prophecy. Generally, the Age of the Father began with the founding of the *Tawantinsuyu*, the Inka Empire, and ended with the deaths of the rival Inkas, Atawallpa and Waskar. The Age of the Son began with the Conquest and ended sometime between August 1, 1990, and August 1, 1993, when the world underwent a cosmic transmutation, a reordering called a *pachakuti*. This cosmic reordering ushered in the Age of the Holy Spirit, which is the age in which we currently live and is the *Taripay Pacha*, a period extending approximately from 1993 to 2012 during which humankind has the potential to evolve spiritually and to manifest a kind of heaven on Earth.

When I queried the Q'ero about Andean prophecy, I began by asking them what they knew about the three ages. Don Mariano was the spokesperson for the group, which discussed my question for several minutes. "The time of God the Father was the beginning; the second time is the time of God the Son, when the world was destroyed by a great flood. Now we are in the time of the Holy Spirit."

"Someone told us," Juan Núñez del Prado said, "that the time of the Holy Spirit is the same as the *Taripay Pacha*. Is that so?"

Juan had purposely asked this question indirectly, as if it were second-hand knowledge to us. He did so because the Q'ero, eager to answer our questions, sometimes speculated in an effort to please us. If they thought we knew something that they did not, they would often struggle to find answers for us. However, if the knowledge seemed to be hearsay, then we were assured of receiving their honest and frank opinions.

After a few minutes of discussion, Juan Pauqar Flores spoke, using a metaphor for time that involved the hours of the day rather the years of an epoch. "My father said that the time of the

Taripay Pacha is the time of day when time will end. After the Day of Judgment comes the Taripay Pacha, when the living and the dead will be together. When this time ends [our present time], we will live with the dead." Then he added, clarifying his answer, "The whole world is now in the time of the Holy Spirit, not just us Q'ero."

As soon as don Juan finished speaking, and while Ricardo and Anamaria were still translating, the Q'ero whispered furiously among themselves. Ricardo and Juan listened and brought us up to speed on the controversy. "They are confused," Juan explained. "They are saying 'perhaps, perhaps,' because they do not know anything for sure. They are just speculating." Finally, don Mariano's voice rose over the others. "Don Mariano says to the others," Ricardo translated, " 'If you know something about this, talk about it.' " But none of the Q'ero volunteered any additional information.

We discussed the situation among ourselves, about how we could best put unambiguous questions to the Q'ero. The double translation process and the peculiarities of the Quechua language were causing confusion and difficulty. In addition, the Q'ero have very pragmatic modes of thinking, and overly broad or abstract questions often confounded them. Sandy suggested that we ask if there would be signs or omens that indicate the Taripay Pacha was imminent, speculating that this kind of question would elicit a concrete response that would reveal parts of the prophecy. Juan reworded the question, and Ricardo asked it. "If the dead people are going to join us when this time ends, then is this time near at hand?"

Juan Pauqar Flores responded for the group. "We do not know. We will only know this when the time arrives."

At this point I thought it best to make things really concrete. I explained the tack I wanted to take with further questioning.

Juan had written an academic article, in Spanish, that gave an overview of the Andean prophecy and described various personages and places involved in the unfolding of the prophecy: terms like *Inka Mallku*, a supreme healer, twelve of whom are prophesied; or the *Sapa Inka* and *Qoya*, enlightened political leaders who would govern the restored Tawantinsuyu during the Taripay Pacha. I suggested asking the Q'ero about these specific terms, because they were inextricably linked with the prophecy. If the Q'ero recognized the terms then it was likely they knew more about the prophecy than they were telling us. Their answers would perhaps more clearly reveal whether they simply did not know about the prophecy or whether they were simply reluctant to discuss it with us. Juan agreed that they would have to know such precise information if they carried the prophecy, but he thought that it was already obvious that they simply did not know about it. Further questions, he implied, would be fruitless. But he translated my question to Ricardo, who put it to the Q'ero. "We have heard that one sign of the time of the Taripay Pacha is the coming of great healers called Inka Mallkus. Have you heard of such a thing?"

The Q'ero response proved Juan correct—they did not know about the Inka Mallkus as they relate to the prophecy. Still, their answer provided some interesting, and amusing, cultural information. Don Agustín explained that an Inka Mallku "is when we are having a fiesta and we visit in groups. When a person goes visiting from one group to the other group, we call to that person, 'How are you, Inka Mallku?' or 'What are you drinking, Inka Mallku?' Or we ask 'Are you having a fine time, Inka Mallku?'"

When our chuckling subsided, Juan explained that don Agustín was describing the custom of *chanq'a*, when during a festival one person makes a ritual visit from one group of partyers to another. The person who comes to visit your group is called an Inka Mallku, "mallku" literally meaning "ancestor" or "relative."

I was beginning to agree with Juan that this group of paqos did not carry the prophecy. I was surprised by this, especially that don Mariano, who had worked with both don Andreas Espinosa and don Manuel Q'espi, both of whom knew at least parts of the prophecy, did not seem to have much information for us. But I was not yet willing to give up. I suggested one more avenue of investigation—the coca leaves. Reading the coca leaves is the primary method of divination in the Andes. Perhaps we could elicit a response about the prophecy by asking if the coca leaves could reveal anything about the times to come.

Juan seemed unsure of what I was getting at. He asked me to be specific. Was I asking about a personal future or about the Taripay Pacha?

"The collective future," I explained. "Let's just throw a general question at them about using the coca leaves for predicting the future of the world. Who knows—maybe they'll laugh at me, but maybe they won't."

Juan discussed my question with Ricardo. He reported back to me that there was some difficulty with accurately phrasing a question about the "world's future" in Quechua. It was not as simple a task as it seemed in English. Ricardo and Juan spent several minutes in discussion with the Q'ero before translating for us.

Finally Juan turned to me and explained. "They are discussing several terms that involve time. It is very interesting. They say that *qhepa pacha* is both future time or future world. *Qhepa* means behind, and for the Q'ero the future time is unknown, like anything that is outside of our line of sight or physically behind us. They explained that ñawpaq pacha is the past, or literally the time before us. For them the past is known, so it is said to be before or in front of us. Then there is the kunan pacha, which is the present time. Now I will ask them if they can know about the qhepa pacha from reading the coca."

The group reached almost immediate consensus. "No," don Mariano replied on the group's behalf, "we cannot. That is not possible."

At that response Sandy, Anamaria, and I looked at one another in disbelief. We had each in the past witnessed don Mariano either reading the coca for an individual and making predictions, or reading a person's energy body during ceremony or the bestowal of a gift and then making predictions. For example, don Mariano had read Sandy's coca leaves in 1994 and foreseen her work with a partner in a shamanic healing practice. Although Sandy had a thriving private healing practice where she combined conventional psychotherapy with body work, such a joint venture was something she had not even considered at that time. But within a year she was, through a series of synchronistic events, indeed in a shamanic healing practice with another woman.

In the introduction to this book, I described the despacho ceremony at Mollomarqa after which five students of the Andean path were called forward and given a khuya from don Mariano's mesa. Sandy and I had been part of the five, and I believe that don Mariano's prediction about my "bringing the word of the Q'ero to the world," words which I had no understanding of then, has come true with this book. My husband had also been called forward. Don Mariano had looked in my husband's eyes and told him he was on a new spiritual path and would soon be on a new job path. My husband did indeed want to change jobs (see chapter 12, where he embodied this desire in a despacho of intention). He very much wanted to move from the Beacon Hill law firm where he managed a huge computer network to a job where he could more openly live his spiritual beliefs and not have to divorce them from his everyday life. Still, he was not actively looking for new work. Occasionally I would clip advertisements from the employment section of the newspaper, but he always found a reason not to send a résumé. One day, about four months after don Mariano's prediction, I clipped a tiny job advertisement for a computer network administrator and, at my urging and with great reluctance, John finally submitted his résumé. The company name was not one we recognized, but it was clear it was a company involved in the alternative health field, which seemed a step in the right direction from the law firm. Within a month John had a new job, working for Dr. Deepak Chopra's organization![1]

Although a skeptic might say that don Mariano simply planted the seeds of ideas that we later nurtured into reality, I believe that don Mariano can read the future in the coca, and I was mystified as to why he was now denying his ability. After all, coca divination is a common practice throughout Peru, and these Q'ero paqos had already related to us the important role coca divination played in their own initiations and mystical activities. I asked Juan to specifically ask don Mariano about his ability to read the coca leaves. Sandy and I explained our experiences to Juan, and Juan recapped them for don Mariano, choosing Sandy's coca leaf reading as the example.

Don Mariano listened intently to Juan's long explanation, and then he replied, "You are right. I did read her coca leaves. But even with that, one cannot see the qhepa pacha."

After some discussion, Juan and Ricardo agreed that a semantic misunderstanding was coloring this entire discussion. "It is only my opinion," Juan explained, "but I think we are talking about two different levels of future." Then he explained his belief that don Mariano and the other Q'ero were trying to make a distinction between an individual's personal future and the collective future. The collective destiny is beyond the scope of the coca, he explained. The individual destiny is not.

Unfortunately, we were interrupted by the hotel owner at this point. Lunch was long overdue and he could no longer hold it. More unfortunate still, we never found the time to resume this line of questioning.

Appendix III

In the Hand of
the Hacendado

The world of the Q'ero cannot be known without first understanding the effects of Spanish colonialism upon them and the syncretization of Catholicism, however heretical, into their ancient cosmology. The Pauqar brothers, both pampa mesayoqs, had come down from Q'ero for just that purpose. Juan Pauqar Flores, the oldest of the group, remembered well the time of his youth when the "hand of the *hacendado*" ruled, for he was ruled by it. Although all the Q'ero were present for this interview, don Juan Pauqar Flores related most of the Q'ero history that follows.

Don Juan leaned forward, his eyes narrowed to slits over his hawkish nose in an otherwise elfin face and the open palm of his right hand gesturing outward to punctuate his words. "It was very difficult during the time of the hacienda period because the *hacendado*, the owner of the hacienda [Luis Angel Yábar], was very violent and brutal. He would beat us. Now is a time of tranquility and quiet, but that was a time of beatings and insults. We were obligated to work for the hacendado, until Juan's father, Oscar [Núñez del Prado], came and liberated us from that slavery. When we opened our eyes [from our birth] we were under that system, but then Oscar came to us and told us that we can get out from under this system, that we can start the land reform here in Q'ero. We will be free from this slavery. He said that to us."

Don Mariano Apasa Marchaqa leaned toward the tape recorder from where he was sitting at the end of the couch, at the end of the line of four Q'ero paqos. He talked in his usual husky but quiet voice. "I remember when I was a child and I saw Oscar arriving to Q'ero with a group of people. When he talked about liberating us, I thought to myself, 'This must be the will of God, because we did not call him to us; he came here on his own.'"

Juan Pauqar Flores took over responsibility for the narrative. "The time of the hacienda was very difficult and at times the hacendado was crazy. One time he intentionally cut down a tree that fell and killed a man! The hacendado was an ugly person. Once he ordered me to go to the pasture to milk the cows and to make cheese. But he rejected the cheese; he broke the cheese over my head and smeared it all over my body! Then he demanded another cheese. I had to replace the rejected cheese, had to bring it from my own home, which meant that my family had none. He did the same with a sheep that died. He took the body, the flesh of the sheep, and beat me with it. Then he told me I had to replace that sheep with one of my own.

"I remember a time when I was working and the hacendado closed me into a room to beat me. He hit me with his fists on both of my cheeks, on my head, and both of my knees. Then he took a stick and hit me with that! The owner became tired from beating me, and just then his wife walked in and she stopped him. But this was the custom. We could not do anything about it. We were always beaten. The owner had affection for only a few men, and these he did not hit. But all the others, he beat them!

"I will tell you another story," don Juan said, his baritone voice erupting from his diminutive body. "This thing happened in a place called Paucartica, where we were working for the hacendado. The ancient tradition was that we Q'ero wear long hair. So we wore our hair long, in a ponytail, as did the ancient Inkas. But one day the hacendado cut off everyone's hair! He did this only to humiliate us! He made us weave our cut hair into ropes, and then he threw the ropes into the garbage!" Don Juan sat back, his hands clasped in his lap, letting his words settle into silence around us.

Juan Núñez del Prado leaned over to me and whispered, "This incident is so important to him that he even remembers the place where it happened!" Then Juan explained that the insult was a grave one, because their long hair was an unmistakable distinction between the Q'ero and the Spaniards, their conquerors. To lose their hair was to lose the last badge of their former independence and the link to their royal Inka lineage.[1]

Juan Pauqar Flores resumed his story. "The violence was not only from the hacendado. The organizer of the work [the overseer] was cruel as well. He was used by the hacendado to carry out violence. But there is one good thing to say about the hacendado. He never abused the women [sexual abuse]. This was only one hacendado. The others were different."

Here Agustín Pauqar Qapa gently indicated that perhaps don Juan was not entirely correct. The Q'ero hesitate to publicly disagree with or correct one another. But don Agustín, in his characteristic soft-spoken manner, said, "I remember hearing stories that there were sexual abuses. I heard that the owner would sometimes arrive at the hacienda, bringing with him bread, fruit, and liquor. Then he would take a woman to a room. He chose the most beautiful woman and forced her to have sexual relations with him. If she resisted, he would banish her and her whole family from the hacienda. Because of this abuse, there were a lot of men of Q'ero who took their families and ran from the hacienda. They ran away and were spread out over the area."

Don Juan spoke of another reason why families fled. "Another thing that happened with frequency, that caused men to leave the hacienda, was that during the time of the potato harvest the hacendado took all the potatoes for himself. Then he sent another man to our villages at Q'ero and he took all the potatoes we picked from our fields! We did not have any potatoes, so we could not live. We suffered much. This kind of thing caused many men to run away."

When I asked what happened to the runaways, Juan Núñez del Prado explained that the hacendado would hunt them down and bring them back, often to very harsh punishment. There really was no place for them to run to, he explained, as the various hacendados controlled almost all the villages in the area. There was no place to go, and few free communities where one could openly live and support a family.

When asked about the obligations of the Q'ero to the hacendado, don Mariano explained that the Q'ero had to work at the hacienda on behalf of the hacendado and also in their own villages in Q'ero, in their own fields. It was very difficult, because the main hacienda was located at Paucartica, which is in the Sacred Valley surrounding Cuzco. But the villages of Q'ero are mostly in the mountains. So the Q'ero had to come to Paucartica to work, a walk of nearly four days. Obviously, they could not often get back to see their families or to work their own fields or tend their few alpacas or llamas. In addition, the hacendado would often hire the Q'ero out, in effect rent them, to other hacendados, to work on their lands. Most of the time the Q'ero were required to provide their own food while they were on the hacienda, as the hacendados were not obligated to either pay or feed their workers.

Don Juan spoke emphatically: "The hacendado kept the money. We were his slaves, his property." But the hacendado was not only a ruthless proprietor, he was an unreasonable one, too. "Once I was ordered to work in the corn fields and to herd the goats," don Juan said. "But we do not have goats in Q'ero, so I did not know how to herd them. When I did not herd them well, the owner beat me. Another type of abuse that happened to me was when I was chosen to be a *pongo*."

Juan Núñez del Prado explained the term. "A pongo is a system within the hacienda where a man must perform special obligatory service for a specified period of time with no pay. He must perform very specific types of labor for the hacendado."

Don Juan resumed his story. "When I was a pongo I was ordered to process potatoes to make *moraya* [dried potatoes]. So the hacendado gave me the potatoes, but when I showed him the moraya I made from them, he claimed that I had not made enough, that it was not all there. 'There must be more!' he claimed. Then he ordered me to give him my own potatoes, from my own fields, to make up for the quantity he thought was missing. If I did not do this, he said he would have me thrown in jail!"

Don Juan was not exaggerating the hacendado's power. Most hacendados' influence extended into the political and civil systems of the surrounding towns, where they were assured the allegiance of the local police.

"This kind of thing happened not only with the moraya but with the sheep," don Juan continued. "The hacendado would give a number of sheep to a pongo to care for, and he would decide that the sheep must double in quantity by the next year." Don Juan left unspoken the punishment received if the flock had not properly multiplied. He hurried on, his voice urgent, to explain the abuses heaped upon pongos. "At another hacienda, in Paucartambo, where we often were forced to work, they had different types of pongos. There was a pongo who must make sure that the birds do not eat the fruits from the trees. He spent the whole day making noises to chase the birds from the trees. Another type of pongo worked in the kitchen. Another took care of the wells and drawing water. He had to get one type of water for [cleaning] plates and another for cooking. He must carry the water for the kitchen and for the all the uses of the household. This pongo, the one in the kitchen, must cook, but he must not allow any smoke into the house. If there is smoke, he is beaten. Another obligation of the pongo is to feed the dogs. The hacendado would come to check that the dogs were given the meat, and not us. We were never given meat.

"Once when I was a pongo, I had to sleep in the main house at the hacienda. The hacendado tied a cord from my finger, in the room where I slept, to his own finger, in the room where he slept. He did this so he could pull the string to wake me up. Not to summon me, but just so I could not sleep—only for that reason. I was always awake! I could not sleep! The hacendado was very old and could not sleep well. So he pulled the cord to keep me awake, too. To be a pongo was very hard, too much!" Don Juan leaned wearily back into the couch cushions, as if exhausted from his tale.

Don Mariano and don Agustín together picked up the story. They are both too young to have served as pongos, but obviously they had heard stories, perhaps from their own fathers or other older relatives, of how it felt to be called to this special obligatory service. "When a person knows he is going to be a pongo, he is as terrorized as when a puma is about to attack. He would shake with terror!

"Sometimes when it was your time to do this service, it was a hard thing to do but you had no choice. You must do it or be punished. It was your obligation to do it. But sometimes, when your moment came to do this service, the hacendado would reject you. Then you must return to Q'ero. You must pay because you could not do your service."

Don Juan perked up and took over the story again, speaking from personal observation. "There was a list of people who had to do their obligation. If you went but were rejected, you must pay from your own pocket for someone else to take your place. The price was usually one llama of your personal property." He sat back to let this fact sink in.

Juan Núñez del Prado explained the significance of the hacendado's price. "That was very expensive. Nowadays, they have a lot of llamas in Q'ero. But in the hacienda times, llamas were scarce. They were very precious."

As if he understood that we now appreciated the significance of the hacendado's demand, don Juan leaned forward to deliver the *coup de grâce*: "If you did not send a man who pleased the hacendado's heart, the hacendado could take all your llamas and all your potato crop. If the hacendado rejected your replacement, he could take all your crops!"

Don Julian interrupted, putting an end to Juan's exhortation, perhaps in an effort to soothe his older brother. "In the time of our grandfather," don Julian said, "you had to serve as a pongo for one month a year. In our generation, things became a little better, because the service was only three weeks."

Taking don Julian's cue, I changed the subject, asking how the hacienda times ended, how the Q'ero gained their freedom.

Once again, don Juan spoke for the group. "The time of the hacienda ended with the arrival of other people, like the people that came with Juan's father, Oscar. [The first modern contact with the Q'ero was in August 1955, when Oscar Núñez del Prado, an anthropologist, mounted an expedition with fifteen others to Q'ero.] It also happened at the same time as another event—with the hacendado's felling of the eucalyptus tree and the death it caused. The death of that man resulted in a legal investigation."

"The case was in the courts for four years," said don Julian. "During this time the villagers chose two men to represent them at the courts. Turibio Q'espi was chosen, along with Florenzo Apasa. So they went to Cuzco to observe the court case. Because of their fear, their terror of the hacendado, they did not go into the town of Paucartambo."

Juan Núñez del Prado provided the explanation of this cryptic remark. "When the Q'ero challenged the hacendado," he explained, "the entire town of Paucartambo became the enemies of the Q'ero, for the hacendado controlled the towns. But to get to Cuzco, the Q'ero had to cross the big river at Paucartambo. There was no other way to go directly from Q'ero to Cuzco. However, because of their fear of the townspeople of Paucartambo, the Q'ero could not do that. They had to sneak across the river in the dark, at night."

Don Julian continued, although he did not pick up the narrative exactly where he left off. "This person, Turibio," he explained, "during the time of the court case, he fell in love with a woman from Pitumarka. He went away to live in this woman's community. But before he did, he completed his responsibilities to Q'ero."

Don Julian seemed proud of the representative's show of integrity. Then he explained how that integrity had been assured. "During the time of the court case, the entire community of Q'ero made offerings to the Apus and Pachamama for the success of the representatives of the community, so that they would have inspiration and be clear thinking and do the right things. So they would be free of all difficulties."

Satisfied that he had accounted for the representative's restraint at waiting until the court case was over before devoting himself to his new love, don Julian continued. "The two representatives of the community also went to Lima, three times. They went to the president of the Republic himself.[2] We still have the photo of this meeting with the president.

"During the time of this court case, we in Q'ero provided the economic support. The rich and the poor gave five or ten *soles*: the poor people put in less money, and the richer people put in more to support the court case. We [the people of the communities that make up Q'ero] had cows, but only a few, perhaps two or three. We had more alpacas and llamas."

Ricardo explained that implicit in Julian's explanation was the understanding that the richer people would provide more money or more llamas or alpacas, because in the event of a favorable legal outcome, they would have more to gain.

Here don Agustín took the opportunity to explain the darker side of the mood within Q'ero. "The time of the hacienda did not end easily, but with much difficulty," he explained. "The community, the men, divided into two groups: those who supported the hacendado, and those who supported the communities of Q'ero. There was a lot of conflict and animosity. Those who were for the community, they became involved in the labor organization movement. They got in touch with Emiliano Waman T'ika."[3]

Don Agustín's articulation of the name Emiliano Waman T'ika was like an invocation. Juan explained its significance. "Emiliano Waman T'ika was a famous and charismatic labor organizer in the Cuzco area. He organized the first federations of *campesinos* [peasants]."

Don Julian picked up the thread of the story. "This leader, Emiliano Waman T'ika, was at one time at Q'ero. This leader started an assembly at Q'ero. He said, 'The hacienda time must end! You will see that you must throw the hacendado into the river and let the river carry him away.'⁴ But when Emiliano Waman T'ika was at Q'ero, the hacendado sent a message to us, saying, 'What is this shit doing in Q'ero?' And to the people of Q'ero who supported the hacendado, he said 'Throw out this shit!' So all the Q'ero who supported the hacendado said we must expel this man. They did not succeed in expelling Emiliano Waman T'ika, but there was a fight between the two groups."

Juan Núñez del Prado filled in the history of the coming of the labor movement to Q'ero. "There were four people who supported the Q'ero, doing all they needed to do in Cuzco. There was Emiliano Waman T'ika, from the Peasants Confederation; there was Demetrio Tupac Yupanqui, a journalist from Lima who went on that first anthropological expedition to Q'ero with my father; there was Mario Vasquez, an anthropologist from Lima who was also on the expedition with my father; and finally there was my father, Oscar Núñez del Prado. These four persons helped the Q'ero community realize their freedom from the hacienda system. All of this happened in a time when agrarian reform was still a utopia in the Peruvian system. The Q'ero, with the help of these four men, had the opportunity to buy their land. This happened around 1958 and was one of the first steps toward agrarian reform in Peru. Widespread agrarian reform started in 1968, ten years later. And for a time Mario Vasquez actually became the vice minister of agrarian reform.

"This is an amazing story," Juan continued, reverting to his professorial mode, "because Mario Vasquez started out working with Allan Holmberg, a North American anthropologist of Cornell University. They started an applied social anthropology program in Vicos. And there they bought a hacienda and eventually gave the peasants their freedom. With the help of the North American university, Cornell University! And Mario Vasquez was a friend of my father. My father started this in Q'ero and Mario Vasquez helped him. He and Tupac Yupanqui and this famous syndicate leader—Emiliano Waman T'ika— became something like a team. Vasquez and Tupac Yupanqui worked in Lima. Waman T'ika and my father worked in Cuzco. They established something like a team to challenge the hacienda system. They together organized this court case in Cuzco because of the death of this man [by the hacendado deliberately felling the eucalyptus tree]. They organized this meeting of the Q'ero leaders with the government and went with them to the government palace. Mario Vasquez also went to Q'ero, to check out the situation."

Just then don Julian interrupted. "But this man, Mario Vasquez," he said, "about five years ago, he was going to a hotel and he was killed. It is a dark thing."

I was unsure of what don Julian was implying—either that Mario Vasquez had committed suicide or that he had been murdered. Ricardo explained the mystery. "The journalists reported that he put on his good suit, went to a hotel, and killed himself." I asked him to query the Q'ero about the journalists' reports. What did they think happened to Mario Vasquez?

Don Julian replied, very simply, "It is not clear."

I pushed Ricardo to get an opinion from them. What did they *think* happened?

There was a short discussion among the five Q'ero paqos. Don Julian answered for the group: "We do not know what happened. We know nothing about it. However," he said, "about the death of Emiliano Waman T'ika, it was written up in a newspaper that there was a car accident because of sabotage by the hacendado. He died going to an assembly [of peasants]."

Although they would not speculate about the circumstances of Mario Vasquez's death, it was evident that they believed Emiliano Waman T'ika had been murdered.

By this point, we were all exhausted. The discussion had gone on for hours and it had been a dark one, dredging up unpleasant memories for most of the Q'ero. I decided to begin to wind down the morning's interview by asking about the outcome of the court case. I still wasn't clear what the charge had been. So I asked Juan Núñez del Prado, who explained that it was indeed a murder charge.

I asked Juan what the hacendado's sentence had been. "If I remember correctly," he said, "it was a totally ambiguous outcome from the court. They did not punish the hacendado. Although he was charged with murder, it was not firmly proved that the felling of the tree was not an accident. I think the hacendado only had to pay civil reparations to the family of the man who was killed."

Don Juan Pauqar Flores summed up the outcome of the case. "We won the court case because of the help of these four men [Waman T'ika, Tupac Yupanqui, Vasquez, and Núñez del Prado]. But there were two outcomes. One was the outcome of the court case. The other was the decision by the government to finally buy the hacienda."

All the Q'eros' efforts, with the help of Waman T'ika, Vasquez, Tupac Yupanqui, and Núñez del Prado, had paid off. The government was putting don Luis Yábar out of business. Although he did not go quietly.

Don Juan picked up his summary of the outcome of the case. "Even after the government bought the hacienda, there remained cows and sheep from the hacienda in Q'ero. The hacendado said, 'The hacienda is in the palm of my hand. And my animals are part of the hacienda.' This [display of power and declaration of ownership] was seen by those associated with the hacendado, and they believed the power of the hacendado was intact. So Daniel Yábar bought the livestock from the hacendado and took all these animals away from Q'ero. Daniel Yábar bought these with his own money. Then we were finally free."

Juan filled in the logic of don Juan's story. "The hacendado said he retained power because his livestock were still on the lands," he explained, "even though the government bought the hacienda from him. But finally he decided to sell his livestock to Daniel Yábar, who removed them from Q'ero. At that moment, with the extraction of the hacendado's animals, everyone felt that they were finally free from his authority."

The obvious question was, who was Daniel Yábar, and was he related to the hacendado, Luis Angel Yábar?

Again, don Juan Pauqar Flores answered. "Daniel Yábar was from Paucartambo, and he was a friend of the Q'ero. He was a government representative to Paucartambo. There were times when we were threatened with arrest and he helped free us. He did not allow the police in Paucartambo to arrest us, often only after much argument. He would tell the police, 'These men are working for me!' Then he would carry us safely to Cuzco in his truck. We do not know more about him."

Juan Núñez del Prado explained again just how much power the hacendados exerted over civil officials. "There was something like an agreement between all the hacendados in the area, in towns like Paucartambo. They controlled the police. Because the Q'ero challenged one hacendado, they were under threat from all of the other hacendados when they traveled to places like Paucartambo. They could be arrested for no reason.

But Daniel Yábar established himself as an authority figure, telling the police that the Q'ero were coming to work for him. In some ways, this was an agreement between the hacendados not to challenge each other. But some of them protected people like the Q'ero in order to go against another hacendado."

Don Juan explained that with the eradication of the hacienda system, the communities of Q'ero came together. "In the time of the hacienda," he related, "there were many internal conflicts and fights. But after the hacienda times, these conflicts ended. There were no conflicts between communities. It was a time of peace. The many communities integrated into one. We became one. We were dispersed, but we came together with one heart."

Don Juan's brother, don Julian, was less sentimental. "[Not long ago] I served as president [rather like a mayor; elected by the people] of Q'ero," he said, not as a boast but to let us know that he had been involved in all the most important issues of Q'ero. "From the end of the hacienda times until now there were only a few internal conflicts. [Immediately after the demise of the hacienda system] a lot of people asked for rights to the land. They said, 'This land belonged to my father and my grandfather. Now I have a right to it. It has been my family's since the time of my great-grandfather. Therefore, this land belongs to me.' So many people asked for land. Villagers had claims to the land from long ago. These conflicts had to be resolved by the community president.

"These conflicts still continue with the young people, but not yesterday or today [they flare up even today but are not common problems]. Now they do not use violence to solve these problems. They do not injure or kill. These problems emerge in the communal assemblies [village meetings], where people speak openly about their land rights. But now the solution is to look at the issue from all different sides, to see all the details, and finally all the conflicts are resolved. We talk about it now, instead of fighting about it."

Endnotes

Preface

1. All quotes from Thomas Mails are from *The Hopi Survival Kit*, 340–341.

2. Our research was generously funded by the Ringing Rocks Foundation, which also supported a team of filmmakers who recorded the Hatun Karpay and the Q'ero's blessing and experience of the whistling vessels.

3. The spellings of a few of these paqos' names may be inaccurate. Most of the Q'ero are illiterate and the spellings given by Quechua and/or Spanish translators are often not reliable. I never did record don Sebástian's and don Bernadino's surnames.

Part I
The Kawsay Pacha: The World of Living Energy

Chapter One
In the Land of the Inkas:
An Overview of Andean Mysticism

1. César Calvo, *The Three Halves of Ino Moxo*, glossary, s.v. "Q'ero."

2. The term *shaman* is rarely used in the Andes. It is mostly westerners who refer to Andean paqos as shamans. Like my teacher, Juan Núñez del Prado, I prefer the term *mystic*. See Appendix I for a more detailed discussion of these terms. We also refer to the paqos as metaphysical "priests," which indicates that there is a structure to the practice of the mystical system and a hierarchy to the training its practitioners receive.

3. A beer-like drink made from maize; it is often served during festivities.

4. *Kawsay*, pronounced rather like "cow-sigh," also is often spelled *kausay*.

5. Perhaps by ingesting their mothers' milk, these children also ingested antibodies against the disease. And, as is obvious, don Juan speaks symbolically, hyperbolically, to emphasize the seriousness of the situation, when he claims that only a few children survived the epidemic.

6. It sounds as if Garibilu Q'espi was using the *hucha mikhuy* technique, which is discussed in chapter 2 and in part III. He used the power of the yellow fever to attract the other sicknesses, then he digested the sicknesses using his energy body and fed them back to the Apus.

7. John Hemming, *The Conquest of the Incas*, 27.

8. Obviously not the same Garibilu Q'espi mentioned in the yellow fever story. There is a Garibilu Q'espi identified in the Q'ero lineage who has become almost a metaphysical figure, a "savior" archetype. Whether one of these two Garibilu Q'espis is that figure is unknown. Q'espi, which means "crystal," is one

of the oldest and most illustrious names among the Q'ero, as is Pauqar. Both are traced back to Inka origins, and these surnames are shared by many people who claim no known blood relation.

9. Because paqos are most often men, I will use only the masculine pronoun in the remainder of this book. I have made this decision only as a matter of semantic convenience, and the reader should infer no bias against female paqos.

10. Saqsawaman is also an ancient fortress and ceremonial site on the outskirts of Cuzco that was built by the Inka Pachakuteq. It was, and continues to be, the site of the Inti Raymi festival, the sacred annual festival honoring *Inti*, the sun.

11. From "The Current Andean Priesthood," by Juan Núñez del Prado and Lida Julia Murillo.

12. It is not clear to me just who or what the *ukhupacharuna*—the beings of the lower world—are within the larger sphere of Andean mysticism. However, the Q'ero speak briefly to this issue in the interviews of part II, where they identify these beings as somewhat diminutive humans who live in a human-like world.

Chapter Two

Children of the Sun: Engaging Your Energy Body

1. See Joan Parisi Wilcox and Elizabeth B. Jenkins, "Journey to Q'ollorit'i."

2. Also commonly spelled Atahualpa and Huascar, respectively.

Chapter Three

Andean Prophecy: The Age of Meeting Ourselves Again

1. I have worked several times with don Manuel, even receiving the *Karpay Ayni* initiation from him in his house at Chua Chua. I was scheduled to meet with don Manuel twice to talk with him for this book, but both times he was unable to attend our meetings because of illness. In his late seventies, don Manuel is in declining health, suffering from bouts of lung congestion and infection.

2. William Sullivan, *The Secret of the Incas*, 29.

3. Also spelled *huaca*. A *waka* is any site or object that is considered the repository of the sacred.

4. It was no surprise to read in newspapers only weeks after the October 1996 meeting during which the "condor of the south" linked energy with the "eagle of the north" that California condors, rare birds in North America, were released into the wild in Arizona for the first time. An additional four condors were released in Arizona in December 1996, in an area where they were last seen in 1924. The news was carried on the major network news broadcasts and in many metropolitan newspapers.

Part II

Walking the Sacred Path: Interviews with Q'ero Mystics

Chapter Four

Ancient Tradition, Modern Practice

1. Estimates by demographic anthropologists Henry F. Dobyns

and Paul L. Doughty reported in *Peru: a country study*, 17.

2. See *Peru: a country study*, 20.

3. See Tony Morrison, *Pathways to the Gods*, 113–114.

4. The Q'ero villages reach from the subtropical jungles to the high mountains; hence, the range of dancers.

5. See "Journey to Q'ollorit'i: Initiation into Andean Mysticism," which I co-wrote with Elizabeth B. Jenkins and which was published as the cover story for the Winter 1996 issue of *Shaman's Drum*.

6. More commonly spelled Qoyllur Rit'i, which means literally "Star of the Snow." In Quechua, *rit'i* means snow, and *qoyllur* can mean star, although it also refers to the planet Venus. The more common word for star is *ch'aska*. Juan Núñez del Prado claims that the term *Qoyllur Rit'i* and the translation "Star of the Snow" is a mistranslation of the real name of the ancient festival, Q'ollorit'i, which means "pure white snow" (from the word *qoyllu/qollo*, which is an adjective that means luminous or resplendent, and *rit'i*, snow). I spell the name of this festival according to Juan's preference.

7. It is a huge responsibility for so few people to have to provide a feast of food and drink for the entire community. The Q'ero struggle to provide for their own families, so such an undertaking is momentous and can be quite a hardship for the hosts.

Chapter Five
The Grandsons of Inkarí

1. Also commonly spelled Manco Capac.

2. There are approximately forty versions of the Inka creation myth recorded in the Spanish chronicles. This is a brief synthesis of several versions.

3. Also commonly spelled Mama Ocllo.

4. In Quechua, *tawa* means "four" and *suyu* means "quarter." These words are joined by *ntin*, a term that designates two different things being brought into unity or merging to create an entity greater than the sum of the parts.

5. The noted anthropologist Juan Ossio has collected versions of the Inkarí myth in his book, *Ideología mesiánica del mundo andino*.

6. An *Intiwatana*, literally a "Hitching Post of the Sun," is a carved rock used as a sun dial and solar observatory. The most famous Intiwatana in Peru is at Machu Picchu. Don Julian here refers to his ancestors somehow using the movement of the sun to determine distance; we did not explore this technique.

7. It is unknown from don Julian's telling of the myth why the woman wanted to camp at these places, if God permitted her to, and what happened to her so that she never arrived to meet Inkarí. I have not seen reference to this incident in any other retelling of the myth.

8. The Christian God, considered synonymous with Jesus. However, for the Q'ero the Christian God is almost always syncretized with the ancient Creator god, Wiraqocha.

9. The llama dung is washed into the river, symbolizing the imperfection of the kay pacha and its hucha, which is at least partly a result of Inkarí's willfulness and hubris at refusing the munay offered by God.

10. What don Julian means here is that when Inkarí sees the
    llama excrement, he is reminded of his grandsons, the Q'ero,
    who herd llamas, and he weeps with longing for them.

11. The civil war that ravaged the empire as a result of
    Atawallpa's and Waskar's struggle for the Inka throne no doubt
    contributed to the ease with which Pizzaro conquered the
    Inkas. Atawallpa was captured by the Spaniards and, despite
    his payment of hordes of gold and silver as ransom, he was
    eventually executed [garroted] by them.

12. Also see chapter 2, where I discuss Atawallpa's and Waskar's
    roles as teachers of ayni to the *ukhupacharuna*, beings of the
    lower world.

Chapter Six

Pampa Mesayoq: Master of the Earth Rituals

1. Don Agustín used the word *phukuy*, suggesting that by blowing
   through the coca leaves, Mother Mary sought to establish an
   energetic connection with her son, Jesus.

2. Implicit in don Agustín's statement is the understanding that
   when one makes an offering to a sacred lagoon, one is seeking
   an estrella. In other words, Agustín's father reconsidered his
   earlier refusal and now sought an estrella so he could become
   a paqo. However, the estrella of the lagoon could not undo
   what had already been decided.

3. Juan Núñez del Prado explained that a misti to an Indian signi-
   fies a mestizo person of power and authority. Many times Jesus
   or an Apu or other sacred personage appears in an Indian's
   dreams as a misti, signifying the call to the mystical path. For a

mestizo, the opposite is true: the personage in the sacred dream is usually an Indian.

4. The man in the dream is asking Agustín to serve him like an alto mesayoq would. The sentence can be read as, "Offer me a despacho from the mountaintop and you will have a good life."

5. Juan Núñez del Prado explained the unstated implication that without parents, Agustín was also left without support. It is expensive to become an alto mesayoq. The training, which can stretch over a decade or more, usually involves payment in livestock and cash to the alto mesayoq teacher. It may also require the service of labor in the alto mesayoq's fields. Without financial support, it would have been almost impossible for Agustín to train as an alto mesayoq. This turn of events no doubt had some bearing on Agustín's decision to follow the path of the pampa mesayoq.

6. Juan Núñez del Prado explained that the estrellas also talked "from a distance" not only because of Agustín's mistake, but also because Bernabe Marchaqa, whose mesa the estrellas were talking through, was a pampa mesayoq, not an alto mesayoq, who can interact much more closely and directly with the Apus.

7. Although one should be aware that the systems are compatible. When an Andean says he is working on the right side, in physical terms associated with the body, that metaphor would mean he was working more with his left brain, because the left hemisphere of the brain controls the right side of the body. With this in mind, the metaphorical systems of North American and South American match: i.e., the "masculine" is more associated with the left brain in the North but is said to be the "right side" in the South. The opposite is true for the "feminine": the right

brain equates with the left side. Also see chapter 7.

8. See Constance Classen, *Inca Cosmology and the Human Body*, 23.

9. This is a metaphoric expression that reveals just how dire their situation was. To make a mistake on the path imperils a paqo's very life.

Chapter Seven

Alto Mesayoq: Master of the Hanaq Pacha

1. Washington Rozas Alvarez, "Los Paqo de Q'ero," 147. All quotes by Rozas are from this article, which I translated into English with the assistance of Cristobál Cornejo.

2. Rozas, 151.

3. When a paqo is called to the path and accepts, he finds or is given a mesa—either by the spirits or by accumulating khuyas from teachers and power spots—that connects the paqo to his power.

4. Anyone who has hiked the Andes, or even traveled on horseback, knows how remarkable it is that an amputee, such as don Martín Herrillo, even with a crutch, could walk to Q'ollorit'i—which is in rugged mountains at an altitude of more than 16,500 feet above sea level.

5. Juan explained that because don Juan had personally met the Lord of Q'ollorit'i, he now had the capacity to read the coca leaves himself.

6. *Wachu* is a Quechua word for something like a furrow. It implies a complicated metaphor equating the seeding of a fur-

row in a field you are trying to cultivate with cultivating your own power as a paqo as you work and gain experience along the sacred path. One must nurture and care for one's progress along the path just as one must nurture and tend to the seedlings in a newly planted field. The *kawsay wachu* is like a field of vital energy, the field of your life in which you plant and cultivate living energy.

7. What don Manuel means is that because these beings follow don Mariano as if they want to establish a connection with him, but they do not actually do so, they are lying.

8. It is quite common for an alto mesayoq to have a pampa mesayoq in service to him. They work together. For many years don Juan Ordoñus was don Mariano's assistant. Now his wife, doña Agustina, works with him.

Chapter Eight

Keepers of the Ancient Knowledge: Kawsay and K'ara

1. The supreme supernatural being, variously called Jesus Christ, the Lord of Q'ollorit'i, and other names depending on the context.

2. There are several paqos of legend who share this name. The story about this particular Garibilu Q'espi and the yellow fever is told in chapter 1.

3. A Peruvian-born teacher of Andean mysticism who lives and teaches in the United States.

4. Remember, there are three "hierarchies" of Apus: the *ayllu Apu*, *llaqta Apu*, and *suyu Apu*.

5. Interestingly, the Black Light energy is often considered the highest energy and the most difficult to master. It is associated, for instance, with the sacred Urubamba river, whose ancient names include Willkamayu or Willkañust'a (River of Black Light or Goddess of Black Light). Obviously, this does not hold true for the k'aras of the Apus, as a black k'ara indicates a low level of power.

Chapter Nine

Keepers of the Ancient Knowledge: The Three Worlds

1. Don Agustín, of course, did not vocalize the animal calls as a North American would, but I would be hard pressed to try to reproduce what these animal calls sound like in Quechua!

2. The implication is that, just as in real life, the size of a family's herd determines its status and wealth.

3. A nutritious grain that is a staple of the Andean diet.

4. Guinea pigs are sacred animals in the Andes. They are raised in most homes, specially fed and well treated, and then eaten on ceremonial days and during feasts. They are also sometimes sacrificed for use in divination.

5. Don Julian is referring to the practice of each church or parish being associated with one patron saint. The saint, though a being of the hanaq pacha, is authorized by God to act with authority in his assigned parish in the kay pacha.

6. A common variation is meeting a drunk on the road; if you are qawaq, you will be able to determine that this drunk is the Apu, come to test you, and possibly to grant your wish.

7. William Sullivan, *The Secret of the Incas*, 5.

Part III

The Flight of the Condor: Putting Andean Shamanic Practices to Work in Your Life

Chapter Ten

Hucha Mikhuy: Cleansing and Digesting Heavy Energy

1. Dr. Deepak Chopra is an M.D. who has combined Western allopathic medicine with Indian Ayurvedic medicine. He is a prolific writer, eloquent speaker, and consummate paradigm-shifter.

2. This admonition is based more upon the shamanic work of Michael Harner than it is on the mystical work of my Peruvian teachers.

3. There is another, more intensive Andean cleansing technique called *kutichi* that is in some ways closer to what Castaneda means by recapitulation. In the kutichi ceremony, you send back all energy, light and heavy, to the people with whom you have interacted until you are left touching only your core, essential self. Then you offer a kutichi despacho. In effect, you are reintroducing yourself to yourself. Andean paqos perform this ritual at least once a year. My husband and I have used this technique and can attest to its efficacy as a deep, comprehensive cleansing.

Appendix II

Lost Knowledge: The Q'ero and Andean Prophecy

1. See note 1, chapter 10.

Appendix III

In the Hand of the Hacendado

1. In Father Bernabe Cobo's tome *Inca Religion and Customs* [Book II, Chapter 2, page 185], he records the following: "The Indians identify their honor with their hair to such an extent that the worst disgrace that one can inflict on them is to cut their hair. . . ."

2. Manuel Prado y Ugarteche, who was president of Peru from 1956 to 1962.

3. Alternative spelling is Emiliano Huamantica.

4. Waman T'ika here displays knowledge of the indigenous mystical system, for hucha—heavy energy—is cleansed and carried away by rivers.

Glossary of Andean Mystical Terms

(with approximate pronuniations as necessary)

Akulliy [ak-wee] The act of choosing and chewing coca leaves in a sacred manner. The Quechua verb from which derives the term for the highest level of Andean paqo, the kuraq akulleq.

Alto mesayoq [al-to ma-sigh-yok] One of two sacred paths in the Andean mystical system, the alto mesayoq works directly with spirits of the kawsay pacha, especially the Apus. The three levels of alto mesayoq—ayllu alto mesayoq, llaqta alto mesayoq, and suyu alto mesayoq—correspond to the level of Apu to which the alto mesayoq is in communication.

Apu [ah-poo] A "Lord of the Mountain." Apus are the spirits of the sacred mountains of Peru, considered the most powerful of all nature spirits. There are three levels of Apus, respectively from least powerful to most powerful: ayllu Apus, llaqta Apus, and suyu Apus.

Ayni [I-nee] The impulse toward sacred interchange and the spirit of reciprocity, which are fundamental operating principles in the social and mystical systems of Peru. In the social system, ayni is shared labor and equates somewhat with the Christian concept of "Do unto others as you would have them do unto you." In the mystical system, ayni is the stance of the shaman and the basis of all ceremony and ritual, for the paqo is always making an "interchange" of energy with the spirit realm.

Chunpi [chun-pee] This Quechua word literally means "belts." According to Andean mysticism, there are four major energy belts, similar to chakras, that surround the human body. These are the yana chunpi, puka chunpi, qori chunpi, qolqe chunpi. The three points of the physical eyes and the third eye form what is sometimes referred to as the fifth belt, the kulli chunpi.

Chunpi Khuyas [chun-pee coo-yas] A special set of five stones that are used to confer the chunpi initiation, an opening of the energy centers of the human body.

Chunpi paqo [chun-pee pa-ko] A paqo who had been initiated with the chunpis and is able to activate these energy centers in others. A chunpi paqo uses a special set of five khuyas, called chunpi khuyas, to activate these centers.

Ch'uspa The woven or animal fur bag in which Andean paqos carry their sacred coca leaves.

Ch'uya To be "clean," that is, to be in a state of physical, emotional, and energetic cleanliness and purity in order to receive an initiation, to perform ceremony, or to communicate with the spirits.

Coca The sacred plant of Peru; its leaves are chewed as a mild stimulant. It is used by almost everyone. Tourists acclimate to altitude by drinking coca tea; peasants exchange coca as an act of friendship and greeting in social situations, and they chew coca when working to alleviate hunger and to increase their stamina. Mystics throw the coca leaves for divination and diagnosis, and use coca in a myriad of sacred contexts, especially when making despachos. A common use of coca is in a k'intu, a fan of three coca leaves used in countless ways in ceremony.

Despacho [day-spach-o] An offering comprised of a variety of natural items, called *recados*, arranged ritually on white paper, prayed over and infused with sami, and then folded into a bundle to be burned or buried. Although there are approximately 250 different kinds of despachos, the two most commonly made are to honor Pachamama or the Apus.

Estrella [estray-ya] The "star," or spirit manifestation, of an Apu. A paqo is called to the sacred path when he or she receives an estrella, that is, when he or she is summoned by an outward manifestation of the Apu. Estrellas commonly take the form of hummingbirds, pumas, bulls, and condors. In dreams an estrella may appear as a man or woman in white clothing who glows. In addition to Apus, sacred lagoons may send estrellas.

Hallpay [hal-pie] The chewing of coca leaves in a social or non-sacred context.

Hanaq pacha [ha-nick pa-cha] Of the three worlds of Andean cosmology, this is the upper world, the place of the most refined energies. It is often symbolized by the condor.

Hucha [who-cha] "Heavy" or "dense" energy that accumulates in a person's poq'po, or energy body. It is one of two kinds of kawsay, and is created only by humans. It is not to be equated with the dualistic Western concepts of "negative" or "bad" energy; rather, it is associated with those things that do not best serve us in our relationship with others or that are incompatible with our own energy. When hucha is cleansed from or released from your poq'po, it becomes food for Pachamama.

Inka Mallku [in-ka myl-coo] An infallible healer, twelve of whom will be revealed, according to Andean prophecy, during the first stage of the Taripay Pacha, signaling the manifestation of the fifth level of the Andean priesthood and the evolution of human consciousness. There will be six males and six females (who are called Ñust'as).

Inti [in-tee] Father Sun; the sun as expressive of the divine masculine principle.

Itu [ē-too] The Spanish term for a physical location or formation of masculine energetic power, such as a mountain, closest to where you were born and to which you are energetically connected. The ancient Quechua term is *saiwa*; the equivalent feminine energy place is called a *paqarina*.

Japu [ha-poo] The union of two perfectly harmonized masculine energies.

Kamaq The supreme creative principle in Andean cosmology. Pachakamaq is the creator of the world.

Karpay [car-pie] An initiation or ceremony during which power is invoked and energy transmitted or exchanged between paqos. A bestowal of the power of the ancient lineage.

Kay pacha [ki pa-cha] Of the three worlds of Andean cosmology, this is middle world—the physical Earth; the mundane, everyday world and awareness, which is often represented by the puma.

Kawsay [cow-sigh] The vital, living energy that animates the cosmos. A paqo is taught to "push" the kawsay for the good of others. Kawsay takes two manifestations: sami and hucha. Hucha, heavy energy, is created only by humans. Also commonly spelled *kausay*.

Kawsay pacha Literally, the "world of living energy," referring to the cosmos as a flow of vital, animating light energy that we are in continual interchange with.

Khuya [coo-ya] A stone that carries particularly fine or abundant kawsay and so is considered a stone of power; it is used for healing and/or communicating with the spirit world. Most Andean mesas are comprised primarily of khuyas. The word itself means "love" or "affection."

K'intu A fan of three perfect coca leaves used in rituals such as despachos and for praying or interchanging energy with others or with the spirit realm, especially the Apus or Pachamama.

Kuraq akulleq [cur-ack a-koolya] Literally, the "Elder Chewer of Coca." A fourth-level paqo, the culminating level of the alto mesayoq path. Currently this is the highest level a paqo can attain; the manifestation of the fifth, sixth, and seventh levels of the sacred path are part of Andean prophecy.

Llank'ay [yan-kī] Of the three "stances" an Andean paqo must integrate—love, knowledge, and labor—this is the physical capacity to perform labor. It also is sometimes seen as the will or the power of intention, and as the body.

Lloq'e [yoke-ē] The "left" side of the Andean path is associated with the feminine and is the aspect of the work that connects one with the "non-ordinary," the place of the "magical" as opposed to the "mystical" techniques. The left side of the mesa is associated with "right-brain" characteristics, that is, with eros and intuition, and it is where one masters the practical aspects of the path, such as healing. A paqo must integrate both sides of the work in order to fully push the kawsay. The left side is associated with the color silver.

Mama Killa [ma-ma key-ya] Mother Moon; the moon as expressive of the divine feminine energy.

Mama Qocha Mother of the Waters, Mother of the Lake or Sea.

Mamarit'i [ma-ma ree-tee] Literally, Mother Snow. Also a Ñust'a, or Princess of the Mountain, especially of a snow-capped sacred mountain. The female counterpart to an Apu.

Masintin A relationship of two similar persons, things, entities, or energies. By examining your masintin relationships, you can quickly see how to form energetic alliances or where there is the potential to attract hucha.

Mesa [may-sa] The ritual bundle containing sacred and powerful objects that a paqo assembles during his work along the sacred path and which he or she uses in ceremony and to heal.

Mikhuy [mee-qwee] A Quechua verb that means, literally, to "digest" or to "eat." In mysticism it refers to the practice of cleansing and digesting hucha from a person, place, or object through one's qosqo, or energy stomach. The hucha is fed directly to Pachamama, who composts it into refined energy. The digestion of heavy energy is specifically called *hucha mikhuy*.

Miscayani [mis-kī-yan-ē] A mythical city that is the feminine counterpart to Paytiti, the abode of Inkarí.

Mosoq Karpay [mō-sock car-pie] Literally the "new initiation." An initiation or transmission of energy that raises one to the fifth level of consciousness. This state of being and karpay are part of Andean prophecy, and we are awaiting their bestowal with the emergence of fifth-level beings called *Inka Mallkus*, who are supreme healers.

Munay [moon-eye] Of the three "stances" an Andean paqo must integrate—love, intellect, and labor—this is love, and the capacity for empathy and selflessness. Also seen as the heart.

Ñawi [nyow-ee] In Quechua, literally an "eye." There are four energy points or centers, rather like vortices of the chakras, in the human energy body, each called a *ñawi* and associated with a broad band or belt of energy called a *chunpi*. These points are the siki ñawi, which is at the base of the spine; the qosqo ñawi, which is at the navel; the sonqo ñawi, which is at the heart; and the kunka ñawi, which is at the throat. There is also the kulli ñawi, which is roughly comprised of the two physical eyes and the third eye, although this point is not recognized by all paqos.

Ñust'a [nwee-sta] Any feminine nature energy; a princess of the mountain, the female counterpart to an Apu. Also a female of the fifth level of consciousness, the counterpart to an Inka Mallku.

Pachakuti [pa-cha-koo-tee] An overturning of space-time or a period of cosmic transformation that affects Earth and human consciousness.

Pachamama Mother Earth; the animating energy of the physical earth; Gaia; the divine feminine principle.

Pago [pah-go] A despacho offered in payment or atonement, often combined with a food offering and chicha (a fermented corn drink).

Pampa mesayoq [pahm-pa ma-sigh-yok] One of the two paths of the Andean mystical system; a pampa mesayoq is an accomplished ceremonialist and is master of the rituals that honor Pachamama.

Paña [pahn-ya] The "right" side of the sacred path that is associated with the masculine energies, the "ordinary," and the "left-brain" characteristics of analysis and logocentrisim. The right side of the mesa connects one more closely to the "mystical" rather than to the "magical" work. It is the side of the mesa where one learns to communicate directly with the spirits. A paqo must integrate both sides of the work in order to fully push the kawsay. The right side is associated with the color gold.

Paqarina [pak-a-reena] See "Itu."

Paqo [pa-ko] The term, which in Quechua also means "male alpaca," for a person who practices the Andean mystical work and walks the sacred path. A mystical practitioner or "priest."

Paytiti [pie-tee-tee] A mythical jungle city where Inkarí, the first Inka, lives and awaits the day he can return to reunite the Tawantinsuyu, the ancient Inka Empire. The masculine counterpart to the feminine mythical city of Miscayani.

Phukuy [poohk-wee] A gentle breath through a k'intu intended to establish an energetic connection between the paqo and another person, place, or object.

Poq'po [poke-po] A Quechua word meaning "bubble." In the mystical system, this refers to the bubble of energy surrounding and infusing our physical body—our energy body.

Q'ollorit'i [koll-yur-ee-tee] An annual sacred festival, perhaps the most important of the year, which is held on a glacial range in the high Andes. The presiding "spirit energy" of the festival is the Lord of Q'ollorit'i.

Qosqo [kos-ko] A Quechua word meaning "stomach" or "navel." In the mystical system, the primary energy center through which we mediate kawsay.

Qoya [koy-ya] The term for the sister-wife of the Inka. In Andean prophecy, the Qoya will rule with the Sapa Inka as a model political leader and represents the female manifestation of the sixth level of human consciousness.

Ranti [rawn-tee] The union of two perfectly harmonized masintin energies.

Recados [ray-ka-doz] The items—such as coca leaves, seeds, shells, tiny gold and silver figurines—selected and ritually placed within a despacho.

Saiwa [sigh-wa] A column of energy, often one that energetically unites the three worlds. Also the Quechua name for an itu, the masculine energy of a place nearest to where you were born.

Samay [sah-may] A strong breath through a k'intu that imparts an energizing influence to that which it is directed.

Sami [sah-mee] Of the two kinds of kawsay, the refined energy that we draw in from the kawsay pacha and that we want flowing through our energy body. The energy that equates with our being in harmony and proper connection with the cosmos. Light energy.

Saminchasqa [sah-min-chas-ka] The general act of blowing through a coca k'intu in order to interchange refined energy with the natural world or with nature spirits. One who performs a sami interchange.

Samiy [sa-my] A gentle breath through a k'intu by which a paqo imparts refined energy to that which it is directed.

Sapa Inka [zah-pa ink-a] The supreme male ruler or Inka. In the prophecy, the Sapa Inka will rule with the Qoya as a model political leader and represents that male manifestation of the sixth level of human consciousness.

Taqe [tah-kay] In the tripartite conception of relationship (tinkuy, tupay, taqe), the third level, where one shares one's finest energy and capacities with others. A joining of energies that creates a state of being greater than the sum of its parts.

Taripay Pacha [tar-ee-pie pa-cha] The "Age of Meeting Ourselves Again," during which humankind has the opportunity to raise its energy level and consciously evolve new modes of being. A golden age of harmony and well-being.

Taytacha [tie-ta-cha] A supreme divine being, usually seen as a masculine energy, with the equivalence of the Christ consciousness. In the Andes, the Lord of Q'ollorit'i and the Earthquake Lord are examples of Taytachas.

Tinkuy [teen-kwee] In the tripartite conception of relationship (tinkuy, tupay, taqe), the first level, where one first encounters another person or thing and touches it energy body to energy body.

Tupay [too-pie] In the tripartite conception of relationship (tinkuy, tupay, taqe), the second level, where one sizes up the other person or thing in the stance of competition and domination.

Tukuy Hampeq [too-kwee hahm-peck] A supreme and infallible healer of the fifth level of human consciousness. This level of healing capacity has not yet manifested; it is part of Andean prophecy. See "Inka Mallku."

Ukhu pacha [oo-hoo pa-cha] Of the three worlds of Andean cosmology, the lower or interior world. The place of the subconscious or unconscious, and of dreams and intuition, often symbolized by the snake.

Unanchasqa [oon-on-cha-ska] One who has been given a sign of power from a divine being, such as Christ or the Lord of Q'ollorit'i. For example, a saint.

Waka [whak-ah] A place or object that is infused with refined energy; a power spot; anything or place that contains sami and so is considered sacred. Also commonly spelled *huaca*.

Yachay [ya-chī] Of the three "stances" an Andean paqo must integrate—love, intellect, and labor—this is the power of the intellect grounded in experience. A mystic relies on personal experience, not book-learning or secondhand teachings, to acquire wisdom. Also seen as the mind.

Yanantin A relationship of two dissimilar persons, things, entities, or energies. By examining your yanantin relationships, you can quickly see how to form energetic alliances or where there is the potential to attract hucha.

Selected Bibliography

Arguedas, José Maria, and Josafat Roel Pineda. "Tres Versiones del Mito de Inkarrí." In Ossio, 219–236.

Bernard, Carmen. *The Incas: People of the Sun*. Trans. Paul G. Bahn. New York: Harry N. Abrams, 1994.

Burndage, Burr Cartwright. *Empire of the Inca*. Norman: University of Oklahoma Press, 1963.

Calvo, César. *The Three Halves of Ino Moxo: Teachings of the Wizard of the Upper Amazon*. Rochester, VT: Inner Traditions, 1995.

Classen, Constance. *Inca Cosmology and the Human Body*. Salt Lake City: University of Utah Press, 1993.

Cobo, Father Bernabe. *Inca Religion and Customs*. Ed. and Trans. Roland Hamilton. Austin, TX: University of Texas Press, 1990. From Historia del Neuvo Mundo [1653].

Cumes, Carol, and Rómulo Lizárraga Valencia. *Pachamama's Children: Mother Earth and Her Children of the Andes of Peru*. St. Paul, MN: Llewellyn, 1995.

Eliade, Mircea. *Shamanism: Archaic Techniques of Ecstasy*. Trans. Willard R. Trask. Bolligen Series 76. Princeton, NJ: Princeton University Press, 1974.

Garcilaso de la Vega, El Inca. *The Royal Commentaries of the Incas*. Vol I. Trans. Harold V. Livermore. Austin, TX: University of Texas Press, 1966.

Gheerbrant, Alain, ed. *The Incas: The Royal Commentaries of the Inca Garcilaso del la Vega, 1539–1616*. Trans. Maria Jolas. New York: Orion Press, 1961.

Harner, Michael. *The Way of the Shaman*. First edition 1980 by Harper & Row. San Francisco: HarperSanFrancisco, 1990.

Hemming, John. *The Conquest of the Incas*. San Diego: Harcourt Brace & Company, 1970.

Highwater, Jamake. "Rulers of the Andes." 1986. *Native Land: Sagas of the Indian Americas*. New York: Barnes & Noble, 1995. 67–110.

Hollzmann, Rodolfo. *Q'ero, pueblo y música*. Lima: Patronato Popular y Porvenir Pro Música Clásica, 1986.

Hudson, Rex A., ed. *Peru: a country study*. 4th ed. Washington, DC: Federal Research Division, Library of Congress, 1993.

Jenkins, Elizabeth B. *Initiation: A Woman's Spiritual Adventure in the Heart of the Andes*. New York: G.P. Putnam, 1997.

Kendall, Anne. *The Everyday Life of the Incas*. New York: G.P. Putnam, 1973.

Lyons, Patricia. "Female Supernaturals in Ancient Peru." *Nawpa Pacha* 16. Berkeley: University of California Press, 1978. 95–137.

Mails, Thomas E. *The Hopi Survival Guide*. New York: Stewart Tabori & Chang, 1996.

McGinn, Bernard. *The Calabrian Abbot: Joachim of Fiore in the History of Western Thought.* New York: MacMillan, 1985.

Morrison, Tony. *Pathways to the Gods: The Mystery of the Andes Lines.* First edition 1978 by Harper & Row. Chicago: Academy Chicago Publishers, 1988.

Núñez del Prado, Juan. "The Supernatural World of the Quechua • of Southern Peru as Seen from the Community of Qotobamba." Ed. Patricia J. Lyons. *Native South American.* Boston: Little, Brown and Co., 1974. 238–251.

———, and Lida J. Murillo. "Preparando un Inca." *Cornicas Urbanas*, n.p., 115–122.

Núñez del Prado, Oscar. *El Hombre y la Familia: Su Matrimonio y Organizacion Politico Social en Q'ero.* Originally published in *Allpanchis Phuturinqa.* Cuzco, 1970.

———. "Version del Mito de Inkarrí en Q'eros." In Ossio, 276–280.

Ochoa, Jorge Flores, and Ana María Fries, eds. *Puna, Qheswa, Yunga: El Hombre y Su Medio en Q'ero.* Collecciones Andinas. Cuzco: Banco Central de Reserva del Perú, 1989.

Ossio A., Juan M., ed. *Ideología mesiánica del mundo andino.* Lima: Edición de Ignacio Prado Pastor, 1973.

Richardson III, James B. *People of the Andes.* Smithsonian Exploring the Ancient World series. Ed. Jeremy A. Sabloff. Washington, DC: Smithsonian Books, 1994.

Rozas Alvarez, Washington. "Los Paqo de Q'ero." *Q'ero: El Último Ayllu Inka: Homenje a Oscar Núñez del Prado.* Ed. Jorge A. Flores, et al. Cuzco: Centro de Estudios Andinos Cuzco, 1983. 143–157.

Sullivan, William. *The Secret of the Incas: Myth, Astronomy, and the War Against Time*. New York: Crown, 1996.

Urton, Gary. *At the Crossroads of Earth and Sky: An Andean Cosmology*. Austin, TX: University of Texas Press, 1981.

_____. *The History of a Myth: Pacariqtambo and the Origin of the Incas*. Austin, TX: University of Texas Press, 1990.

Wilcox, Joan Parisi, and Elizabeth B. Jenkins. "Journey to Q'ollorit'i: Initiation into Andean Mysticism." *Shaman's Drum*, 40 (Winter 1996): 34–49.

Index